SEVERN TUNNEL JUNCTION

SEVERN TUNNEL JUNCTION

P. D. RENDALL

The Crowood Press

First published in 2020 by
The Crowood Press Ltd
Ramsbury, Marlborough
Wiltshire SN8 2HR

enquiries@crowood.com

www.crowood.com

British Library Cataloguing-in-Publication Data
A catalogue record for this book is available from the British Library.

ISBN 978 1 78500 737 8

FRONTISPIECE: 37147 has the road away from the Down goods loop. Weeds are now beginning to encroach the reception roads… AUTHOR'S COLLECTION

Designed and typeset by Guy Croton Publishing Services, West Malling, Kent

Printed and bound in India by Replika Press Pvt Ltd

Contents

Dedication and Acknowledgements

To all staff who worked at 'The Tunnel' 1886–1987

Special thanks are due to the following who have given their time to help me with the preparation of this book:

Terry Bruton, ex-Newport panel supervisor; Peter Payne, ex-Undy hump chargeman, guard at STJ and Caldicot Crossing signalman; Graham Darby, ex-area freight assistant, Bristol TOPS 1980s; Maureen Rendall, for recalling memories of Crossway; Terry Winter, for permission to reproduce parts of his father, William Winter's essay to STJ staff on closure of the yard in 1987; Monmouthshire County Council; the staff of the Ebbw Vale Records Office, Ebbw Vale and the Wiltshire History Centre, Chippenham, Wiltshire; Tim Rendall for loan of photographs; D. J. Tomkiss and Ray Caston of the Welsh Railway Research Circle.

Photographs by the author except where otherwise credited. All photographs are credited to the photographer where known.

Note on diagrams: Many of the diagrams and plans in this book are up to 133 years old. The quality of some of them is as can be expected for their age.

Introduction

On 12 October 1987, Severn Tunnel Junction marshalling yards were closed. The feelings of the staff then employed at Severn Tunnel Junction were summed up in a short essay written and circulated to all staff by diesel depot roster clerk, the late William Winter, on the occasion of a gathering of staff at closure.

Severn Tunnel Junction Marshalling Yards 1886–12 October 1987

Dear Colleagues,

As the Severn Tunnel Junction marshalling yards close, I cannot allow such an historic occasion to pass without expressing a few words of comment on the event.

The first railway to run through the village (of Rogiet) was the tracks of the South Wales Railway which opened for traffic the 75 miles [120km] between Chepstow and Swansea on 18 June 1850. There was no station then, as Rogiet had only a few inhabitants, mostly farmers, farm workers and a few quarrymen. This line remained alone until it was joined in 1886 by the Severn Tunnel Railway, an act of parliament for which was passed in 1872. The railway was to run the 8 miles [13km] from Pilning to Rogiet under the River Severn. You will all know the dramatic history of the building of that subsequent tunnel. It was to coincide with its opening that a station was built to be known as Severn Tunnel Junction and the first siding for the marshalling yards formed.

From that time up to and including World War I, the yards were increasing in size and use. The 'History of the Great Western Railway' records that traffic increased through the tunnel from 18,099 trains in 1913 to 24,027 in 1917 – mostly coal for the southern ports and docks. There was a Chief Inspector then stationed at the yard, one of whom, Mr Williams, retired in 1922. His son, Archie, who died a few years ago, was a railwayman all his working life.

Up to the end of the Great War most workers employed came from the half-circle of Magor in the west to Portskewett in the east, excluding Rogiet, although Ifton Terrace, Rogiet Terrace and Sea View Terrace had been built almost as soon as the station or very shortly afterwards. Around the same time Lord Tredegar financed the erection of the Roggiet Hotel.

The Chepstow Rural District Council built its first houses in Ifton Road and the Caldicot Road under the Housing Act 1919 and they were occupied in 1921. Shortly after this, the Great Western Garden Village Society commenced its programme of house building for railway employees with financial aid from both the Exchequer and the district council. Both these sites were the basis for the strong community spirit founded on railway service.

Sometime between the wars, a hostel was built between the station and the loco shed. This may have been purpose built but was in any case used later as a 'double home' lodge. At least one marriage was made in this building when a member of the female staff married a fireman and settled in a society house to raise a family.

Early in World War II, fifty concrete prefabs were built to accommodate railway personnel and for a time there were sleeping coaches in the car dock. The hostel, now the Moors hostel for homeless families, was built in 1941. Many will remember their time in residence on transferring to the depot and later settling down to family life in the area. It is believed that at the commencement of the war, 1,050 people were employed in all departments.

The first loco shed – a Great Western standard shed with four roads – was opened in what was later the car dock in 1908 followed by the opening of the new shed in, I believe, 1921. My father worked in the former shed until dismissed in 1911 for smoking on the footplate. He then joined the regular army until invalided out in 1919. Later he again worked on the railway as a platelayer in the tunnel from 1935 to 1937.

In 1947, one year before nationalization, a census of engines revealed Severn Tunnel Junction as being the third in the table of totals in the old Newport Division with ninety-three. Ebbw Junction was top with 140 followed by Canton with 121.

From the turn of the century until 1963 all was expansion and consolidation. When I started work the Great Western Railway still had six years to run, although the paternalism of that railway was inevitably under strain during the war years. Following nationalization almost imperceptibly things began to change. This continued until Dr Beeching decided that the railways as we knew them would never be the same again. Not content

with the closure of so many lines, he seemed determined that, however the climate changed in future years, there would be no opportunity for expansion should the need arise.

The appointment of Dr Beeching, however, may have been a consequence of the increase in private car ownership and the massive motorway building programme to accommodate the ever increasing number of lorries, which were also becoming larger in size and axle weight. The 'dream' following nationalization of a fully integrated transport system never came to fruition due to the failure of all governments to stand up to the road lobby and insist on its implementation. Until 1963, through two world wars, every small lineside factory had its own sidings forming brooks, which formed streams until, reaching marshalling yards like ours, formed rivers of traffic of all descriptions being delivered without problems. BR now seem to lose in the competition, with fewer trains chasing fewer goods available to both, leading to the need for reductions in staff.

The railway was always in our consciousness from an early age. The whistle of a train heard on a restless night. The clang-clang of steel wagons buffering up against others off the hump. The whistles of the engines welcoming in each New Year.

A Sunday evening walk with my family sometimes brought us over the railway bridge from the Moors. This always seemed to coincide with the passing of the Carmarthen milk train. Milk traffic commenced in the 1880s, with the liquid being carried in thousands of churns in open trucks until, in 1906, the first glass-lined 3,000-gallon tankers were brought into use. Traffic now lost, as are the fish trains which I used to shunt with the fish pilot, killed by the formation of the deep freezing industry. Cigarette and chocolate traffic carried through the tunnel on the 8.08pm Bristol–Manchester for many years are other goods that have gone.

I have heard it said that all people coming to work at the depot are accepted without question or reservation. Perhaps I have indicated our long history of acceptance into our working community, and, where appropriate, our domestic environment. There are still examples in the area of long-term service on the railway in addition to all those who followed their grandfathers.

For example, Ken Margrett's great-grandfather was a signalman, his grandfather was the Chief Inspector mentioned earlier who retired in 1922 and his father, Bill, was a driver before him. Another is a sprightly ninety-one-year-old ex-foreman, Mr Jack May, whose father was a chief inspector at Aberbeeg. His son, Herbert, has just retired as a supervisor and his granddaughter is in higher management on the Eastern Region. This latter is an indication of the changing attitudes brought about by various sex discrimination laws.

It is, perhaps, invidious of me to mention people as I have not the time or memory to recall all the varying characters I have met and worked with over the years. I may be forgiven, however, if I mention some of those from my early years. My first Station Master for instance, Mr Richard 'Dicky' George. He was a great fan of the hunting field and, in 1938, under a title 'Station Master George goes Hunting every Monday' an article appeared in the *Daily Express* about him. What the directors may have thought I cannot imagine, but it may have been considered a public relations exercise. There was Jack Davies, 'Top End' Inspector, who was so annoyed at the slowness of his signalman in the Middle box, George Foulkes, to transfer bankers from arrival trains to departure that he wrote a long poem about him. One does not know if this failure to work quickly was plain laziness or downright awkwardness for he (Foulkes) was very eccentric. I suspect the former as George liked a little nap on the night turn.

My second mate, with whom I worked for five years, must be mentioned. This was Bill Andrews, the Timekeeper in the office which once stood on the site of the present amenity block. Bill had lost a leg at the time of World War I when attempting to jump on a brake van to get to work. The vehicle had no step, being a plough van, which caused the accident in the darkness. Following his return to work he was employed for eighteen years on nights in the Newport telegraph office, before returning to the depot. Bill was an expert on all types of engines, particularly that of his Ariel Square Four motorcycle. I remember Chief Inspector Jenkins from Swindon always visited him when at the depot to talk about the latest development of steam engines. Bill I remember as a very great gentleman.

My first mate, for a short while, was Inspector Raffel, an expert gardener whose brother was a head gardener at Kew. Before I worked with him he used to sport a beard and there's a rude story about him which I cannot repeat here in relation to his nickname of 'Beaver'. When I worked with him he had a walrus moustache and chewed twist. The surplus juices were usually deposited in the mouthpiece of the telephone during a long conversation or spat accurately to fry on the top of the red hot stove in the corner of the office.

I remember Guard Albert Edwards who, no matter what time of night he booked off duty, would always wait for someone to ride home with him to Magor as he was reluctant to pass the barn at Llanviangel, believing it to be haunted.

Then there were the prodigious users of expletives, Stan Powell and Ivor Pritchard, who could string four letter words together like pearls in a necklace. These two were exceptional in what is generally a swearing industry. And finally, Signalman Ted Pippin, who, dressed one night as an Indian Brave, relieved his mate Fred Boon at 10pm having left a fancy dress dance early as Fred would not stay on for him.

Tales could be told of so many more, such as Horace Edwards, Bill Sheppard, Charlie Avery, Adrian 'Doctor' Crawley etc. The list of personalities is endless, but time and space does not allow such liberties.

From 12 October all that will be left will be memories. Some of you – most I hope – will have happy ones. Some, a few who may have been involved in accidents or other incidents, may have memories they would rather forget. All I believe must have experienced something of an attachment to the depot that will remain with you wherever you go or how long you live in retirement.

My own particular memories are the day I started work learning duties in the Bristol yard on 21 December 1941, having left school at the age of fourteen the Friday before. I was allowed Christmas Day off but had to report for work on Boxing Day. I remember seeing my first fatality when I found Guard Tozer of Maesglas dead across the rail early one wet June morning in 1943. Another memory is the camaraderie of the Down side shunting gang, particularly on a wet night with the rain driving in from the moors. Strangely enough, one never seemed to get so wet and miserable whilst working all night as one felt after one or two hours in daytime. And later, when on light duties in East box, I well remember the sound of bird song in the very early morning in spring, mixed with the slight hiss of steam from an engine waiting at the shed signal. For our depot is possibly unique in the whole BR system in that, except where it is touched by the few houses in the area of the church, the vast acres of the yards are entirely surrounded by countryside.

And so, after 101 years, an era ends, and the railway through Rogiet reverts to the line of the Severn Tunnel Railway. When the yard rails are recovered, all that will remain for the hard work, spirit and dedication of countless men and women over generations will be one unmanned passenger station. In this high-tech age of computers and microchips I wonder what industry could replace the railway in which we could prove that our children and our children's children were able, in the next hundred years, to build on the traditions of the past.

Whilst it is true that you will meet Mr Davidson (Area Manager) for a farewell interview if you are leaving the service, this may not be enough for some as there are several strong emotions to consider. Frustration for instance, that you could do nothing to prevent the loss of your jobs. Anger that your life's work has gone and that some of you must leave earlier than you would wish, and others uproot their homes and families and find jobs at other depots where you may find the atmosphere will not be as relaxed as ours has been. And finally, deep sadness at the loss of the friendship and companionship of your mates. True, friendships can continue, if loyal, but it will not be the same as the levity of cabin life and the 'All OK, mate' when relieving each other on engine or brake van.

I trust it will not be thought presumptuous of me, therefore, to supplement what the Area Manager may say to you, with these words of my own. I feel qualified with my long service to the community and depot and by my long association with you, to do so.

I am leaving after forty-six years and in farewell would like to say how much I have enjoyed working with you. To those with whom I attended school and who started work around the same time in the war, all who subsequently joined and those of you who came from Ebbw Junction that October Sunday in 1982 with, perhaps, some trepidation, believing you were arriving at a depot where you could work contentedly until retirement. Some of these, I believe, will have regrets that they cannot stay and may even wish they had joined our 'family' earlier.

I am grateful for the privilege of working for the Great Western and BR as, whatever the circumstances that can be levelled, the industry, as far as I know, never failed to look after staff who had fallen down in health in some way, and were found alternative positions.

Whether you are retiring or have found a new depot at which to work, I wish you all good luck and all the very best in health, happiness and prosperity, especially the former, for without that, the other two are meaningless. To close, perhaps a quotation from Lord Lytton would be apt:

Ah, Never can fall from the days that have been
A gleam on the years that shall be…

W. C. Winter, 1 September 1987

Two miles (3km) inland from the small village of Portskewett on the Welsh side of the River Severn, 4 miles (6km) southwest of the town of Chepstow and 4 miles (6km) east of Newport was what was once the largest goods marshalling yard in the area once run by the Great Western Railway Company. It lay just a few hundred yards of where, until 2019, stood the toll booths of the M4 motorway. The River Severn itself was, at its closest to the yards, a mere quarter of a mile (400m) away.

This was Severn Tunnel Junction; a name now known to twenty-first-century commuters as an unstaffed junction station on the South Wales main line in Monmouthshire, but to older railwaymen and women and railway enthusiasts it was the site of the largest freight marshalling yard in the Western Region of British Railways. At its height, it boasted four yards and a locomotive depot, and stretched for over 2 miles (3km) along the Welsh bank of the River Severn between the town of Caldicot and the village of Undy. Opened in 1886 along with the Severn Tunnel, the yard was the hub of freight traffic for South Wales. Enlarged in 1930, when it became a 'hump' yard, enlarged again in 1937 and once more in 1960, it was finally closed in 1987 and most of the traffic that once passed through 'STJ' was either lost all together or moved onto the roads. In the past, to many railway enthusiasts and photographers, Severn Tunnel Junction meant a vast railway marshalling and hump yard first, and a station and junction between the Gloucester and Bristol main lines second, with the steam loco and (later) diesel depot third.

In order to understand the working of the yards and loco depot, plus the community that sprang up around them, it is necessary to take into account the approaches to the yards from either side. Thus this book will take in an area bounded by Bishton to the west, and on the east side, Caldicot Junction on the Gloucester lines and Severn Tunnel East signal box on the London lines and the English side of the river. Also included, as both were of importance to Severn Tunnel Junction, will be the short branch to Sudbrook and the longer branch to Caerwent Royal Navy depot.

It's important to remember that Severn Tunnel Junction yard wasn't just a railway yard, junction, station and loco depot. As the reader can see from William Winter's words above, Severn Tunnel Junction was a railway community; the village of Rogiet was taken over by railway staff who moved there to take jobs at the 'Junction'. Houses were built by and for them, making the one-time hamlet into a small town.

This is its story.

Map of area covered

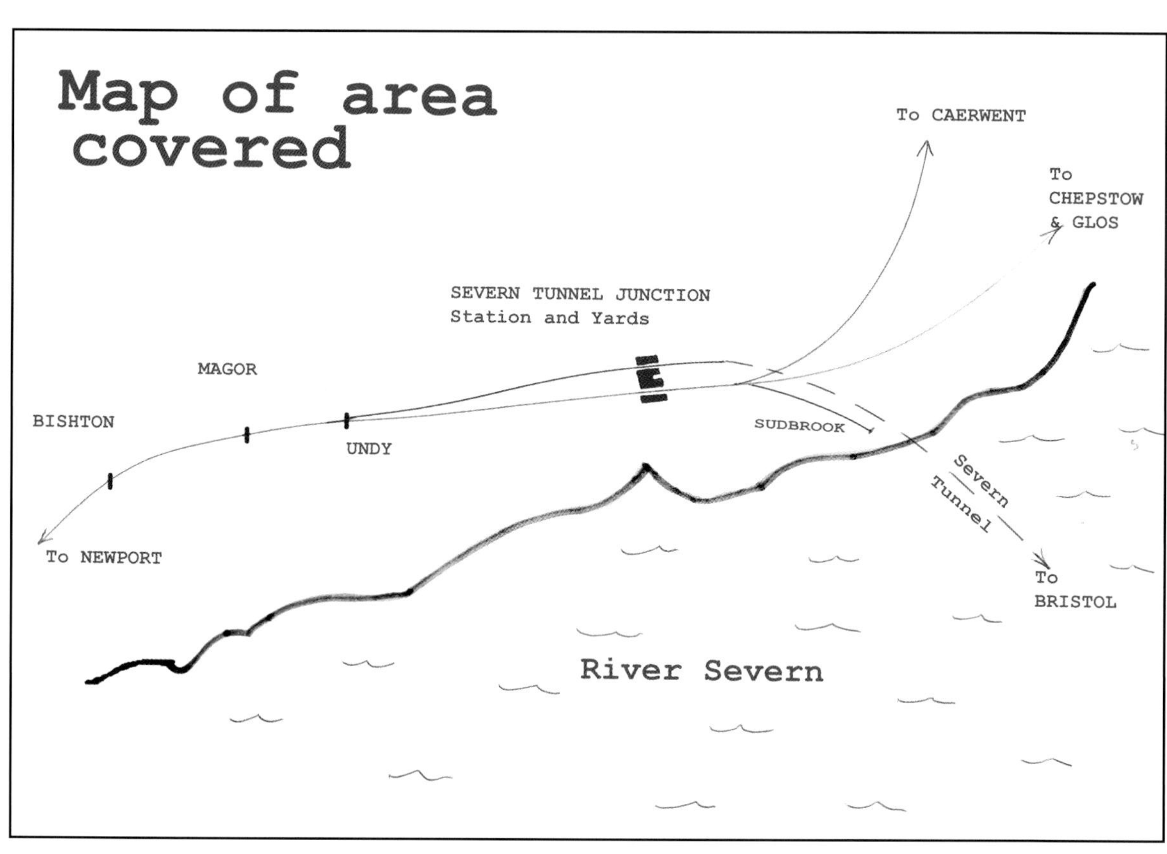

CHAPTER I

The Beginnings

The year 1870 had begun with mixed prospects. In Europe, the Prussian prime minister, Otto von Bismarck, was whipping up nationalistic fervour in order to unite the independent German states with Prussia. The French were against such ideas and this led to the Franco-Prussian War, which started in July 1870. In the United Kingdom, Queen Victoria was continuing to rule alone; her consort, Prince Albert, had been dead for nine years and Victoria was still in mourning. It was not all gloom though. Joseph Lister had invented the sterilization process for surgical instruments and the Education Act had been passed.

In Britain, the railway age was in full swing. Whilst many railway lines and companies were making their presence felt in the country, in the southwest of the UK the Great Western Railway was finding things difficult. Brunel, its iconic engineer, had been dead for eleven years. Brunel's engineer Daniel Gooch still held the flag for the GW 'old guard' but his age was telling on him. The company may have boasted the longest main line in the country, but there was the ongoing 'Battle of the Gauges': Brunel's 'out on a limb' broad gauge versus Stephenson's almost universally adopted narrow (4ft 8.5in) gauge. The broad gauge was losing and large parts of the GW network were already 'mixed gauge'.

Elsewhere on the GWR system, capacity was challenged by the fast-growing coal industry. Economics dictated where many of the new lines went and this was especially so in South Wales, where the economic mainstay was coal. South Wales, having outstripped the north of England for coal production (at the expense of the men and boys working in the mines), was on its way to becoming the biggest exporter of coal in the world. Railways not only moved the stuff but railway loco-motives would become one of the largest users along with domestic markets.

The South Wales Railway

The GWR began moving coal by rail out of South Wales. It had its line out of South Wales, the South Wales railway (now the main line from Gloucester to Swansea via Chepstow), which had opened between Chepstow and Swansea in 1850. This was initially a main line of two parts, with another section of the South Wales Railway running from Gloucester to, at first, Grange Court, along the western bank of the Severn and then to a tempo-rary station on the Gloucester side of Chepstow. The 'missing link' was a bridge over the River Wye. The poor old passengers had to detrain and cross the river by means of a road bridge until Brunel successfully bridged the Wye with his unique sus-

An old print showing Brunel's unique bridge at Chepstow, which completed the missing link in the South Wales Railway. It was replaced in the 1950s.

pension bridge, and the railway, now owned by the Great Western, opened throughout on 19 July 1852.

From picturesque Chepstow the line took a sharp turn to the southeast and followed the River Wye before turning southwest and following the coast for a couple of miles and turning slightly inland towards Newport just after the village of Portskewett, where a small station was built. This line was, for a time, adequate for goods traffic, but not for passengers. It could take a couple of days to travel from Cardiff or Newport to Gloucester and from Gloucester to the rest of the GW system or to a port, for example Southampton. Not for nothing had the GWR been given the nickname of 'Great Way Round'.

Crossing the Severn

The GWR sought to alleviate the delays and to speed up the movement of coal traffic and passengers into and (mainly) out of South Wales. But there was a snag: the River Severn. Not the widest or deepest river in the country, the Severn

was, perhaps, the most unpredictable. There was the problem of the tides, for example: the Severn had the second highest rise and fall of tides in the world: 14ft (4m) on average, up to 50ft (15m) on those occasions when the famous tidal wave known as the Severn Bore rushes up the river. Then there were numerous underground springs, mudbanks and deep freshwater pools. Crossing the river was not an easy challenge to overcome. Engineers wrung their hands in despair at the thought of building a bridge.

Whilst this industrial wringing of hands was going on, the Bristol and South Wales Union Railway was built from Bristol to New Passage on the English banks of the Severn, opening in 1863. A pier was built and from here passengers could detrain and embark on a ship to cross the river. This was fine as long as the weather and the tides played ball, and the new Passage Hotel built nearby was in much demand on such occasions when they didn't. This service could also only carry passengers, not goods.

Those engineers, meanwhile, had stopped wringing their hands long enough to produce

The River Severn. It has the second highest rise and fall of tides in the world. The fishermen are on the old Beachley–Aust ferry landing stage.

plans for bridges over the Severn. They needed to be high bridges, because ships (which in those days had high masts carrying sails) needed to be able to pass underneath on their way upriver to Sharpness and Gloucester docks. One engineer, Sir John Fowler, planned such a bridge: 100ft (30m) above high water and 2.75 miles (4.4km) long, it would stride across the Severn. Possibly out of a sense of desperation, the GWR board of directors approved this bridge in 1865.

Bridge or Tunnel?

Like all such schemes, it took time to draw plans and survey ground, and by 1870, whilst the world – and other railway companies – was moving on, the GWR found themselves treading water. The South Wales coalfields, having been tapped, were now gushing and if the GWR didn't get their act in order, they could well lose out to rivals. The LNWR had already made inroads into the South Wales coalfields. The bridge was still the preferred option but all the time another voice was advocating a plan that could reduce the travelling distance between South Wales and Southampton by 61 miles (98km).

It could knock an hour off the journey time between Cardiff and London and wouldn't need to be at the mercy of high tides and tall ships. It all came about because of an idea to speed up railway services between South Wales and the rest of the United Kingdom, and the idea was a tunnel: a tunnel under the mighty River Severn.

Whilst many engineers had balked at the idea of tunnelling under the Severn, one man, Charles Richardson, surveyed the route and planned his tunnel. The route would run from Pilning (where it would leave the course of the Bristol and South Wales Union line) and descend through a deepening cutting until plunging into a tunnel under the River Severn at a falling gradient of 1 in 100, changing to a rising gradient of 1 in 100 halfway through, and rising up to emerge into another deep cutting near Caldicot. This line would meet the line from Gloucester at a place called Rogiet on the Monmouthshire side of the river. The new line would be almost 8 miles (13km) long, of which 4 miles 624 yards (7km) were to be in tunnel, 2.25 miles (3.6km) of which would be underneath the River Severn.

The Welsh side of the Severn Tunnel was approached via a deep rocky cutting. This illustration is from an old commemorative cigarette card.

Daniel Gooch and the GW board listened to Richardson and liked what they heard. The bridge plans were dropped. Richardson's plans were deposited in 1871 and the tunnel got its Act of Parliament in 1872. Work commenced in 1873 and, thirteen years later, Daniel Gooch was one of the people who rode on the first train to pass through the tunnel from west to east on 5 September 1885, after completion of the works. The tunnel opened for goods traffic in 1886. On 9 January 1886, an experimental coal train ran from Aberdare to Southampton through the tunnel, with the result that coal was delivered at the port in the evening of the same day. The opening for traffic was delayed pending completion of the new pumping station arrangements at Sudbrook, to contain the underground river known as the 'Great Spring', which had broken into and flooded the workings during construction. The Sudbrook pumps moved approximately 30 million gallons (136 million litres) of water a day (*see* Chapter 9).

On 1 September 1886, the line was opened for goods traffic and passenger trains began to run between Bristol and Cardiff three months later. The new line and tunnel cut 60 miles (97km) off the journey between London and Cardiff. This was shortened further in 1904 by the opening of the South Wales Direct line between Wootton Bassett and Patchway.

The junction of the Gloucester–Newport lines with those of the new lines from Bristol was near Rogiet. At the time the South Wales Railway Gloucester–Newport line arrived in the area in 1850, Rogiet was merely a tiny hamlet on the 'Caldicot Levels' – the flat lands just inland of the River Severn. Rogiet was at that time a village and community in Gwent (now Monmouthshire), southeast Wales, between Caldicot and Magor. It is 8 miles (13km) west of Chepstow and 11

EXTRACT FROM KELLY'S LOCAL DIRECTORY
OF MONMOUTHSHIRE 1901

ROGGIETT (Severn Tunnel Junction station on the Great Western Railway South Wales line) is a parish on the shore of the Bristol Channel 7½ miles southwest from Chepstow, and 142½ from London, in the Southern division of the county, hundred of Caldicot, petty sessional division, union and county court district of Chepstow, rural deanery of Netherwent, archdeaconry of Monmouth, and diocese of Llandaff.

miles (18km) east of Newport. The area also encompasses the hamlet and separate parish of Llanfihangel Rogiet (located immediately west of Rogiet and which derives its name from the Welsh name for the church of St Michael) and the land immediately east of Rogiet, which once formed the separate small parish of Ifton. The origin of the name Rogiet is not known and it has been spelt 'Roggiatt', 'Roggiett' or 'Roggiet' in its time, the latter two variations being used within living memory. The church of St Mary is the parish church. (An earlier dedication was apparently to St Hilary, a man who seems to have little connection with South Wales other than being thought of highly by St Augustine, who apparently held him in some esteem. St Augustine, of course, is said to have held a conference with early British bishops at Aust, on the English side of the Severn, in AD 603.) Much of the church dates from about the fourteenth century.

Much has been written about the construction of the Severn Tunnel and I do not propose to go over old ground; however, its working is part of the story of Severn Tunnel Junction. The completion of the tunnel under the Severn proved to be a winner so far as the fortunes of the GWR in the South Wales area were concerned. Yet, whilst its existence brought many benefits to the Great Western and unlocked the potential of South Wales traffic, being 4.5 miles (7km) long and double track between Severn Tunnel Junction on the Welsh side of the River Severn and Pilning on the English side, once the tunnel began to be heavily used it proved a bottleneck. Over the years goods loops were added at both sides of the tunnel but that 4.5-mile (7km) block section was a pinch point; slow freight trains could take 10 minutes to pass through the tunnel. As I mention later in the book, intermediate block signals were often contemplated to break the long section, but any proposed benefits were always outweighed by the horror of a collision in the tunnel; it took a world war to change that way of thinking, but only whilst the crisis was ongoing (*see* Chapter 4).

CHAPTER 2

Severn Tunnel Junction Station

At the time of the opening of the Severn Tunnel, the nearest railway station was 2 miles (3km) away, at Portskewett. With the arrival of the line from Bristol, a junction station was built at Rogiet to serve the new Severn Tunnel. The GWR must, at that early stage, have had great foresight to build a big junction station where the lines met. Yes, there would inevitably be exchange of both passengers and goods between the Bristol and Gloucester lines, but the tiny community at Rogiet hardly warranted a four-platform station and sidings when it first opened.

The Station Buildings

The station at Severn Tunnel Junction was a neat station with the main buildings on the north, or 'Up' side. The station approach road – on the north side of which stood Seaview Terrace – split into two roads, one of which climbed up to the bridge that crossed the tracks at the west end of the station, which was the spot where many, many railway Imagegraphs were taken, the majority of the yard and loco facilities being out of range for most Imagegraphers and trainspotters.

The road over the bridge led to the area known locally as 'the Moors' and access to the wagon

The station 'totem' sign from Severn Tunnel Junction.

Severn Tunnel Junction station in the 1940s, looking west. The loco stands in the Wye Valley bay. AUTHOR'S COLLECTION

An old postcard showing the Wye Valley bay and all platforms. The train is on the Bristol line.

repair works could be gained on the river side of the tracks. The station access road ran along to the north side of the railway and accessed the station and carriage/car loading bay. Along this road were sited various buildings belonging to railway departments: permanent way, electricians, and an oil store. There was also a long, low single-storey wooden building. This was the first railwaymen's hostel and was built sometime around the end of World War I. Later it was used as a 'double home' hostel for railwaymen needing somewhere to stay whilst they waited for their return working.

The layout catered for the four main tracks – Bristol lines to the north, Gloucester lines to the south. There were four main platforms linked by a covered footbridge, and a bay platform at the eastern end of Platforms 2 and 3 to accommodate the Wye Valley service. The platforms were numbered as follows: the Up Bristol platform was No. 1, the Down Bristol platform No. 2; Platform 3 was

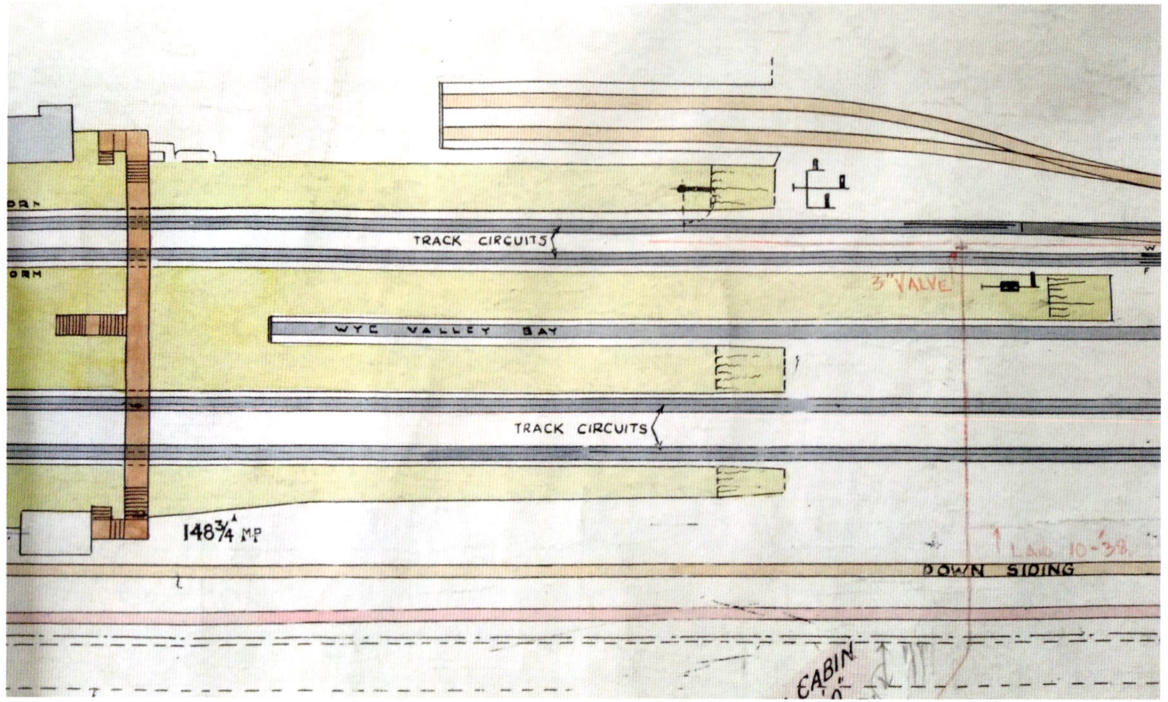

Plan of the east end of the station showing the final arrangement of the car-loading dock. WILTSHIRE HISTORY CENTRE

the Up Gloucester and Platform 4 the Wye Valley Bay (always known to staff as 'the bay' rather than its platform number). Platform 5 was the Down Gloucester.

The main station buildings comprised a ladies' waiting room, general waiting room, booking office, and Station Master's office. Slightly separate from the last was a bike shed and porters' room. There was a canopy from the station building. There was a letterbox in the wall outside the station which was cleared at 5.25pm daily.

The footbridge steps began adjacent to the ladies' waiting room. There was a urinal east of the footbridge. An additional siding at the east end of Platform 1 was originally known as the 'Carriage Loading' siding and was where carriages and early cars were loaded on to flat wagons to be carried to Pilning station on the English side of the river. In later years there was an additional siding added here. A water column stood at the end of the platform.

Severn Tunnel Junction's middle platform buildings comprised a lavatory, ladies' waiting room, general waiting room, refreshment room (run during World War II by manager Lilian Hawthorn) and a (later) porters' room. A coal store stood just off the west end of the platform. Platform 2, the Down Bristol line, had a water column at the west end and another one approximately halfway along the platform. The Wye Valley bay, Platform 4, was at the east end. The Platform 4 face, Up Gloucester line, had a water column that stood off the end of the platform.

Platform 5 was the poor relation of the others; standing adjacent to the Down Bristol line, its facilities were sparse. The first waiting room was originally described in GWR plans as a 'Waiting Shed'! This was later a 'proper' waiting room but in reality only slightly better than a shelter. Next to it stood a urinal. Platform 5's water column stood at the west end of the platform.

On the west side of the Moors road bridge was the main bulk of the yards. Here were the Bristol yard on the Up side and the Down yard. On the north side, close by the bridge, stood the cattle

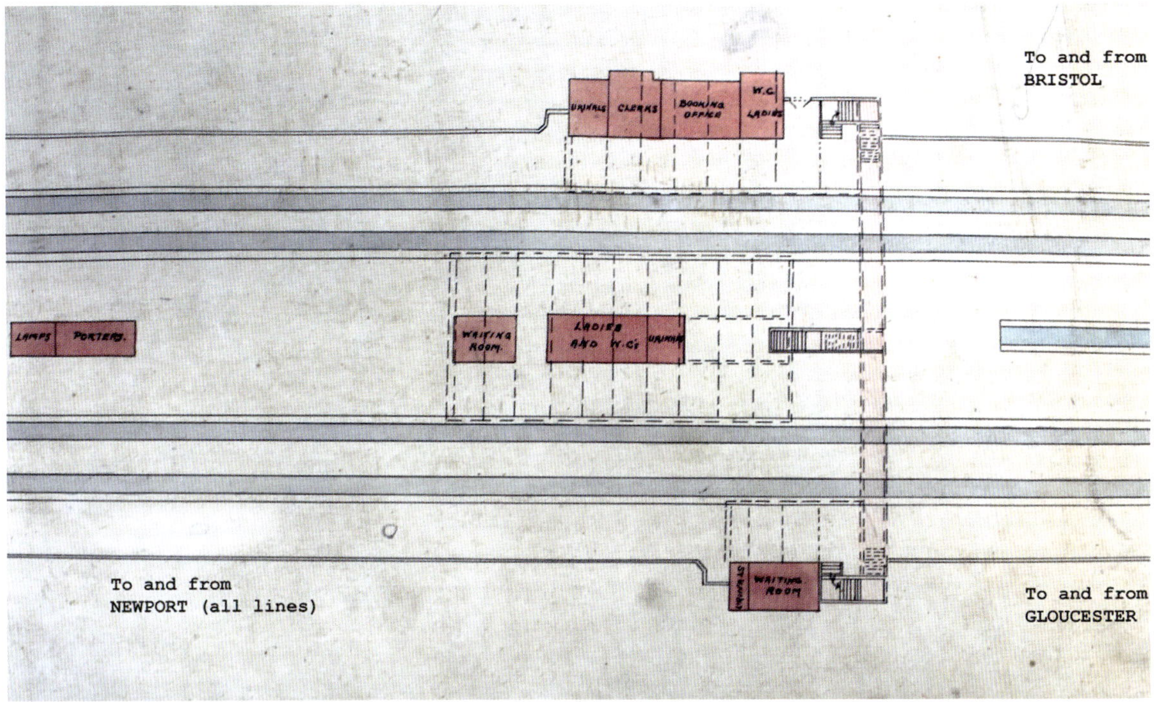

The arrangement of buildings on the middle platforms. WILTSHIRE HISTORY CENTRE

pens, served by a siding. Beyond the pens was the wooden amenity block, where the yard foreman had his office. Here also was the guards' accommodation and shunters' mess room. The yard timekeeper had his office here.

Severn Tunnel Junction station was always busy; in addition to the regular passenger traffic of workers in factories and offices in Bristol, Gloucester and Newport catching the trains, there was regular parcel reception and delivery. Special trains ran (and still do) calling at Severn Tunnel Junction to pick up fans travelling to football and rugby matches and even, on occasion, Speedway events.

It wasn't just train loads that arrived at STJ. There was a goods shed in the Up yard with a 2-tonne crane. Up to nationalization, there was a lot of local 'pick-up' goods working, whereby stopping goods trains picked up and dropped off individual wagons at small local sidings. In the 1950s, moves were made to centralize this sort of traffic . The Railway Executive (a forerunner of the British Railways Board) established regional commercial centres, each run by a District Commercial Officer. Local traders were sent information about the freight services and facilities available to them in their respective BR regions. All freight services available at stations and depots were listed for the traders and every effort made to encourage them to use the local facilities. A road vehicle collection service was advertised to collect goods from local villages within a usual radius of 10 miles (16km) from the local railhead. Railheads were established where goods were delivered by rail and taken onward to customers by road up to 20 or 30 miles (32–48km) from the railhead. Items included almost everything from small items to bulk loads, livestock and agricultural machinery.

In British Railways days, Severn Tunnel Junction station and goods shed was one of the Western Region depots and came under the direction of the District Commercial Superintendent at the Newport Railhead, N. D. Jenkins. Mr Jenkins' area included sub-railheads at Abergavenny,

G. W. R.

Severn Tunnel Junction

A GWR luggage label. AUTHOR'S COLLECTION

Abertillery, Blackwood, Brynmawr, Ebbw Vale and Pontypool (Crane Street.) These railheads served a total of seventy-three stations and other depots. It was a good system – imagine how much less traffic there would be on the roads if only such a system were in use today. Today, it's not unusual for a 50-tonne articulated lorry to deliver a small parcel to your house if that parcel is part of its delivery round; a small lorry or van would have delivered that parcel before, and it would have come from a railhead, having got there by rail.

Alas, almost every station in the Newport and STJ area lost its goods facilities over the ten or fifteen years after this plan was published in 1953 and all the stations either closed or unmanned. Traffic lost was handed to the road haulage industry. Taking into consideration that this lost traffic was handled by rail, there must have been an enormous financial loss to BR over the years during which the Beeching plan for the reshaping of BR was being actioned.

The Staff

The Station Master

As a busy station at the junction of the Bristol and Gloucester lines, Severn Tunnel Junction had its share of porters, telegraphists and clerks, all over-seen by a station master. In 1901 the station master was Alfred Edward Arnold. Arnold had been born in Caldicot in 1864, the son of a local builder. He began work at the age of fourteen, joining the GWR as a lad passenger clerk at Portskewett station. In December 1886, Arnold became passenger clerk at the new station of Severn Tunnel Junction. Six years later he moved to Lydney, still as passenger clerk. In 1892, he started work in the District Superintendent's Office at Cardiff and in January 1901 he was appointed to the post of station master at Severn Tunnel Junction. Alfred Arnold was still in post in 1911 and unmarried.

By 1923, Alfred Arnold had been succeeded as station master by William Albert Capron. Capron had been born in Talaton, Devon, in 1863 and was a far more experienced railwayman by the time he arrived at STJ. His first job on the GWR was as lad telegraph clerk at Castle Hill, Hereford, a post he took up in 1878. By 1881 he was working as telegraph clerk at Stourbridge, from where he moved to the District Superintendent's Office, Birmingham, in 1886. Promotion followed and he was appointed station master at Hartlebury in December 1896. In October 1909, he moved to the post of station master at Cwmbran and from there he moved to succeed Alfred Arnold at Severn Tunnel Junction.

Early station staff at STJ. The photo was taken from the information sign at the park which now covers the Down side yard.

William Capron's successor when he retired in 1928 was Richard Wright George, a man who had started work on the GWR at the age of fifteen as a lad clerk. Born in Pembroke in 1882, Richard George moved to Nantymoel, then Tondu before arriving at Severn Tunnel Junction. He and his wife, Ethel, lived in a pleasant detached cottage in Caldicot. Station master Wright was a colourful character; during his time at the station, he was renowned for his love of fox-hunting, which even led to an article in a 1938 edition of the *Daily Express* (*see* Winter's letter in the Introduction). 'Dicky' George died in November 1958.

It would seem that the post of station master at Severn Tunnel Junction attracted a certain type of personality. Other than the hunting, all three men mentioned above had similar off-duty interests; they were all freemasons. Arnold was initiated into Chepstow Lodge Striguil No. 2186 in March 1905, and Capron joined Kidderminster Lodge of Hope and Charity No. 377 in 1894. George joined a Pembroke Lodge, Castlemartin Lodge No 1748, in May 1909 and transferred to Striguil Lodge at Chepstow in 1921.

It has been claimed that one Thomas Strange was station master at STJ in 1901. Kelly's 1901 local directory also has him listed as Station Master at STJ, but it seems that he wasn't. He may have had a brief appointment to Severn Tunnel Junction, but census returns from 1901 and 1911 show that Strange was station master at Pontypool Road. Prior to 1901 he was district relief clerk at Newport. The mix-up may have arisen through the 1901 census, which shows Mr Strange living at Llanvihangel, in the Station House. But this was Llanvihangel Pontymoile, which is near Pontypool, not the Llanfihangel at Rogiet.

Other staff known to have worked at Severn Tunnel Junction station over the years include C. F. Angell, who was employed here as a telegraph messenger in 1907. One early staff member at 'the Tunnel' was porter John Branchflower. He was employed here in 1899. He was given an official caution at a disciplinary hearing on 26 March 1900 for 'causing an engine to get off the road'. Sadly the records do not give any further details.

The Depression Years

The years after World War I saw the Depression of the 1930s. Railway staff, many of whom had been exempt from service in the forces between 1914 and 1919 as they were needed to run the railways, now found that they were not exempt from the effects of the Depression. Staff were laid off from work without pay for anything up to three years, although they were given the promise of being re-employed when the economy picked up. It seemed to be the least important posts that were chosen for redundancy. The following staff, all employed at Severn Tunnel Junction (STJ), were laid off:

H. F. Bullock, Grade 2 porter, laid off 1930, re-employed as Grade 2 porter at Portskewett station 1934

W. Chivers, goods porter, laid off 1930, reinstated 1934 at STJ

S. C. Evans, telephonist, laid off 1930, re-employed as junior points cleaner at Cardiff docks in 1932

A. E. Howells, goods porter; laid off in 1930 and reinstated at Chepstow station in 1933

H. T. Margrett, Grade 2 Porter, laid off 1930, reinstated at STJ 1934

J. Peppin, Grade 2 porter; laid off 1930, reinstated 1933 at STJ

F. Sheen, telephonist, laid off 1930, re-employed as a lad porter at Newport, Ebbw Vale, in 1933

H. Smith, Grade 2 porter, laid off 1930, reinstated at STJ 1934

N. G. Sparks, Grade 2 porter, laid off 1930, reinstated at STJ 1932

E. Workman, telephonist, laid off 1932, not recorded as being re-employed on one record, but shown as being reinstated in 1934 on another

As can be seen from the above examples, times were indeed hard for the railway staff in the area. Here the railway was the main employer; there were few pits east of Newport. It can also been seen that some staff took 'menial' jobs in order to continue drawing a wage to feed their families. It's also worth noting that the records do not appear to show any managers being laid off.

Vehicle Transport Service

Being, as it was, the junction between two main lines into and out of Wales, Severn Tunnel Junction station always had a good passenger service. Although Rogiet was mainly a railwaymen's town, adjacent Caldicot was a little bigger; there were also several villages and hamlets within the station's catchment area. Even in years past, people commuted to Newport, Cardiff, Gloucester and Bristol for work.

From 1924 to 1966, Severn Tunnel Junction was the terminus of a motor vehicle transport service through the tunnel to Pilning. Any type of private motor car, motorcycle or motorcycle and sidecar which was capable of being loaded onto a standard railway vehicle could be carried at competitive rates. As the alternative was either the Aust–Beachley car ferry or a three-hour drive via Lydney and Gloucester, any rate could be said to be competitive! In early days, there was just a single siding at the east end of the Up platform. This siding was approached from the road by a ramp up which carriages could be driven and loaded onto rail wagons via an end-on dock. This facility was quaintly described as a 'carriage landing'.

A magnificent photo looking east. There's a wealth of information to be seen, from the signals, the GWR tin sheds, the steam loco depot with water-softening plant and the coaches in the Wye Valley bay. AUTHOR'S COLLECTION

A Gloucester bound express speeds through Platform 4. Note the two goods loops behind Platform 5 – these are on the site of the Ifton sidings. J. NEMETH COLLECTION

After the 1920s, the plans show two sidings and it appears that side loading onto rail wagons was enabled. Car-carrying flat wagons (some converted from carriage underframes) would be shunted into the end-on loading dock adjacent to the Up platform at Severn Tunnel Junction station. Cars would be driven onto these wagons, usually by designated station porters, and, when the loading was complete, the train engine – usually a Prairie tank loco – would couple up to one or two passenger coaches for the occupants of the cars

and these would be shunted onto the train. The train was then shunted to Platform 1 for the passengers to board, the car flats being formed up at the rear of the car trains. Shunters were allocated to the station for such shunting moves. It was quite common to have the train made up of six or seven bogie flat wagons, each conveying three cars. Motorcycles with sidecars could also be carried, but no more than a quart (2 pints) of petrol was allowed in the bike's petrol tank. Instructions stated that cars so carried need not have their

An earlier GWR plan of the east end of the station. Note the 'carriage landing' and the two Ifton sidings. WILTSHIRE HISTORY CENTRE

A British Railways handbill advertising the motor vehicle carrying service. AUTHOR

petrol tanks emptied as long as there were no leaks and the pressure had been released by loosening the petrol filler cap and tightening it again. Additionally, the car engine had to 'be run by the person in charge of the car until the carburettor has become exhausted and the engine stops automatically' – a process that could not happen with cars today.

Cars thus transported through the tunnel would be offloaded at Pilning station. On weekdays, the car train left Severn Tunnel Junction at 09.10 and arrived at Pilning station on the English side of the Severn 17 minutes later. An 'evening' train left STJ at 16.40, arriving at Pilning at 16.57.

EXTRACT FROM BRITISH RAILWAYS WESTERN REGION, CARDIFF DIVISION SECTIONAL APPENDIX, OCTOBER 1960

Conveyance of Motor-Cars with Spare Wheel Attached
When a spare wheel forms part of the external equipment of a motor-car, senders must secure the wheel by a strap or other equally suitable fastening, or remove and place it in the body of the car in such a position that it cannot fall out.

Class 37 No. 37229 runs light diesel through Platform 1 in the 1980s, whilst 37298 and an unidentified Cl 47 are stabled on the siding. Note the rather tatty Severn Tunnel emergency train behind the platform. AUTHOR'S COLLECTION

Corresponding services left Pilning for Severn Tunnel Junction at 08.15 (Mondays only), 10.00 and 18.45, arriving in South Wales at 08.33 (Mon), 10.18 and 19.03. Sunday services left Pilning at 10.50 and 19.20, with return services arriving back there at 09.32 and 19.32. The 10.50 outwards and 09.32 return Sunday trains were conditional and ran during September and October, plus on selected dates during December. Services were also liable to alteration on public and bank holidays. There were two trains each way on Sundays, the morning services being 'conditional', running certain times of the year only.

Fares for carrying a car were 15 shillings (75p) for a single journey and 25 shillings (£1.05) for a return. In addition, the passenger fare was 1 shilling and 9 pence (about 8p) first class and 1 shilling and 2 pence (6p) second class. If you wanted a waterproof sheet to cover your car/motorbike, that would be an extra 2 shillings (10p). Cars had

to arrive at the station of departure 'leaving sufficient time to admit to loading 30 minutes before the train is due to depart…'. It was advisable to book in advance, such was the popularity of the service. This could be done by letter, telegram or by phoning Severn Tunnel Junction on Caldicot 210 (or Pilning 206).

The service was made redundant by the opening of the Severn Bridge in 1966. When the new Severn and Wye road bridges opened in 1966, car trains (and the Aust ferry) became less well used and soon ceased to run. On the English side, the loading bay at Pilning station became occupied by the Fire Service emergency train, which would be taken over by the fire brigade in the event of mishap and used for transporting them into the tunnel. This train had been withdrawn from Pilning and stationed at Severn Tunnel Junction by the time it was needed for the December 1991 Severn Tunnel rail crash.

Passenger Services

Taking 1972 as an example year under BR management, we can see that the train service was still quite good; even though the car trains no longer ran, people were happy to leave their cars at home and use the train, rather than pay a daily toll to use the Severn bridge (there was only one bridge until 1994.) Many people worked at the aircraft works at Filton, near Bristol, and used the train to Patchway station, where they would alight for the short walk to the Rolls-Royce aero engine factory or a longer walk to the Brabazon hangar, where Concorde was being built.

In 1972, there were seventeen Up and seventeen Down trains every weekday which stopped at the Junction. Of the seventeen Up trains, ten went to Bristol, five to Gloucester and one only went as far as Chepstow before returning. The odd one out was the first Up train of the day, the 04.50 from Cardiff Canton sidings. This train did not appear in public timetables. It comprised a single diesel power car that ran empty from Canton to Newport, where it picked up railway staff and parcels, before moving on to Severn Tunnel Junction where it stopped for two minutes between 05.40 and 05.42. After leaving, the diesel unit stopped again at Severn Tunnel West end, where permanent way staff alighted. The diesel unit then carried on to Bristol.

The next departure was the 06.39 for Bristol. This started as the 06.10 Cardiff and comprised a loco and coaches. There were then departures at, 07.13½ for Chepstow and 07.32½ for Gloucester. Further departures for Bristol left at 07.49 and 08.39, after which there was a gap until 10.02½, when there was a departure to Gloucester. The 11.08 departure was another train for Bristol and the 12.35½ for Gloucester.

Then there was a gap of two hours before the 15.08 departure, again for Bristol. The 16.13½ went to Gloucester and the 18.19 to Bristol again. There was an 18.30 service to Gloucester. Another two-hour gap now occurred before the arrival at 20.16 of the 19.48 Cardiff to Bristol at 20.15½, leaving at 20.16. The next service was again to Bristol; the 21.47 departure. This was effectively the last train of the day so far as the public were concerned. All these advertised trains were diesel multiple units. The very last stopping train was again a loco and coaches; this was the 23.00 Cardiff–Bristol service, which arrived at 23.42, leaving a minute later. It was advertised in timetables as: 'Calls at Severn Tunnel Junction to set down passengers and pick up/set down train crew'. Therefore passengers – other than railway staff – who may want a late return to Bristol stations should not have got on the train. However, it's certain that it happened on more than one occasion.

Severn Tunnel Junction station was also well served for Down trains to Newport and Cardiff. Of the seventeen trains per weekday that stopped

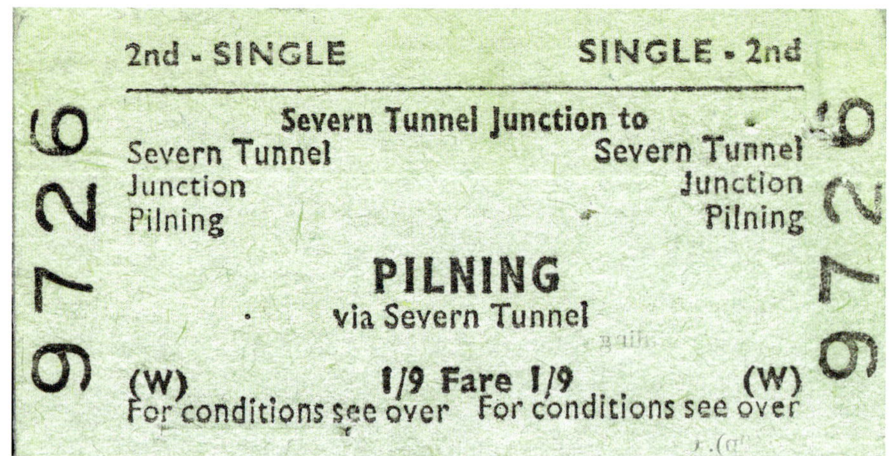

A BR single fare ticket to Pilning.

A GWR return ticket to Newport.

here, eight ran to Cardiff and seven to Newport. One ran to Swansea.

The daily service began with the arrival of the 06.00 Bristol–Newport train, which arrived at 06.32½ and left for Newport at 06.33. The 06.30 from Chepstow was next, arriving at 07.02 and leaving for Newport at 07.03. The next train to arrive also started from Chepstow and left STJ for Cardiff at 07.47½. The 08.08 departure was somewhat different in that it started from Weston-super-Mare and ran to Swansea. The 08.42 was a train for Cardiff and the 09.22½ started from Gloucester at 08.38 and ran to Newport. Next there were two departures to Cardiff, at 10.27½ and 11.27½; both started from Bristol.

The afternoon departures now alternated destinations. The 12.04½ started from Gloucester and ran to Newport; the 13.27½ departure started

The diesel 'South Wales Pullman' seen here at Pilning after passing through the Severn Tunnel. WILF STANLEY

Caldicolt Halt in 2019.

Undy Halt in the 1950s. AUTHOR'S COLLECTION

from Bristol and ran to Cardiff, with the 14.24½ again starting from Gloucester and running to Newport. The 15.27 was a Bristol–Cardiff train. Trains continued to alternate into commuter time; the 17.39 departure was Bristol–Cardiff and the 17.54½ a Gloucester–Newport service. The 18.27½ ran Bristol–Cardiff again, and then there was an evening lull before the 21.30 Bristol–Cardiff arrived at 21.52, leaving again half a minute later. The last stopping train of the day was the 23.00 Bristol–Cardiff, which arrived at Severn Tunnel Junction at 23.26 and left at 23.27.

During the course of the day, many expresses rushed through the station, but two in particular always drew attention from waiting passengers and staff alike. These were the Up and Down South Wales Pullman services, operated in steam days mainly by Castle or King class locos, or British Railways standard Britannia class locos (it was known for class 9F 2-10-0 freight locos to also appear on occasions, mostly 92220 'Evening Star'. This loco was also a favourite to head the 'Red Dragon' express.) In

diesel days the services became the duty of the diesel Pullman sets, firstly in the Nanking blue and white livery, later in grey and blue with yellow fronts. The latter would speed though the station at 08.26 (Up) and 10.38 (Down) and again later in the day at 17.55 (Up) and 19.12 (Down).

The main junction station wasn't the only station in the immediate area. Caldicot Halt was situated on the Gloucester lines 59 chains (1.2km) east of Severn Tunnel Junction station and Undy Halt stood on the west side of the bridge that carried the road called 'The Causeway' over the railway only half a mile to the east of Magor station. Opened on 11 September 1933, Undy Halt served the main lines only, as the quadrupling of the lines in the wartime expansion meant that the building of the relief lines left the platforms isolated between the tracks, accessed only by a footbridge. Like Caldicot, Undy Halt consisted of two wooden platforms made from old sleepers. Both Halts were unstaffed. Undy Halt closed in November 1964 but Caldicot Halt remains open, the sleeper platforms replaced by concrete years ago.

CHAPTER 3

Severn Tunnel Junction Yards 1886–1936

Records indicate that there were a couple of sidings already at Severn Tunnel Junction when the station opened. This is not surprising, as tunnel construction works and contractors would have needed siding accommodation, and that these were kept after the tunnel was finished and the station opened would be expected at a junction such as this. An eye to the future in 1886 could see that the South Wales coal traffic would expand greatly with the Severn Tunnel was open. There was also the traffic to and from Bristol and the south and west, plus the existing traffic to and from Gloucester and the Midlands to consider. Owing to its location, Newport station was limited in how much it could expand to accommodate extra sidings or through roads. Docks traffic took up much of the vast yards at Alexandra Dock, west of Newport. It was logical therefore, that with a junction between two major routes at Rogiet, there would have been marshalling sidings of some sort from the beginning.

Early Sidings

Sources suggest that the first sidings specifically for goods were laid at Severn Tunnel Junction not long after the opening of the tunnel in 1886. When I started to research the origins of the railway yards here, most commercially available (but sec-ondary) sources appeared to say that the yards at Severn Tunnel Junction were first constructed in the 1930s, expanded in the 1940s and again in the 1960s (the latter in line with the 1955 modernization plan) then closed in 1987 after Dr Beeching and Ernest Marple's successors closed the coal mines and eventually won the battle to remove most freight traffic from railways. Certainly the construction and design of the Up and Down hump control cabins seemed to bear out the 1930s theory, both being obvious 1930s design. But, considering that the later steam engine shed at Severn Tunnel Junction had been opened in 1908 and was obviously meant to house more than just a few engines for local goods and passenger work and some bankers to assist trains through the tunnel and up to Patchway on the English side of the Severn, it seemed obvious that from the beginning there must have been a larger goods presence at Severn Tunnel Junction than seemed to be recorded.

Could it have been, perhaps, that the 1908 loco shed was an 'outstation' depot, providing engines for all the Newport goods traffic, as St Philip's Marsh shed did at Bristol? No; the 1908 shed was too small to fulfil the role of a 'goods engines only' depot for Newport. Newport originally had a four-road shed at High Street station, built by the South Wales Railway, and other sheds at Dock Street and Newport Pill. In 1915 the large Ebbw Junction shed opened and in 1929 Dock Street shed closed, with its locos transferred to Newport Pill. This group of sheds provided engines for most work.

Research proved the Great Western Railway built a major goods yard at the junction between the Gloucester and Bristol lines. Traffic from west of Bridgend went to Stoke Gifford sidings to be sorted into trains for the London area; traffic from the Newport and Cardiff areas was sorted at Severn Tunnel Junction into trains for the south and west of England and London. Traffic from Swansea was sorted into trains for the south and west of England only. The yards at STJ sorted coal traffic coming from the South Wales valleys coalfields into trains for London and the Midlands. Conversely, it sorted goods traffic from the rest of the UK into trains bound for destinations in South Wales.

Reference to Ordnance Survey maps for 1902 show that there was a junction at Undy Crossing, approximately half a mile (1km) west of the Rogiet houses known as Railway Terrace and close to Great House farm near Undy village. Up and Down goods loops ran east from here towards the station. Near to Rogiet St Mary's church, the loops entered sidings; six sidings lay between the main lines and three on the Down side. A further four sidings were laid on the Up side to the east of Railway Terrace, where there was a 2-tonne crane in the yard. These last sidings also served a goods shed. To the east of the sidings and before Rogiet road bridge at the station, there was a further junction. Here the Gloucester and Bristol lines split. East of the road bridge stood Severn Tunnel Junction station, beyond which was a small 'engine house' and a turntable.

Further information gleaned from the GWR internal publication 'Classification of Signal Boxes and Relief Signalmen's Posts', dated 1925, showed that by 1925 there were three large signal boxes at Severn Tunnel Junction (see Chapter 10) so there must have been more than just a station, a junction between two routes, and a loco shed to deal with. Signal boxes were awarded 'marks' per hour for things like each lever movement, how many bells, how many times the phones were answered and so on. The Severn Tunnel Junction boxes were busy: East, Middle and West boxes were, individually, as busy as boxes at major railway centres in other areas. Severn Tunnel Junction East (299 marks) and Middle (288 marks) boxes were shown to be busier than Paddington station Departure signal box (266 marks), whilst Severn Tunnel Junction West box (338 marks) was busier than Westbury South box (128 marks) so there was obviously a lot of traffic in that area by then. By way of further comparison, in 1925 Stoke Gifford West box on the Badminton line, which controlled one end of a busy marshalling yard and junctions to Bristol, South Wales and Avonmouth was, at 218 marks, almost 25 per cent less busy than Severn Tunnel Junction East box.

By the 1920s, the sidings had expanded. There were twelve sidings on the Up side of the lines and the Up goods loop passed through the Up yard between sidings 6 and 7. It was a 'dead-end' yard,

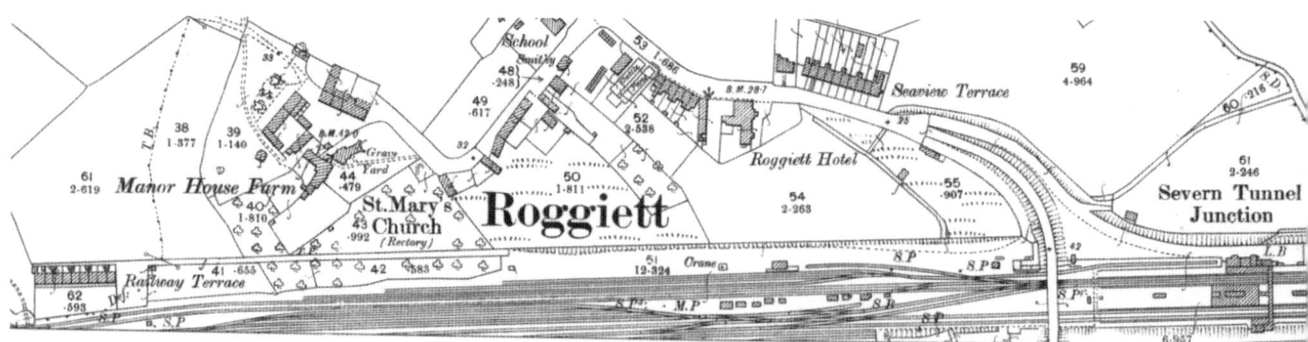

On this 1902 OS map, the Severn Tunnel Junction area is right on the edge of the sheet; nonetheless it shows the goods facilities there at the time. Also shown are the earliest railway houses, in Railway Terrace and Seaview Terrace. (Reproduced with the permission of the National Library of Scotland under a Creative Commons licence.)

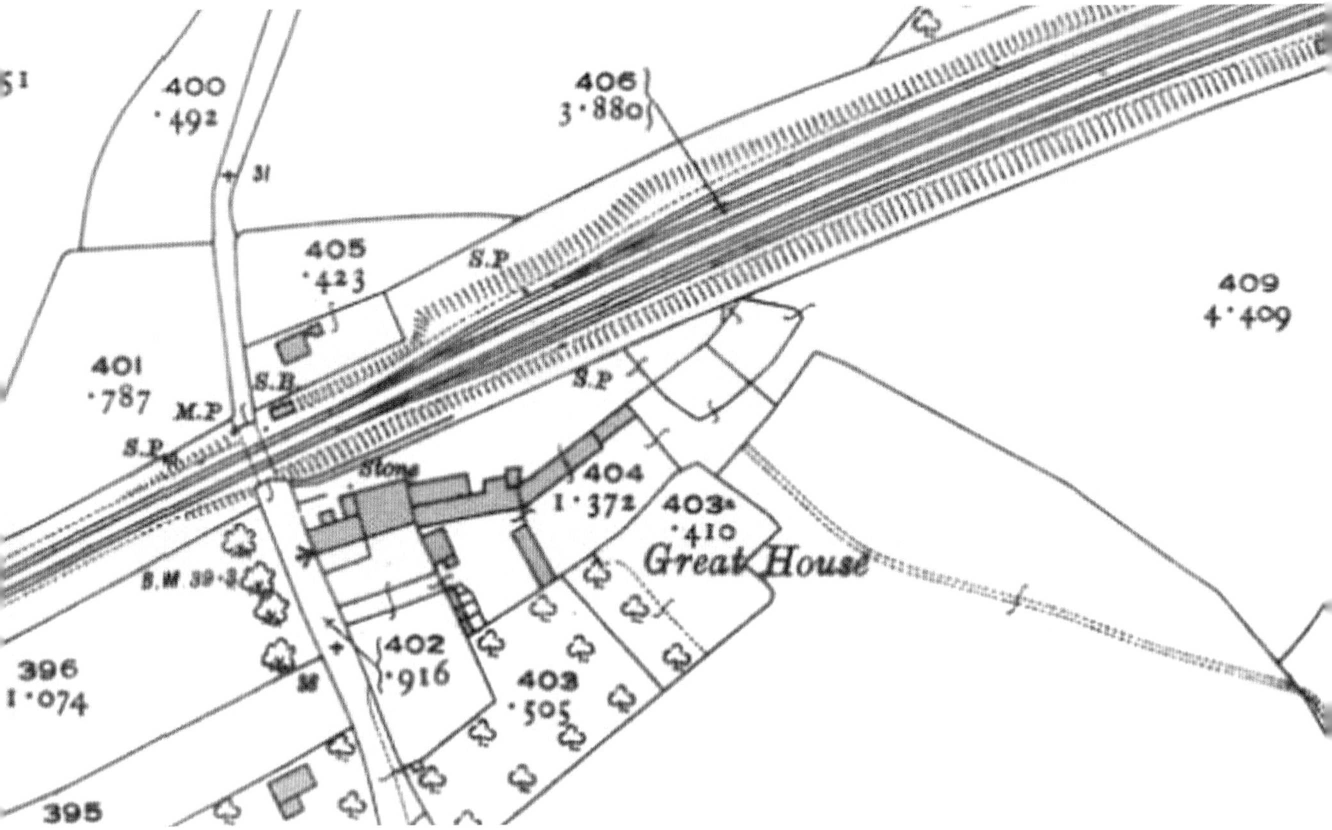

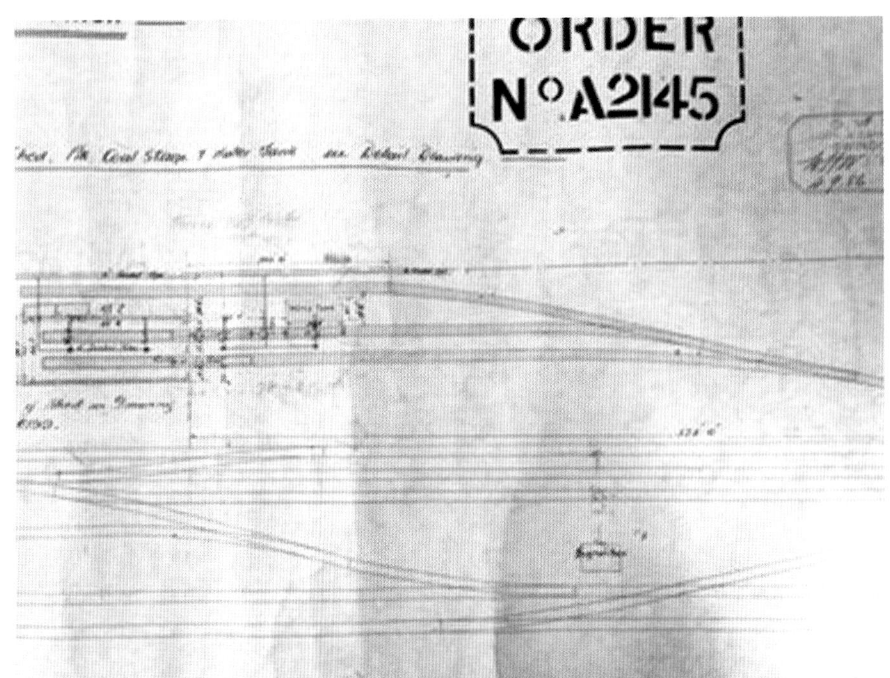

Undy Halt in the 1950s, looking east. AUTHOR

This plan, dated 2 September 1886, shows the layout of the original GWR locomotive shed close to the station platforms at the east end. WILTSHIRE HISTORY CENTRE

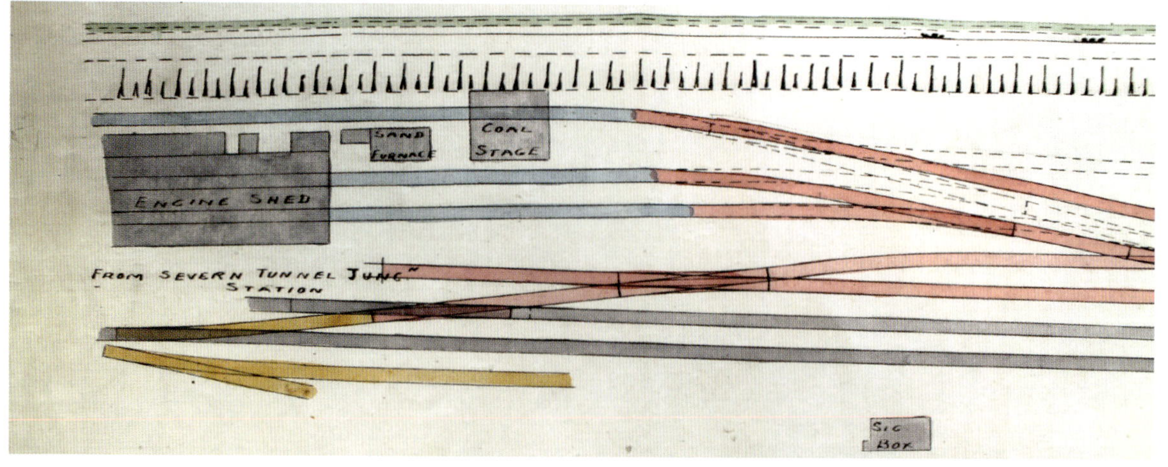

Undy Crossing, 1902. Note the original position of the signal box and the Up goods loops. There are no Down good loops yet. (Reproduced with the permission of the National Library of Scotland under a Creative Commons licence.)

EXTRACT FROM GREAT WESTERN RAILWAY GENERAL APPENDIX TO THE RULE BOOK, AUGUST 1936

Definition of the Several Mode of Shunting Wagons

In order that there may be no misunderstanding as to the meaning of the shunting terms Double Shunt and Fly Shunt in common use among Shunters, Guards and others, the following definitions are to be noted:

Double Shunt: This means the propelling of two lots of wagons (uncoupled from the engine propelling them, but coupled together in two lots) from one line of rails on to two different lines of rails; that is one lot going through one set of points on to one line of rails and the other lot going through another set of points on to another line of rails. The term 'Double Shunt' also applies to the case of an engine propelling wagons when the wagons are turned on to one line of rail and the engine turned on to another line.

Fly Shunt: This means that while an engine is drawing wagons attached to it towards a set of facing points, the wagons are uncoupled from the engine or from each other, and the engine, or engine and trucks, is run on to one line of rails, after which the following wagons are run on to another line of rails.

Double Shunting is strictly prohibited except when done by engines used specially for the purpose of shunting, attended by experienced shunters.

Fly Shunting is strictly prohibited unless the circumstances do not permit of the shunt being performed in any other manner, and, even then, the operation must be performed by an engine specially used for shunting and attended by an experienced shunter.

that is, there were buffer stops on all roads at the east end. During this period, the goods sidings were shunted at what was known as a 'flat yard'. This was the normal layout for goods yards in the United Kingdom.

Goods yards generally consisted of a series of sidings on either side of a main line. Trains were received on goods loops and/or reception lines. Usually the train engine was uncoupled and stood clear, whilst a shunting engine, or pilot, removed and added wagons as necessary. Wagons shunted into the sidings were pushed against others by the pilot, which marshalled the vehicles into new formations for other destinations. There was another method of shunting, whereby the wagons were uncoupled from the pilot, which pushed them rapidly into the siding and applied its brakes, leaving the wagons to run under their own momentum into the siding and against their train. This was known as 'fly shunting' and was not generally permitted. There was a gravity-assisted yard in the UK as early as 1873, that at Liverpool Edge Hill, but this type of yard was not common.

From the beginning, local trade sought to use the yard. Local quarry company the Ifton Limestone Company Limited, which had quarries immediately to the northeast of Rogiet between

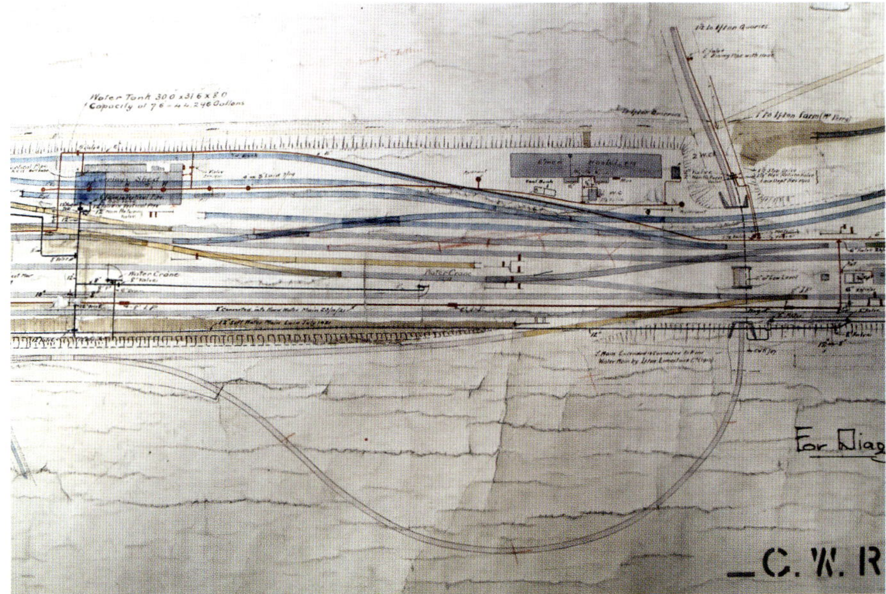

Extracted from an old GWR plan, this shows the junction at the east end of the station where the Ifton siding access the Up Gloucester line via a ground frame. It also shows the very sharp curve of the Ifton Limestone quarry line as it leaves the Ifton sidings and arcs round to pass under the GWR lines. Above the underbridge of the Ifton quarry line is the site of the old East ground frame.
WILTSHIRE HISTORY CENTRE

Rogiet and Caldicot, wanted rail access to the GWR sidings. They wrote to the GWR asking for an agreement to lay sidings for the transportation of limestone dug from their quarry. An agreement was drawn up dated 19 May 1901.

In this agreement, the Ifton Limestone Co., as the licensee, agreed to pay the GWR the sum of £1 on 1 January each year, by way of easement for the land over which the 'various junctions, sidings and works' were constructed. Two sidings – one a runround loop – were laid alongside the down platform at Severn Tunnel Junction station. A short, standard-gauge branch line led from the Down sidings, along the river side of the station, first turning due south, then curving back north on a radius of 240ft (73m) and passing under the main lines, after which it ran to Ifton quarry. At the east end of the quarry sidings a line ran up to and joined the up Gloucester line by means of a trailing connection. This connection was worked by a ground frame, released from Severn Tunnel Junction East signal box. There were gates at the western and eastern end of the quarry's lines. The quarry was in the press in 1908 when several ancient skeletons were discovered during quarrying operations. Traffic from the quarry was regular although never heavy.

World War I

We must now return to the earlier years of the twentieth century. Whilst the goods yards at Severn Tunnel Junction were working round the clock and the loco shed was proving to be a major employer in the area, other factors were coming into play. With the advent of war in France in 1914, many young men hastened to enlist in the army for the adventure, on the famous promise that it would be 'over by Christmas'. Railways were to play an important part in the conflict, both at home and abroad. The government took the railways under its control for the duration of the conflict and designated railway service as a 'reserved occupation'. This forbade railwaymen from signing up as they would be needed to run the trains at home, although many enlisted before the order banning them from joining up came into force.

Severn Tunnel Junction was not heavily involved in the war preparations as at that time it was not the huge employer it would later become. Nonetheless it was not possible to remain unaffected by the dreadful conflict; the massive casualty lists bore the names of so many young men that it was inevitable that everyone knew somebody who had lost a friend or relative. William Atwell was a

The original GWR Roll of Honour 1914–18, which once hung at Severn Tunnel Junction and is now at Norchard on the Dean Forest railway. AUTHOR'S COLLECTION

The war commemorative garden and plaque at Rogiet. AUTHOR'S COLLECTION

locomotive fire cleaner at Severn Tunnel Junction shed. He came from nearby Undy and was nineteen when he enlisted in the army. He died in France in 1915. Aubrey Blight of Portskewett had joined the GWR as a loco cleaner in 1912, when he was fifteen. His elder brother was a loco cleaner as well. Aubrey left the Great Western a year later in November 1913, and signed up for the Territorial Army 1st Battalion, the Monmouthshire Regiment.

Rifleman Blight died in Flanders in 1915. John Cox, a fitter's labourer at the loco who was lodging at Railway Terrace in 1911 with the Preece family, joined the 6th Battalion, the South Wales Borderers, and went to France. Private Cox was killed in France on 19 May 1916. William Jenner of the Traffic Department and son of a railway construction engineer also joined up with the 6th Battalion, the South Wales Borderers. He, too, was killed in action in France, on 10 October 1916. Charles Stringer, a 'shed sweeper' at the loco also went to France and was killed on 29 September 1917. Other railwaymen lost relatives. Bert Beasley was a shipbuilder, son of a GWR employee, a pumpman at Sudbrook. Bert died in France. Edwin Peach was a goods guard on the GWR at STJ. His son, Harry Peach, died at Flanders in 1915. Stanley Spencer, killed in France, was the son of a GWR platelayer. One who survived was Ebenezer Flook. Ebenezer served in the Royal Navy as Petty Officer during the war and afterwards until 1929. He was employed as a member of the loco department after his navy service.

All in all, 25,479 employees of the Great Western Railway joined up in the 1914–1918 war, and 2,544 men and boys paid the supreme sacrifice. After the war, the GWR made a Roll of Honour celebrating all Great Western employees who had laid down their lives for their country. Copies of the Roll of Honour were displayed at many railway stations across the GWR system. Many can still be seen at major railway stations today. The Roll of Honour once so proudly displayed at Severn Tunnel Junction 'lest we forget', is now displayed at the Dean Forest Railway museum at Norchard, near Lydney. Soldiers Cox, Jenner and Stringer are commemorated on the GWR Roll of Honour under the heading 'Severn Tunnel Junction'.

It's good that the roll is preserved, but sad that it (or a safely protected copy of it…) isn't on show at STJ station today, or at least, with the Rogiet community war memorial which is kept at the village sports hall. Yet, as gaining access to see the Rogiet memorial is very difficult – when I went there on a Saturday afternoon, everything was locked up apart from a stone plinth in the grounds and some memorial benches – perhaps the roll is best where it is.

Post-War Recession

Back at Severn Tunnel Junction, as the railways recovered from the war, freight traffic began to settle down to a routine again. Ifton quarry was still in business in 1920 when the GWR wrote to the company advising them that they wished to

**LETTER FROM IFTON QUARRY
CO. TO GWR**

Telegram 'LEX' Newport
The Ifton Limestone Company Limited, Kings Chambers, 67 High Street, Newport
9 March 1920
Quarries at Ifton Station: Severn Tunnel Junction
To: H. J. Balter esq, Great Western Railway Co. Divisional Superintendent's Office, Cardiff

Dear Sir,
In further reply to your favour (sic) of the 1st inst. We have the pleasure to assent and to thank you for your proposal that you should relay with heavier class material about 40ft [12m] of the siding inside the gate at Severn Tunnel Junction and that you also undertake the annual maintenance of this 40ft.
Yours faithfully, J. Guthrie
Managing Director

relay track at the western end of the sidings, presumably as heavier goods locos were now running on the GW system.

As the 1920s wore on, goods traffic increased and so did the siding accommodation at Severn Tunnel Junction. By 1921 the Down side included the two Ifton sidings. So far as the GWR and their proactive General Manager Felix Pole were concerned, things were ripe for improvement. Pole was a great modernizer and had been responsible for the introduction of new 20-tonne coal trucks in place of the old and obsolete 10-tonners. The Great Western ordered 1,000 new 20-tonne wagons and these were first delivered to Severn Tunnel Junction in 1924.

Sadly, optimism alone could not prevail when other factors were involved. The Royal Navy, for instance, had begun to abandon coal-firing of its ships in favour of fuel oil. Much of the coal had come from South Wales coalfields. This loss, in conjunction with the general post-World War I decline in coal exports from South Wales had a marked effect on the railway coal traffic. Frank Booker, in his book *The Great Western Railway – a New History*, reveals that by September 1924 the export of coal from Bristol Channel ports had

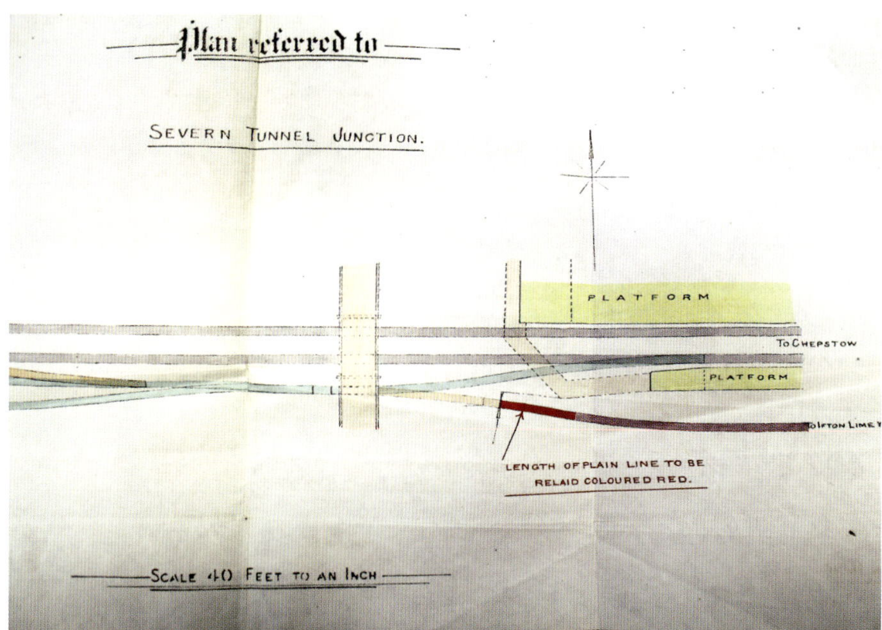

In 1920, this was all there was on the Down side east end at Severn Tunnel Junction. The Ifton limestone siding stands alone behind Platform 5. Note the Moors Road bridge. WILTSHIRE HISTORY CENTRE

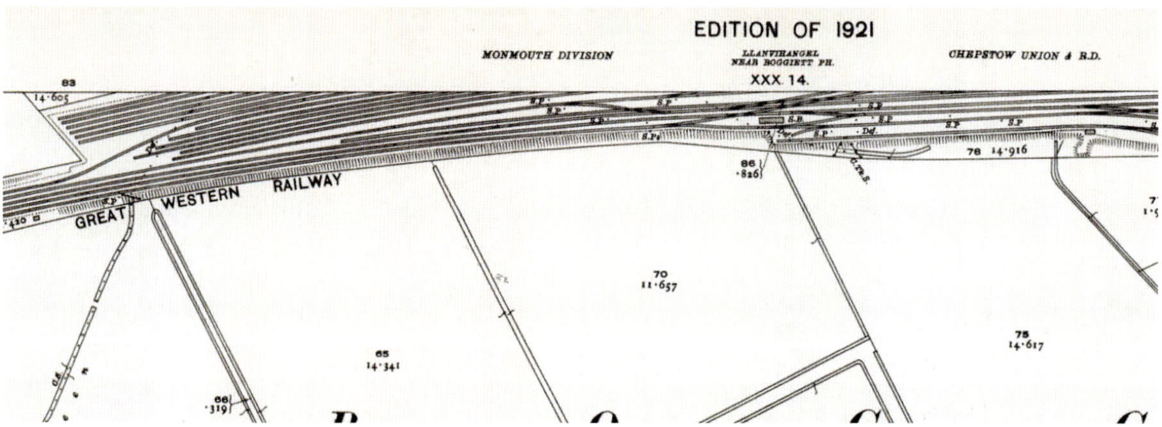

This OS map shows the extent of the western end of the Up yards in 1921. Note that there is not yet a hump yard. (Reproduced with the permission of the National Library of Scotland under a Creative Commons licence.)

fallen by 3 million tonnes. By 1926 the GWR as a whole had lost almost 6 million tonnes of goods traffic, much of it coal. There was also further economic downfall looming ahead in the shape of the Depression and 1926 General Strike (*see* Chapter 11). To add to the gloomy outlook, in October 1929 the Wall Street Crash caused stock markets to fall dramatically across the western world.

Because of the rather pessimistic economic outlook, the UK government introduced the Development (Loans, Guarantees and Grants) Act 1929, to finance schemes of work for the relief of unemployed men and to stimulate the economy. At Paddington the Great Western Railway identified a programme of works costing £8m over five years and, taking the view that it was better to 'speculate to accumulate', took advantage of the Act to finance alterations and modernization of facilities across the system. The decision was taken to improve the facili-

Nor did fortune continue to favour the Ifton Limestone Co. Before the decade was out, the traffic generated by the quarry had dropped off and they had ceased trading. The GWR Estates Office ascertained that the limestone company had ceased to trade and wrote to the railway company's Deeds Office advising them that the Ifton Limestone Co. had no longer any interest in their sidings at Severn Tunnel Junction.

Expansion

The land occupied by the limestone quarry sidings was needed for future Down side expansion. The GWR approached the quarry company to ascertain if they were likely to need the sidings and branch. If not, the Private Sidings Agreement (PSA) needed to be terminated. This was fortuitous for the Great Western's future expansion of the sidings accommodation at STJ. As the twentieth century began, over on the Continent, where there was more space for railway yards, they had invented the 'hump' yard. At this type of yard, trains were

ties at Severn Tunnel Junction by constructing a hump yard there on the Up side.

Based on Continental practice, this is what a modern British hump yard looked like: the massive Sheffield Tinsley Hump yard in the 1980s. TIM RENDALL

It's 1931 and the new Up hump yard at Severn Tunnel Junction is complete. This view is from the Undy end of the yard. It looks as if the points are all hand worked at this point in time. There's no Down side yard other than a few 'dead-end' sidings in the distance, but work appears to be taking place to extend the Down side facilities. AUTHOR'S COLLECTION

received at reception sidings, where they were broken up and wagons pushed up a short slope by the pilot engine. The pilot stopped at the top, leaving the uncoupled wagons to roll down the other side, where they were directed into their destination sidings by shunting staff; a type of legal fly shunting. This type of yard also had mechanical retarders, a sort of braking system to slow wagons down. Whilst hump yards were subsequently built in Britain, those fitted with retarders were not common.

Accordingly land west of Railway Terrace was purchased from the church commissioners and work commenced to clear the ground. With the land cleared and levelled, a hump was constructed with a base of old locomotive ash and earth and a fan of sixteen sidings was laid east of the hump summit. A thirty-five-wagon spur stood at the Magor end of the sidings. This spur ended close to the road north of Undy Crossing. From sources it would appear that all points in the new yard were at first hand operated. Later, a ground-level cabin was built and this was named 'Severn Tunnel Hump Yard West signal box' on some plans of the works, and 'Severn Tunnel West Yard Ground Frame' on others. According to GWR paperwork, this frame electrically controlled the west end entrance points to the new Up sidings.

A new Up goods loop was provided between Undy Crossing and Severn Tunnel Junction West. Trains for the yard pulled into the goods reception line and the wagons would be removed and pulled back into the spur, from where they would be shunted over the hump summit and onto the appropriate sidings. Pilot engines were paired with a small, four-wheeled wagon equipped with

EXTRACT FROM GREAT WESTERN RAILWAY GENERAL APPENDIX TO THE RULE BOOK, AUGUST 1936

Head and Tail Lamps on Shunting Engines and Shunting Trucks

Shunting engines, when at work in shunting yards, must carry a red light at each end, in front, at foot of chimney, and at rear on top lamp stand on bunker or tender.

Shunting trucks, where provided, must carry a lamp similar to the one which would be placed on the engine if no shunting truck were attached, and the shunter is responsible for seeing that the proper lamp is carried.

If a shunting truck is attached to a shunting engine, the tail lamp of the engine must be transferred by the shunter from the engine to the truck, where it will remain until the engine is detached from the truck, when the shunter must replace the lamp on the engine.

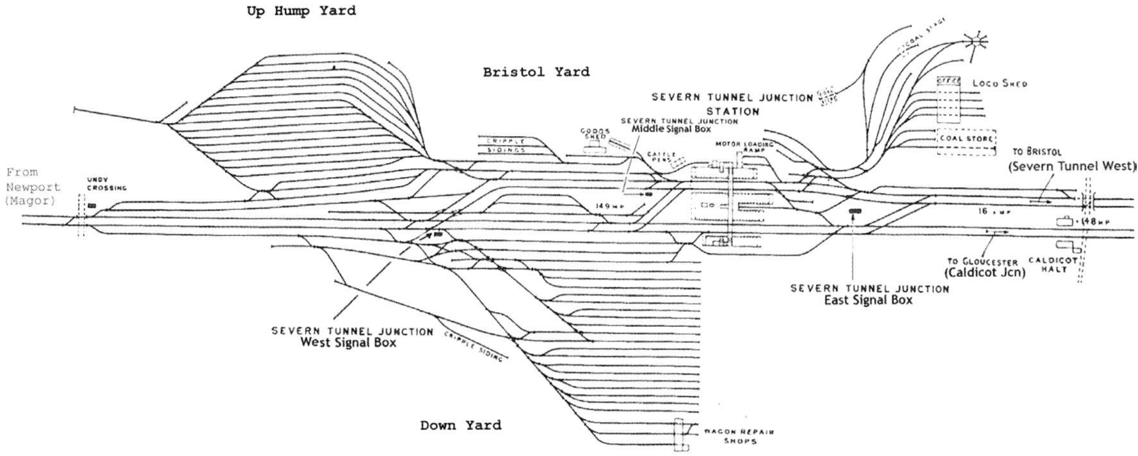

The complete layout at STJ after the Down sidings had been extended. They are still dead-end sidings though. BRITISH RAILWAYS

a tool locker and footboards. This was a shunter's truck (known at some yards as a 'backer' or 'jockey'). It contained shunting poles and brakesticks and the facility for shunters to ride on the footboards.

Wagons running loose into the siding would be followed by the 'runner' shunter on foot and wagon handbrakes – controlled by a long lever – applied by the shunter using his shunting pole or a brakestick.

The Down sidings were also expanded: from the three sidings there in 1901 and the twelve in 1921, further sidings in two sections west of the station platforms brought the Down side total to nineteen. The two sidings to the south side of the Down platforms, originally laid for the use of the Ifton Limestone Co., were officially known as the 'Ifton sidings' almost to the end of the yards, although the southernmost one later became the 'Down goods running loop'. There were also three additional sidings on the south side for wagon repairs at the works owned by the Bradbury Wagon Co. Previously accommodating 1,405 wagons, Severn Tunnel Junction now had the capacity for 2,652 wagons.

At this point in time, whilst the Up yard was a double-ended hump yard, the Down yard was still a dead-end yard.

The *Railway Gazette* of 8 December 1933 described the work as having permitted 'more economical working', as the freight traffic previously concentrated on several yards was now dealt with at one. The *Gazette* also pointed out that timekeeping of other traffic had improved owing to a reduction in occupation of the Severn Tunnel.

Severn Tunnel Junction was, therefore, now well on its way to eventually becoming the largest hump marshalling yard on the GWR system.

TOTAL CAPACITY OF UP SIDINGS AT SEVERN TUNNEL JUNCTION AFTER 1937	
Siding No. 1	65 wagons
Siding No. 2	65 wagons
Siding No. 3	60 wagons
Siding No. 4	70 wagons
	(or 56 clear of point C)
Siding No. 5	75 wagons
Siding No. 6	79 wagons
Siding No. 7	80 wagons
Siding No. 8	75 wagons

CHAPTER 4

World War II

Further Expansion of the Yards

During the 1930s, it was becoming obvious to many that, with the rise of National Socialism in Germany and the activities of Herr Hitler, another war was very likely. In 1937 a committee was set up to advise the railway companies on what steps to take in the event of air raids. The committee was named the 'Railway Technical Committee on Air Raid Precautions'. Its brief was to investigate and make recommendations on how to protect railway infrastructure and keep traffic moving during raids. A sub-committee was set up to advise on lighting. This was known as the Lighting Restrictions committee. Three levels of blackout were laid down after trials: Category A – total darkness; Category B – fully restricted; and Category C – exempted. In Category C, signal boxes, goods yards and passenger stations were to have lamps screened so that they would not show any light above the horizontal, colours should be between blue and green and should be sprayed with a dye which should last for the life of the bulb!

Other preparations for war involved alterations to the sidings accommodation with additional sidings being laid in at Severn Tunnel Junction. On 8 February 1937, Mr J. Wildsmith of the District Goods Manager's Office at Newport wrote to the Cambrian Wagon Works concerning the effect some alterations were to have on that company's accommodation in the Down sidings:

Gentlemen, Sidings, Severn Tunnel Junction. As you are aware, the scheme of alterations which this Company are carrying out at Severn Tunnel Junction, has involved the surrender of an agreed portion of the land held by you under lease from the Company and the slewing of the three sidings serving the wagon works, as indicated on the enclosed plan. In addition, at your request two of the sidings have been shortened to the extent of 66ft [20m]. The necessary document to provide for the surrender of the land is being negotiated with your Solicitors, but with regard to the variation in the siding layout, it is considered that the position will be met by an exchange of letters between us. I propose, therefore (subject to your agreeing) to attach a copy of this communication and the plan, together with your reply, to the siding agreements dated 29 March 1924 and 9 May 1930 with Bradbury, Son and Co. Ltd, which agreements were transferred to you by agreement dated 25 March 1936. I shall be glad to hear at your convenience that you agree the plan and the suggested procedure, when I shall be pleased to send you a copy for record purposes.

Close-up view of the Down sidings and loops, plus the Bradbury Co. Wagon works. WILTSHIRE HISTORY CENTRE

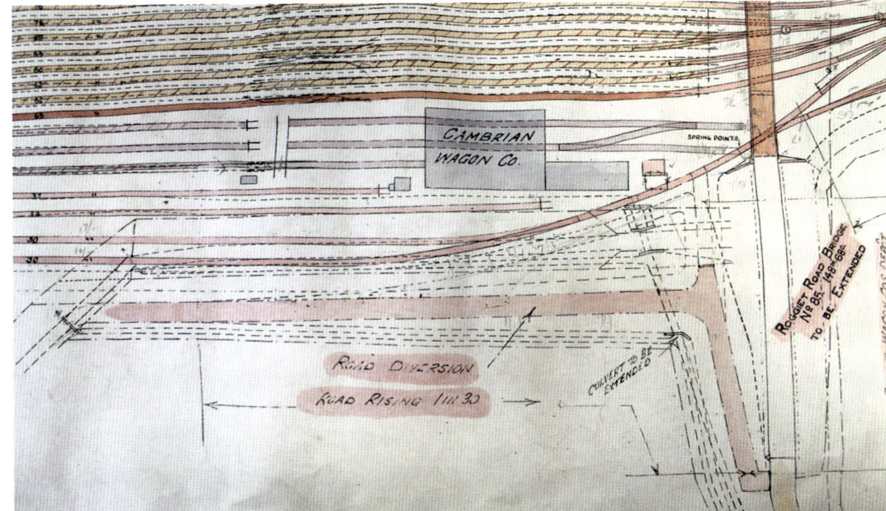

Plan showing the diversion of roads and alteration to sidings around the wagon works (now Cambrian Wagon Works) ahead of the eastwards extension of the Down yard. WILTSHIRE HISTORY CENTRE

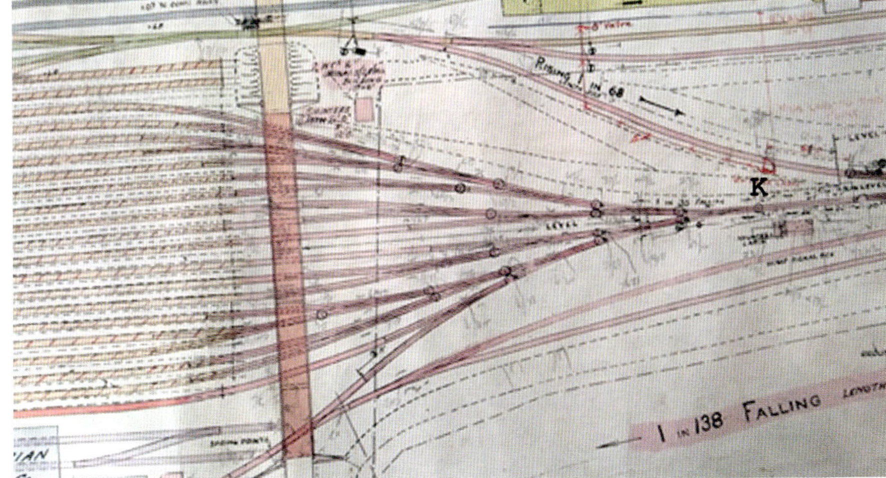

Plan showing the Down sidings extending eastwards into the hump 'summit'. WILTSHIRE HISTORY CENTRE

The Down hump control cabin seen here in 1982.
AUTHOR

Even in the preparations for war, the polite way of making agreements prevailed. The same would be unlikely to happen today. Sadly, the actual plan doesn't appear to have survived, but the plan shown here covers the content of the letter.

In preparation for the expansion of the yards, an area of land '2 acres, 3 rods and 17 poles' was purchased on the Up side of the line west of Railway Terrace – the latter row of houses becoming an oasis in a sea of railway sidings (rods and poles are old surveyor's measurements and are equal to 16.5ft or 5m). Here the Up side yard was extended to include six new dead-end sidings, accommodating an additional 392 wagons. Two extra sidings at the east end of this new layout contained eighteen and twenty-seven wagons respectively, making a total of 437 extra wagons. These new sidings were numbered 20–25 plus 26 and 27.

On the Down side the expansion was far greater. Three new reception sidings were laid at the east end of the station, accessed from the Down Gloucester lines. A new connection from the Up side east of the station led to the Ifton sidings behind Platform 5. A new Down hump was built close to the station. The Rogiet Road (Moors) bridge was extended southwards and the road realigned on the river side of the new extension. This was to accommodate extra sidings leading from the Down Hump to the Down yard, in particular those running behind the wagons works. The wagon works access road was also realigned. Dead-end Down sidings Nos. 3–18 plus one new road were extended eastwards to the hump. Siding No. 1 became a reception line and one stayed a dead-end siding.

The existing Down shunting spur was extended to Undy to form a Down goods loop.

New control cabins were built at both hump summits. Severn Tunnel Junction Down hump and Severn Tunnel Junction Up hump boxes both opened in 1939 and contained a Westinghouse Brake and Signal Co. control 'panel' with thumb switches rather than levers. These were both built from brick and concrete with flat roofs. They were not dissimilar to Southern Railway boxes constructed in the 1930s.

Defensive Measures

In September 1939, with the commencement of hostilities for the second time in twenty-one years, it was clear that Severn Tunnel Junction would be an obvious target for enemy bombers. Being of the opinion that enemy air raids would commence at once, the government placed restrictions on night-time lighting. In total blackout, working at a large yard such as Severn Tunnel Junction was fraught with danger. Signal wires and hand point levers became lethal in the dark, and hump shunting became a very dangerous occupation. Hand point levers were painted white and at the station, the platform edges were painted white.

With the main lines to South Wales, Gloucester and Bristol, plus the railway tunnel to be protected, some form of defence was needed. The consequences of bombs landing on any of the tunnel pumping stations, the junctions or blocking the tunnel itself would be massively disruptive to the war effort and economy. Accordingly, heavy anti-aircraft guns (HAA) comprising of 3in, 3.7in and 4.5in guns were positioned at Portskewett and Caldicot to protect not just the yards but the Severn estuary as well. Further defences were positioned at Shirenewton (Mynders Farm) near Crick – just above the Caerwent munitions factory. These guns and nearby searchlights were manned at first by members of the 45th Anti-Aircraft Brigade, but the 9th AA Brigade, formed from the Monmouthshire Regiment TA in November 1940, took over the sites. The 9th were responsible for the South Wales, Herefordshire and Gloucestershire areas.

The advent of war meant that some alterations were made to the loco shed as well. It had been common practice for loco fires to be dropped by shovelling the hot ashes from the firebox and throwing them on the ground. Naturally, the ashes would still be glowing and this was unacceptable in wartime. Precautions were taken. To the shed side of the coal stage, an 'ash shelter' was built. This covered two sidings and consisted of two brick walls approximately 6ft (1.8m) high, with the rest of the

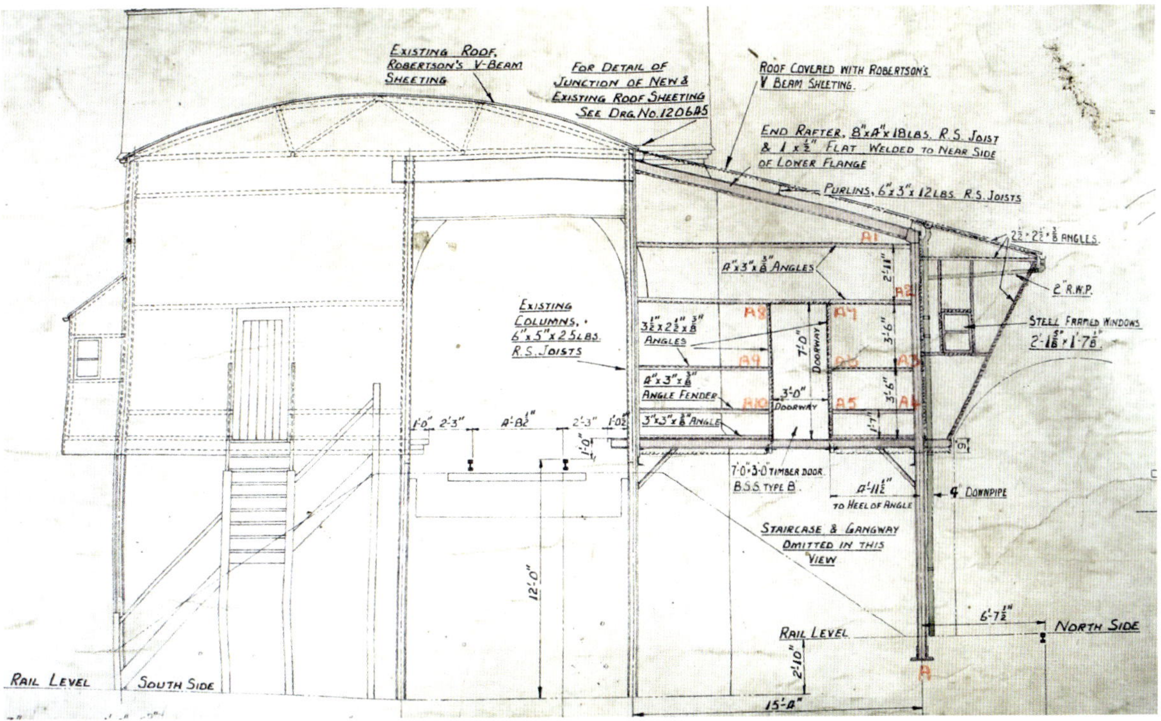

The plan of the extension to the coal stage in preparation for wartime traffic in World War II. WILTSHIRE HISTORY CENTRE

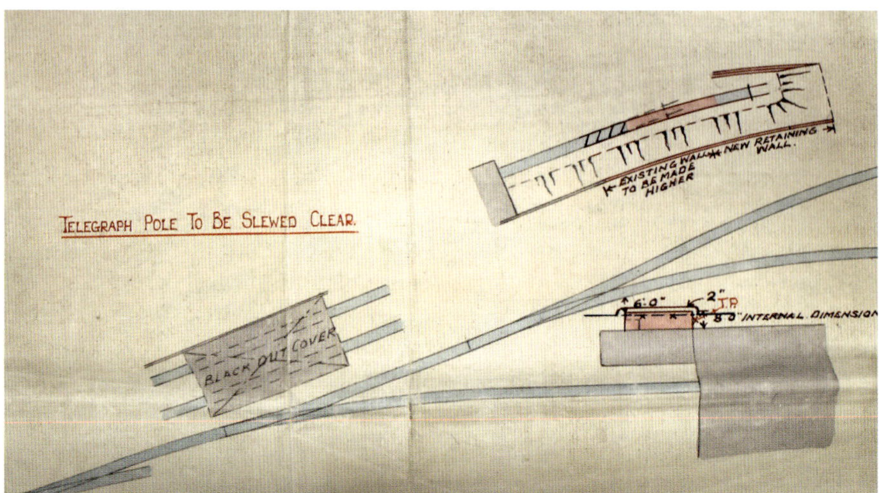

An overlay to the previous picture showing the ash shelter (blackout cover) and other alterations. WILTSHIRE HISTORY CENTRE

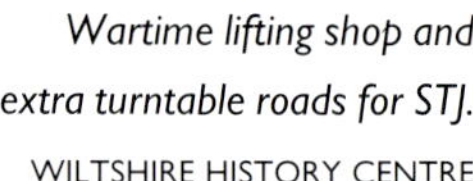

Wartime lifting shop and extra turntable roads for STJ. WILTSHIRE HISTORY CENTRE

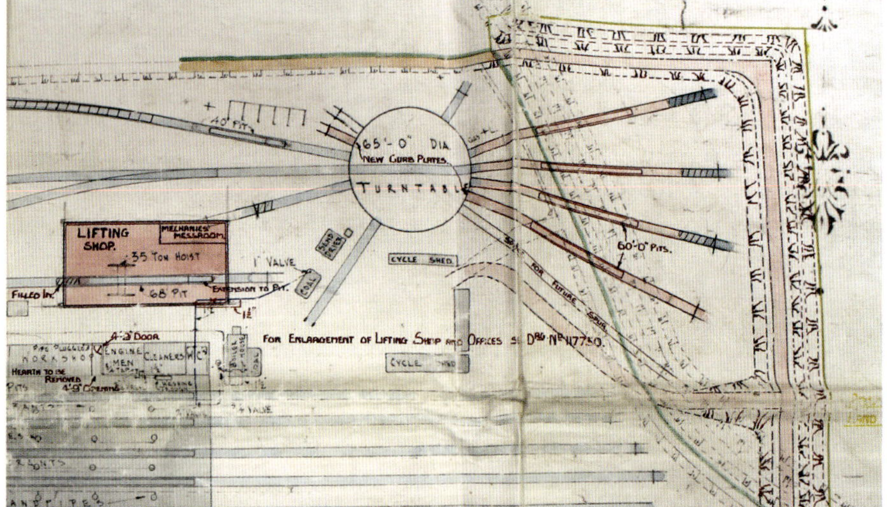

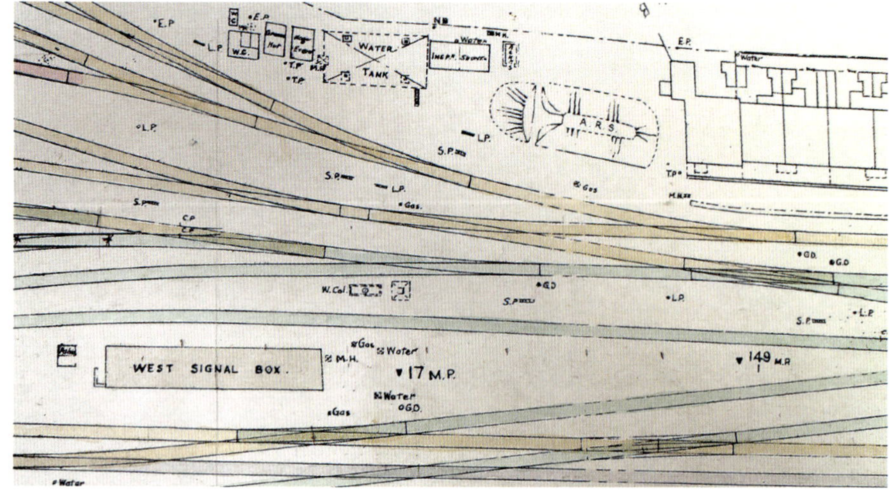

Provision of an air raid shelter adjacent to Railway Terrace. WILTSHIRE HISTORY CENTRE

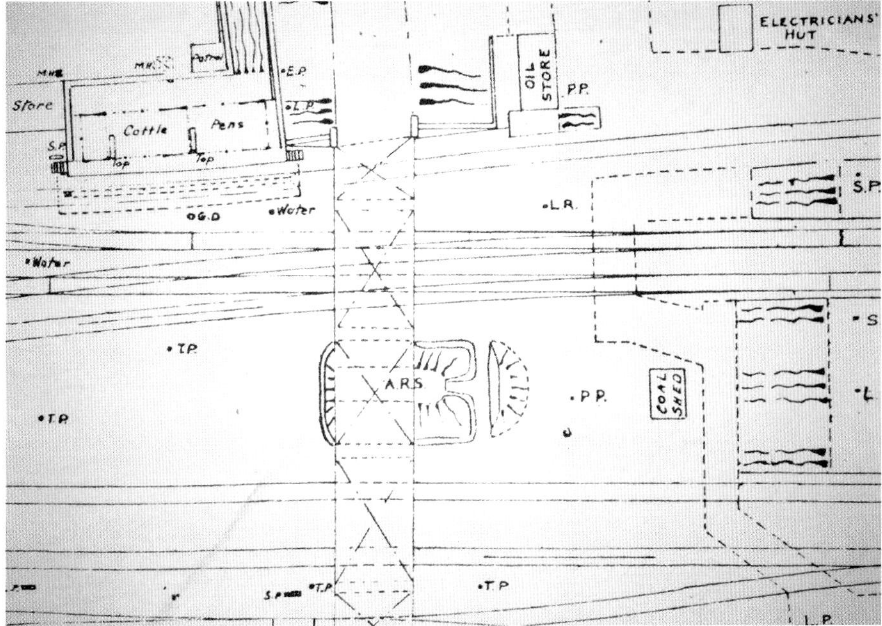

Provision of an air raid shelter right underneath Moors Road bridge at the west end of the station.
WILTSHIRE HISTORY CENTRE

walls and roof being made of corrugated asbestos sheets. Locos requiring their fire to be dropped or ash shovelled out would stand under this construction, the idea being that it would shield the glowing ashes from any enemy aircraft flying overhead.

Severn Tunnel Junction station, yards and the Rogiet community were in the flight path of Luftwaffe bombers targeting not just the railway, but Bristol, Newport and Cardiff as well. The huge goods yards were an obvious strategic target for German bombers and almost impossible to camouflage. Air raid shelters were built in and around the yards. One shelter was built under the road overbridge to the west of the station platforms, between the Bristol and Gloucester lines. Another was built to the south side of the lines, near to Severn Tunnel Junction West signal box and a third close to the Up hump summit. A further shelter was built close to the west end of Railway Terrace.

Wartime Works

During World War II around £6.5 million was spent on improvements to the national railway system. Around half of that went to the Great Western for the provision of additional tracks and sidings. Money was also spent on improving the engine shed at Severn Tunnel Junction and a new housing scheme for the Rogiet area. This included a new hostel to be built opposite Seaview Terrace, near the entrance to Severn Tunnel Junction station. This hostel was for the use of railway staff. Over a thousand men and women worked at Severn Tunnel Junction by the outbreak of the war. Duties for train crews were long and often meant long hours away from home. Sometimes these shifts entailed staying at the destination overnight and returning the following day with another train. This was known as 'double home' working. To accommodate trainmen, the GWR first stabled two sleeping coaches in the car dock adjacent to Platform 1, then built the new hostel for train crew. The hostel was a brick two-storey building and was run by a manageress and several female staff. One of the first manageresses was Evelyn Pole. Her staff included Ellen Miles, Margaret Reasden and Lucy Card.

In 1939, prior to the outbreak of war, a national census was taken and this reveals that two drivers, William Roper and Herbert Len, were staying at the old hostel when the census was taken. Four firemen were there as well: Gwyn Evans, William

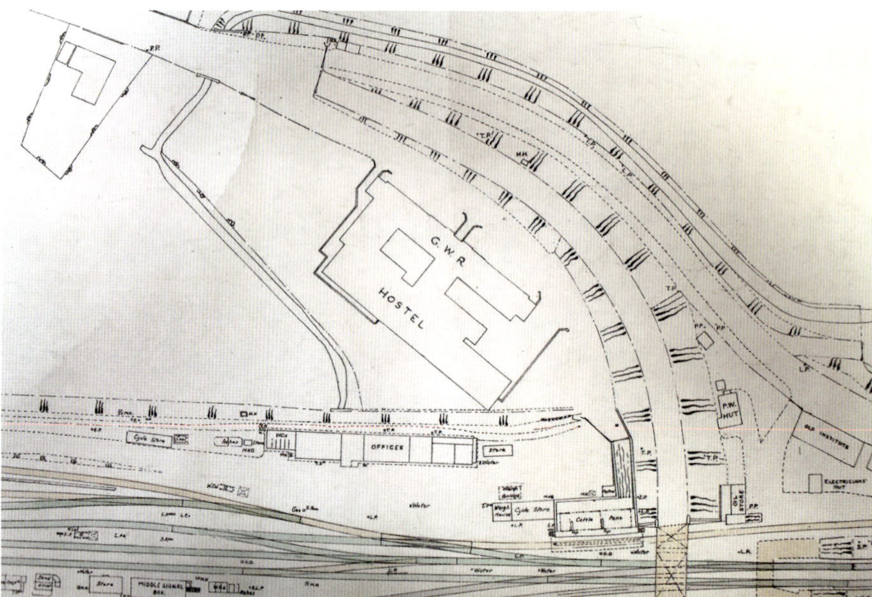

The GWR hostel built close to the yards and station approach road. WILTSHIRE HISTORY CENTRE

Southcott, Les Willmott and Herbert Broad. Guards Walter Thomas, William Allen and Francis Goodfellow were also there that day.

Signal Box Upgrades

Other wartime railway works involved the quadrupling of the main lines between Newport and Severn Tunnel Junction. This work entailed the provision of goods lines between Severn Tunnel Junction and Newport, necessitating new signalling works throughout. The existing signal box at Severn Tunnel East (on the English side of the tunnel) was replaced by a brick structure with a flat, reinforced concrete roof. This new box opened in 1942. The existing box at Severn Tunnel West was, for some as yet undisclosed reason, never replaced. The busy boxes at Severn Tunnel Junction East, Middle and West were also subject to wartime works. That at Severn Tunnel Junction East which had opened in 1906, was reconstructed as a brick and reinforced concrete structure with blast walls to protect the ground floor doors. It had its lever frame extended from 100 levers to 132 levers in 1938. Severn Tunnel Junction Middle box had been opened in 1901 and had 85 levers. It appears to have remained unaltered by the wartime changes.

Severn Tunnel Junction West box, which was the second box on its site when it opened in 1901

with ninety-one levers, had been extended in 1920 to allow for a longer lever frame of 130 levers. It was eventually replaced in 1945 by a much larger version of the ARP design at Tunnel East box, also with a concrete roof. It had 146 levers.

West of the goods yards stood Undy Crossing signal box, a timber structure originally from Margam Moors and opened in 1901 with an eighteen-lever frame replaced by a thirty-lever frame in 1930). This box was closed and replaced by another brick and concrete box on an adjacent site. The new box controlled the level crossing and the two new lines in addition to the existing main lines. It had a forty-seven-lever frame.

Further towards Newport was the small station of Magor. During the months of September and October 1941 a major change occurred when work commenced to quadruple the lines eastwards and westwards through Magor. The work was completed by September 1941, causing the platforms to become 'islands', which in turn necessitated the rebuilding of Magor station. The station building was replaced by a separate booking office built in the station yard. The signal box, built in 1884 with twenty-five levers, was extended to 23ft 8in long (7.2m) – almost double its original length – to accommodate a larger lever frame of forty-seven levers. The small level crossing to the east of

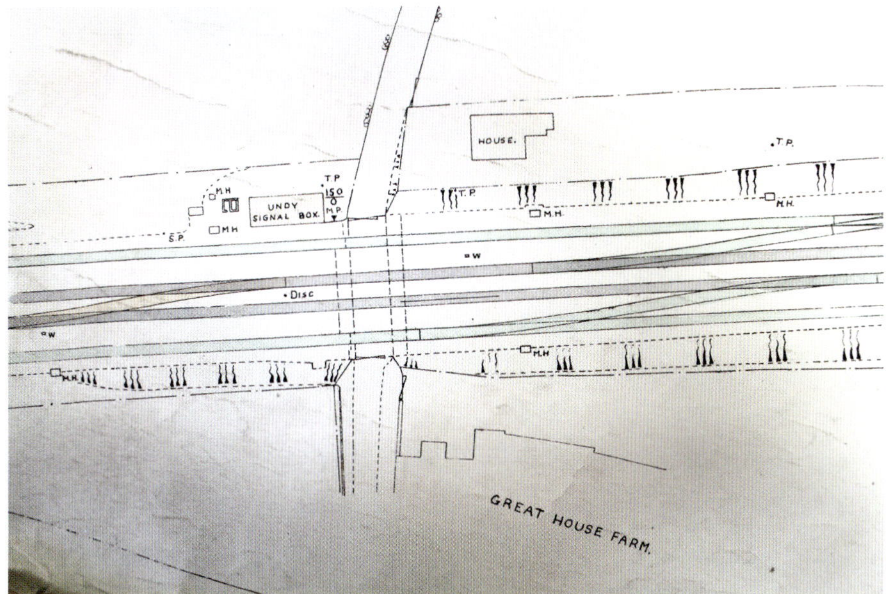

The wartime quadrupling at Undy Crossing: new running lines are in place and a new signal box erected on the west side of the crossing. WILTSHIRE HISTORY CENTRE

Magor station before quadrupling. Both platforms became island platforms when the new lines were laid in. AUTHOR'S COLLECTION

Bishton signal box. AUTHOR

Bishton level crossing. AUTHOR

Bishton level crossing gates: still there at the time of writing! AUTHOR

Magor station was closed as a result of the wartime quadrupling of the lines here.

Further west towards Newport, Bishton Crossing box (24 levers) closed on 2nd February 1941 and was replaced by a larger box which contained 38 levers and was named 'Bishton West'. This controlled the level crossing as well as the main and goods lines. Bishton East (21 levers) closed on 2 September 1941 as the quadrupling of the main lines progressed eastwards from Newport. Its functions were taken over by the new Bishton East box.

With all the extra traffic generated by the four lines and extra sidings, plus the need for ammunition trains to run from South Wales to England, the Severn Tunnel was once again a bottleneck to traffic. Trains loaded with domestic and loco-motive coal from South Wales coalfields rattled downhill into the tunnel and struggled up the steep incline on the English side. With both coal and express passenger traffic demanding prec-edence, the additional pressure of wartime traffic flagged up the need for some extra margin space between trains. Accordingly, the idea of installing intermediate block signals in the tunnel was born.

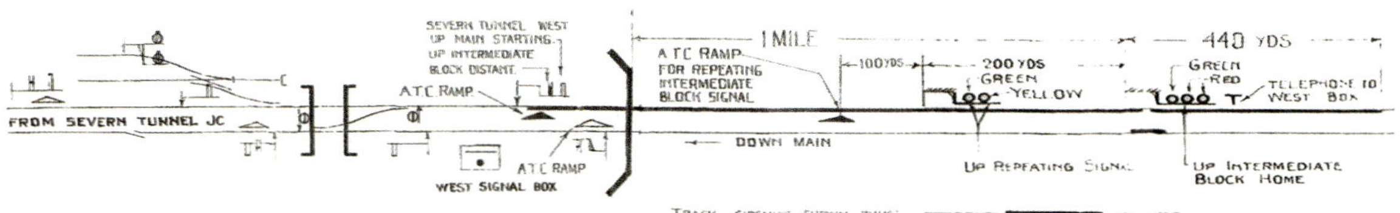

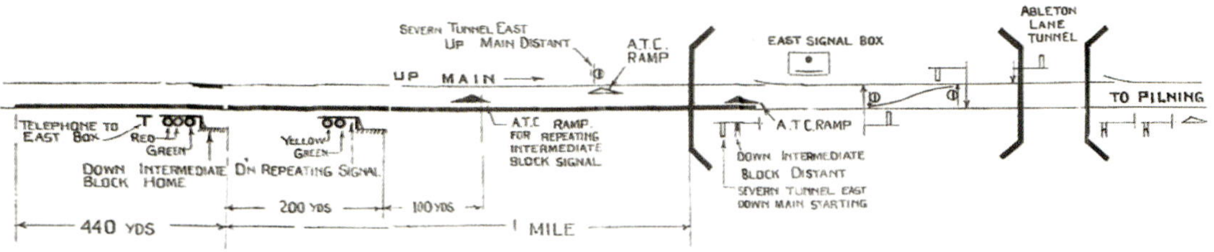

ABOVE TOP: *Wartime intermediate block signals in the Severn Tunnel: the west end layout.* GWR/AUTHOR'S COLLECTION

ABOVE BOTTOM: *Wartime intermediate block signals in the Severn Tunnel: the east end layout.* GWR/AUTHOR'S COLLECTION

This plan had been suggested before but had been swiftly dismissed. Collision in the tunnel, deep under the river, was a spine-chilling thought. The smoke generated by steam locomotives was always present in spite of extract fans, and it was not hard to imagine a train, steaming hard, the driver's view obscured by smoke and steam, missing a red signal and crashing into a stationary train ahead. Such catastrophe would block a major route and causes untold delays in wartime.

Nonetheless, plans began to be made for the installation of intermediate block signals (IBS) in the tunnel. In March 1943, at the new Severn Tunnel West signal box, the Up main starting signal, by the mouth of the tunnel, had a lower distant signal fitted below it. This was the distant signal for the new intermediate block signal, which was installed 1 mile (1.6km) into the tunnel. This signal, known as the 'Up intermediate block (IBS) home' was in the form of a three-lens colour light signal; the upper two lights being red, the lower aspect being green. Two hundred yards in the rear of this signal was a two-aspect repeater signal – green below yellow. The Up IBS home had a telephone communicating with Severn Tunnel West box.

In the opposite direction, a semaphore lower arm distant signal was fitted below the Down starting signal for Severn Tunnel East box. In similar arrangements to the Up line set-up, the Down IBS home signal, again a three-lens colour light signal, was installed 1 mile (1.6km) into the tunnel and had a two-aspect repeater situated 200 yards in the rear. In this instance, the telephone communication was with Severn Tunnel East box.

Both IBS home signals and their repeaters were fixed to the wall of the tunnel.

Safety Precautions and Contingency Plans

As a safety measure, the Severn Tunnel 'tell-tale' wire was extended into Sudbrook pumping station. The 'tell-tale' was a wire that ran the length of the tunnel, attached to the tunnel wall. In the event of a train becoming disabled in the tunnel or if a per-

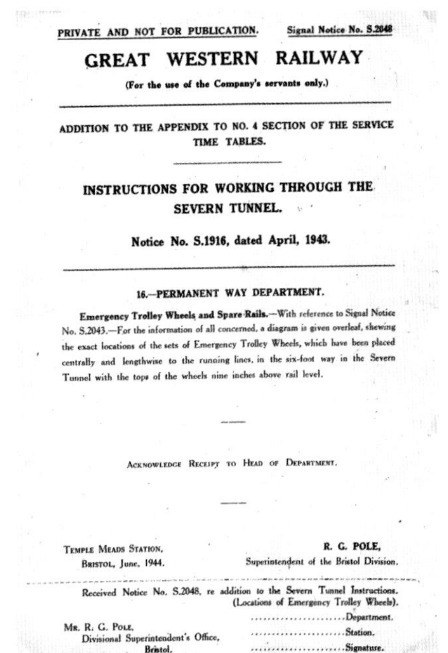

Wartime notice appertaining to the provision of emergency trolley wheels in the Severn Tunnel. GWR/AUTHOR'S COLLECTION

manent way patrolman found a problem, the wire could be broken. This would sound an alarm in Severn Tunnel East and West signal boxes and the signalman could alert the necessary authorities. The wartime extension of this wire into Sudbrook pumping station took place on 9 March 1941. The idea was that should enemy action disable the Sudbrook pumps, a member of staff there would cut the wire and this would alert the respective East and West signalmen, who would immediately stop trains entering the tunnel until they had ascertained the problem.

Another wartime measure was the provision of trolley wheels and base in the tunnel, to be used in case of emergency. The wheels were to be kept in the 'six-foot' – that is, between the tracks.

The GWR made plans for the diversion of trains in the event of lines being blocked by enemy action. If the lines between Severn Tunnel Junction and Newport became blocked, passenger trains running north and west between Bristol and Crewe via the Severn Tunnel would be diverted through Stoke Gifford, taking the Badminton

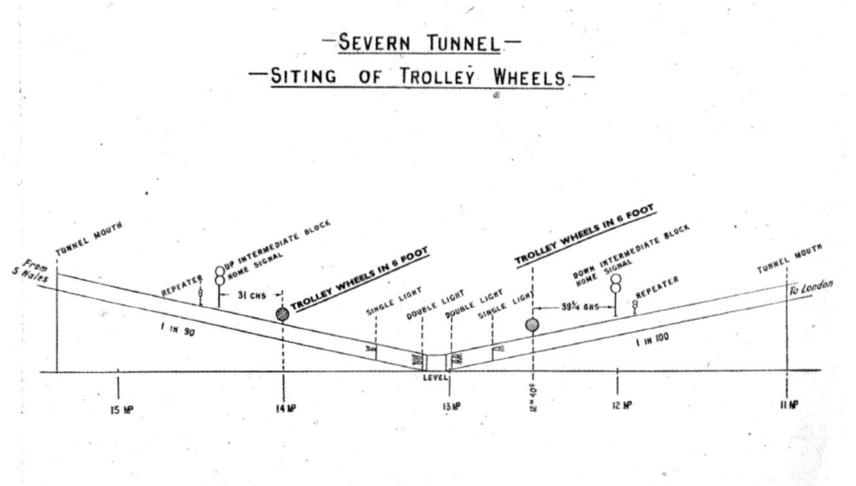

Wartime notice showing the location of emergency trolley wheels in the Severn Tunnel.
GWR/AUTHOR'S COLLECTION

route as far as Westerleigh West Junction, where they would take the spur to the LMSR Bristol–Gloucester main line to Yate. From Yate the trains would run via Gloucester and the Honeybourne line to Stratford-upon-Avon, Birmingham and Market Drayton to Crewe. Trains to and from Cardiff, which usually connected with the Bristol trains at either Pontypool Road or Hereford, would run independently between Cardiff and Crewe via Shrewsbury and Wem. Portsmouth–Cardiff services would run via Melksham and Swindon, to Gloucester, thence via Ross-on-Wye, Hereford and Pontypool Road.

Should the obstruction be at Severn Tunnel Junction itself, then trains to and from the Bristol and Gloucester lines would be diverted via Stoke Gifford, Yate, Gloucester, Ross-on-Wye and Hereford to Pontypool Road and thence to Cardiff and Newport. Some other services would be diverted to run via the Severn rail bridge, but as this was single line only, these diversions were restricted. There were locomotive restrictions on the bridge: the only GW locos permitted to work over the structure were 0-6-0 locos of class 2301–2360, 2381–2490 and 2511–2580, and 0-6-0 tank engines of class 2021–2160. In addition, locos were not allowed to work in multiple.

Elsewhere, diverted trains faced loco restrictions between Gloucester and Hereford via Ross-on-Wye; Castle, Saint and Hall classes were restricted to 20mph (32km/h) over these routes.

All goods trains were diverted according to control instructions. These diversions and restrictions needed to be taken into account in case an air raid resulted in a sudden blockage. For the yards at Severn Tunnel Junction, this could result in trains arriving the 'wrong way round' with traffic for, say, Newport, at the Bristol end of the train. There was also the loco watering and servicing to take into account.

Bombing 1940–41

This seems to be the appropriate place to look into often-repeated stories both in print (and more recently, in 2010 by a Network Rail director), which is that Severn Tunnel Junction yards and surrounding area were 'heavily bombed' during World War II. The director of Network Rail was quoted as saying that:

The £150m Newport area re-signalling scheme is set to deliver a twenty-first-century railway to South Wales and will also reverse the history of Severn Tunnel Junction. The railway around Severn Tunnel Junction suffered years of decline after it was bombed in World War II. While this work will significantly boost per-

formance, it will also provide the potential for more trains to travel through in the future.

That's an interesting statement, and totally incorrect; where he got the idea that the biggest marshalling yard in the west and Wales 'suffered years of decline' after being bombed in the 1939–45 war is a mystery. It is a statement that would lead people to believe that Severn Tunnel Junction yards suffered the sort of bombing that devastated German railway yards in the war.

That being the case, where are the reports and pictures of the devastation? Where are the images of the wrecked sidings, damaged locos, battered signal boxes? Where are the reports of the huge delays to rail traffic caused by the 'heavy bombing'? And where are the pictures and reports of damage to local properties? I spent many years mixing and working with railwaymen from both sides of the River Severn, from my mid-teens to the present day. I've spent time sitting in signal boxes and loco depots talking to old colleagues who have told me tales of the war years in Bristol and of the bombing of that city along with raids on Newport, Cardiff and Swansea. I've heard of raids on Avonmouth, but nobody has ever mentioned extensive bombing of Severn Tunnel Junction. Furthermore, William Winter's letter to staff at the

yards' closure mentions nothing about the area being bombed.

I have searched records and files; spent time with locals who have lived in Caldicot and Rogiet all their lives; talked with people whose families lived in the area: all have expressed surprise at the news that Severn Tunnel Junction was apparently 'heavily bombed'. The only reference I have found is in an online account of the war years by a local resident, Dennis Harper, who contributed to the BBC's WW2 People's War archive, and he only mentions that some bombs fell on the railway yards but little damage was done.

Had the yards and surrounding town been subjected to heavy bombing then one could reasonably expect a large amount of unexploded ordnance to lie in and around the railway there. A recent intensive survey carried out by private company BACTEC for the Newport M4 diversion, which was planned to commence close to the site of the Undy yard and run through an area south of Newport docks, found nothing. The report notes that the army had, in the past, looked into reports of unexploded devices south and east of the steam shed site but found nothing.

However, there's no doubting that the Severn Tunnel, STJ yards and loco shed, along with Sudbrook pumping station, *were* strategic targets for the Germans. Had any of them been badly damaged,

Seaview Terrace, Rogiet.
AUTHOR

St Mary's church, Rogiet.
AUTHOR

it would have caused severe problems for the railways in the area. There were some bombs dropped in the area: after the so-called 'phony war' period which occurred after the declaration of war in September 1939, air raids on Britain began in earnest. Bombs fell in the Severn Tunnel Junction area in August 1940. Some fell in 'the Minnetts', an area of woodland northwest of Rogiet. Others fell in or around the Bristol yard but caused little damage – some windows in the West signal box were shattered by blast. In this latter raid, at around 05.15 on the morning of Thursday 8 August1940, one bomb fell near Seaview Terrace, close to the Roggiet Hotel. A thirteen-year old boy, Grenville Pritchard, son of a GW platelayer, had left his bed during the blackout to go outside to see the searchlights at work. He was caught by the blast of the bomb and killed outright. His mother, Gwladys, a district nurse, was about to go on day duty when she discovered his body in the front garden. Grenville was buried in the graveyard of St Mary's Church, Rogiet, and his death is recorded under Civilian War Dead on the online Newport Roll of Honour.

Decoy Sites

So, why were the railway yards not damaged or destroyed during the Blitz? The answer may lie with the Caerwent munitions factory and Newport docks. The docks in particular imported large amounts of materials, and so the Luftwaffe raided Newport docks several times before switching to bombing the city itself. These raids caused much damage and loss of life. However, further research revealed that there were several 'decoy' sites between Severn Tunnel Junction and Newport. These were sites set up to decoy enemy aircraft away from strategic targets by simulating railway yards and towns and imitating the results of bombs being dropped. The idea was that the bombers would see what they thought were other bombs going off and fires starting and drop their bombs on them.

These sites stemmed from a 1939 meeting held at RAF Bomber Command HQ where it was decided that dummy targets would attract bombers and would result in less damage to railways and towns.

Accordingly, a national decoy authority headed by Colonel John Fisher Turner was set up in July 1940 and, following earlier experiments elsewhere, a system of urban lighting decoys was set up. The sites were known as 'Civil' sites: Civil 'QL' for urban lighting simulation, and Civil 'QF' for dummy fires. 'Q' sites were equipped with assorted electrical and pyrotechnical apparatus to simulate the flare given from furnace doors, steel-making, railway marshalling yards, and light given off by inefficient blackout precautions. Other sites simulated small fires started by incendiary bombs, while oil-storage fires were simulated near large oil installations. A further variation on fire decoy sites were the 'SF', or 'Special Fires' sites. A larger, longer-burning type of fire was provided at these sites – known as 'Starfish' sites – to draw incendiary bombs, and hopefully as a consequence the full enemy bombload, from falling on the larger towns, railway yards and defence installations during heavy air raids.

One of these decoy sites was set up at Blackdown, in the Mendip Hills, and simulated Bristol railway yards at East and West depots, Pylle Hill and Temple Meads. In the area of Severn Tunnel Junction and Caerwent there were nine such decoy sites between Undy and the western side of Newport. One was near the coast, south of Undy, and another closer to Llanwern. These would have drawn enemy air raids away from Severn Tunnel Junction and the eastern yards of Newport, as well as protecting the Caerwent factory. BACTEC's report says that in '1940 alone 'Q' and 'Starfish' sites received nearly 200 attacks. However no specific records listing enemy raids over Monmouthshire were located'.

Luftflotte 3 of the German Air Force was responsible for attacking ports and airfields in the west of England and South Wales, prior to the concentrated attacks planned for 14 August 1940, raids that were intended to begin the destruction of the Royal Air Force ahead of Germany's invasion of Britain. Records show no concentrated attacks on any targets in the area on the night of 8 August, although there were a few nuisance raids across the country. It's possible that the bombs came from an aircraft intending to raid shipping in the Bristol Channel but jettisoned its bombs over land after finding no target. Another possibility is that the bombers may have seen the decoy site on the coast near Undy and bombed that, thinking it was Newport docks or Severn Tunnel Junction. Bombing at that stage of the war was not very precise and bombs aimed

in a hurry at the decoy may well have overshot the 'target' and landed close to the Bristol yard.

As the Luftwaffe were intent on bombing Avonmouth docks on the English side of the Severn, plus Newport and Swansea as well, there was, in the early years of the war, much enemy air activity over the Severn estuary and the South Wales coast on most nights, but initially these were reconnaissance or just nuisance raids. In January 1941 and continuing into February, heavier raids were carried out by the Luftwaffe against Cardiff and Swansea.

After a busy period for the anti-aircraft defences of South Wales in early May 1941, the main Blitz ended in the middle of the month, although sporadic nuisance raiding continued through June and July. The gaps in AA defences were now being rapidly filled as more equipment and units became available. Searchlights, now assisted by searchlight control (SLC) radar, were reorganized, with a 'Killer Belt' established between the Cardiff and Bristol (the 8th AA Division). In May 1942, further bombs fell in an area north of Rogiet known as Dewstow Road. These were initially thought at the time to have been aimed at Severn Tunnel Junction railway yards. However, in later years it was discovered that, rather than being an intentional raid on the yards, the bombs were dropped by aircraft attempting to bomb Avonmouth on the English side of the Severn. Seven Heinkel 111 bombers had made their way to Avonmouth in bad weather. One was shot down and the other six lost their way in the cloud and rain. Thus it was that the nearest they got to bombing Avonmouth docks on this occasion was farmland at Rogiet.

Many trains that passed through STJ carried prisoners of war to the many POW camps in South and Mid Wales. There were two such camps near Rogiet, one at Chepstow and one at Llanmartin, near Magor. Two other camps existed at Abergavenny.

During the war, a goods train was derailed near Undy and one of the damaged wagons contained bananas – these were eagerly seized on by the local children!

STJ Staff in the War

As with the 1914–18 conflict – only twenty-one years previously – railwaymen were generally held in a reserved occupation status. However, many did go to war and several failed to return, killed in action. Roy Edwards was employed as a loco cleaner from July 1939 to December 1940, when he became an acting fireman. He joined the merchant navy in 1942 and was killed when the SS *Empire Mica* was torpedoed and sunk by a U-boat off the coast of America on 29 June 1942. Another possible victim of the war was a man who had been a greaser at STJ since 1934, becoming a loco cleaner in 1936 and fireman at another depot in 1938. He served in the armed forces from 1939 to 1947, when he returned to the GWR. However, he failed his rules exams several times and was given a job as shed labourer. His records note that he was 'not to lose his seniority'. It can be surmised that his war service may have affected him and he was given a job with no loss of seniority by a sympathetic management.

Glyn Clements joined the GWR in 1936 as a loco cleaner at Severn Tunnel Junction shed. In 1938 he became 'acting fireman' for a few months before resuming his cleaning duties. When war came, many staff were moved to fill position left by those who had joined the forces or were needed to fulfill jobs that had come about as a result of the growing war effort. In May 1939 Glyn was posted to Honeybourne to fill a fireman's vacancy, returning to STJ shortly afterwards.

Another man who was moved away was Roy Nancekievill. Roy, like many other young men, joined the GWR in 1941 as a cleaner. Eight months later he was made up to fireman and sent to Hereford. He returned to STJ in December 1941. Len Foster, who joined in 1937, spent some time as a fireman at Banbury before returning to STJ, where he eventually became a driver. Rob Hollway went to Gloucester in 1941 as a fireman; he stayed there for two years before coming back to STJ. Arthur Sheppard of Magor spent two years at Bristol as acting fireman. He managed to move back to STJ in 1942. William Duddridge, who joined as loco cleaner in 1937, was transferred to Newport Pill shed as acting fireman in early 1939. He was moved to Bristol in September 1939 and back to Newport Pill again in April 1940.

Other railway staff served in the Home Guard or as Air Raid Prevention (ARP) wardens. Such a post was filled by Caldicot Road resident Harry Carter Selwood, a shunter at the yards by day and ARP warden by night.

Many railway staff lived in Rogiet as mentioned above, but others lived in Caldicot and Undy. Still more were temporarily housed in the GWR hostel, which was sited on the station approach road, almost opposite Seaview Terrace. The roads in Caldicot where railway staff lived were almost as full of railwaymen and their families as those in Rogiet. In 1939, in The Avenue in Caldicot, a road of neat short terraces of houses and semi-detached homes, lived Charles Edwards, engine driver, Albert Raffill, yard inspector, Thomas Davis, driver, David Wallis, loco fitter and Harry Higgs, guard. Drivers Charles Fowler, William Lovesay, George Terry, Richard Smith lived here as well, as did firemen Wyndham Lockyear and Arnold King. Retired drivers Jim Crowley and George Gillins were residents, as were fitters George Langham and Gilbert King. Shed labourer Phil Holloway lived here too.

Arthur Stanfield Williams lived in Ferney Cross, Caldicot in 1939 with his family. Williams was employed as a shunter at the yards.

> **GWR INSTRUCTION FOR TRAIN DRIVERS, 1942**
>
> GREAT WESTERN RAILWAY
> ENGINE WHISTLES – SEVERN TUNNEL WEST
> Drivers of trains for the Badminton line must give two whistles when passing Severn Tunnel WEST box.
> This amends the instruction shown on page 32 of the Appendix to No. 4 Section of the Service Time Tables.
> R. G. Pole
> Divisional Superintendent's Office
> Bristol. August 1942

CHAPTER 5

Severn Tunnel Junction Yards 1945–87

One of the first things to be done after the war was to remove the intermediate block signals in the tunnel. This was undertaken on Sunday 11 May 1947, when all the IBS signals, their repeaters and ATC ramps were removed. Train operating instructions were amended accordingly.

By the late 1950s, a new source of traffic for the yards was being planned and this would bring a large increase in work. Richard Thomas & Baldwin Company Ltd were planning to build a steelworks on a new site at Llanwern, south of the main lines between Magor and Bishton. The site was extensive and ranged over 3 miles (5km).

Work began in 1958 and was completed in 1962. Known as 'RTB' and then the Spencer works, the steelworks – an 'integrated' steelworks that comprised a blast furnace and coke oven complex, hot and cold continuous strip mills and galvanizing plant – was expected to generate over 1 million tonnes of steel per year. This was to be made on site, and finished products such as steel coil and hot-rolled strip steel would be going out. Together with Port Talbot works, at its height of output the plant produced up to 3.5 million tons of hot-rolled steel strip per year. Plate steel going out was transported directly to the Midlands car construction

Stanier 8F No. 48415 heads west through Cardiff station with rolled coil steel from the Spencer works. AUTHOR'S COLLECTION

Rolled coil steel is heavy, so is loaded over the bogies.
AUTHOR'S COLLECTION

industry or to places like Shotton for coating, to Trostre works at Swansea for tin plating and to Ebbw Vale for rolling and coating.

The steelworks traffic was marshalled at Severn Tunnel Junction yards. Plans were made for 3 million tonnes of coke per year to be imported through Newport docks, to be transported to the steelworks along with other raw materials coming in.

Naturally, all this new traffic would need extra accommodation at Severn Tunnel Junction and new works were carried out to take the extra wagons.

Expansion in the Early 1960s

BR staff and management morale was high, mostly on the back of the 1955 modernization plan and the subsequent new fleet of steam locomotives. Coal was still a staple of traffic through Severn Tunnel Junction; both the locomotive department and domestic markets for coal ensured a steady flow of coal traffic into England from South Wales. Steel, oil and other imports from Newport docks were also moved through STJ and the tunnel. Raw materials and other traffic such as pit props flowed into Wales. There were three main routes into and out of South Wales for this traffic and Severn Tunnel Junction served two of them – via Gloucester and Lydney and via the Severn Tunnel. The third route was via Hereford.

Severn Tunnel Junction was one of five large marshalling yards in South Wales at this time, the others being at East Usk and Alexandra Dock in Newport on the main line; Pontypool Road on the Hereford line and Rogerstone on the west side of Newport. Although a new hump yard was planned for Margam, Severn Tunnel Junction was the largest WR hump yard at that time.

Undy Works

As if the yards weren't large enough already, in the wake of the British Railways modernization plan, plans were made to expand the yards further. Land west of Undy Crossing was acquired and was to be used for the building of a new yard of reception sidings. Undy level crossing was closed. The ground was built up to rail level using mining waste and ash from locomotive depots. New sidings were laid and in July 1960, work began to connect these to the existing layout. At the same time, other changes to the layout were to be carried out.

Accordingly, work commenced on Sunday 10 July 1960. On the Up (north) side, at the Up hump yard, a new engine release line was laid in prior to the work commencing. This led from the existing Up hump reception line to the existing No. 1 Up reception siding. For the time being, this was maintained out of use. The existing Nos. 2, 3 and 4 Up reception sidings were connected to the hump yard sidings. These, too, remained out of use until they could be connected to the Up hump control cabin.

At Undy Crossing, the wartime signal box was closed and all associated signalling taken out of use. All points previously worked by the box were taken out of use, except those leading from the No. 2 Down goods running loop to No. 1 Down goods running loop. These were disconnected from Undy box and worked temporarily by a hand signalman.

Still at Undy but further towards the existing yard, new crossovers were laid in between the engine line and the Up goods line near the existing Undy ground frame. These points remained out of use for a few hours after installation. Eventually, Undy ground frame was recovered and the facing connections there to the Up reception were clamped out of use. All other points worked by the old ground frame were recovered. The existing Up reception line was taken out of use and would later be reinstated as No. 2 Up goods line.

To the west of Undy and opposite the water tank on the Magor side of Church Road bridge, a new facing connection was laid in on the Up goods line. This connection led to ten new reception sidings and a hump engine return line. At first the new connection was temporarily worked by a hand sig-

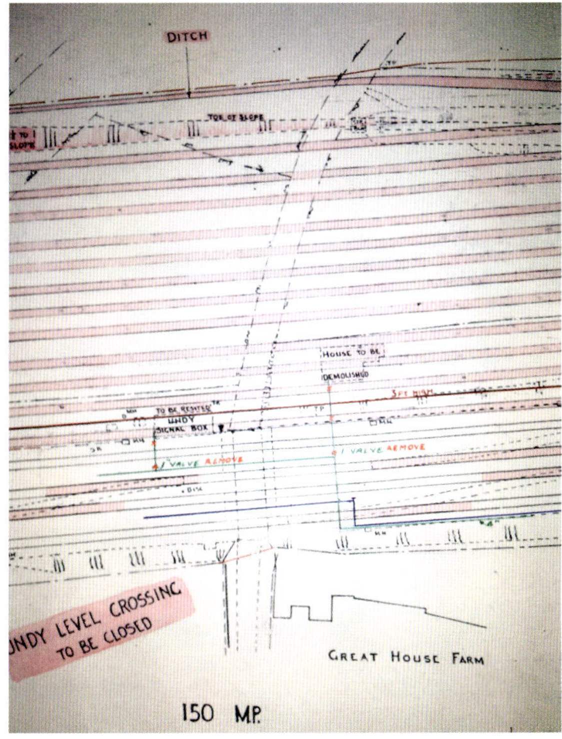

BR 1958 plans for the creation of the new Undy yard. The crossing was to be closed and the old crossing keeper's house to be demolished. The wartime Undy Crossing signal box was to be resited but it never was, being demolished instead. WILTSHIRE HISTORY CENTRE

The layout at Undy Crossing before it was closed. SIGNALLING RECORD SOCIETY

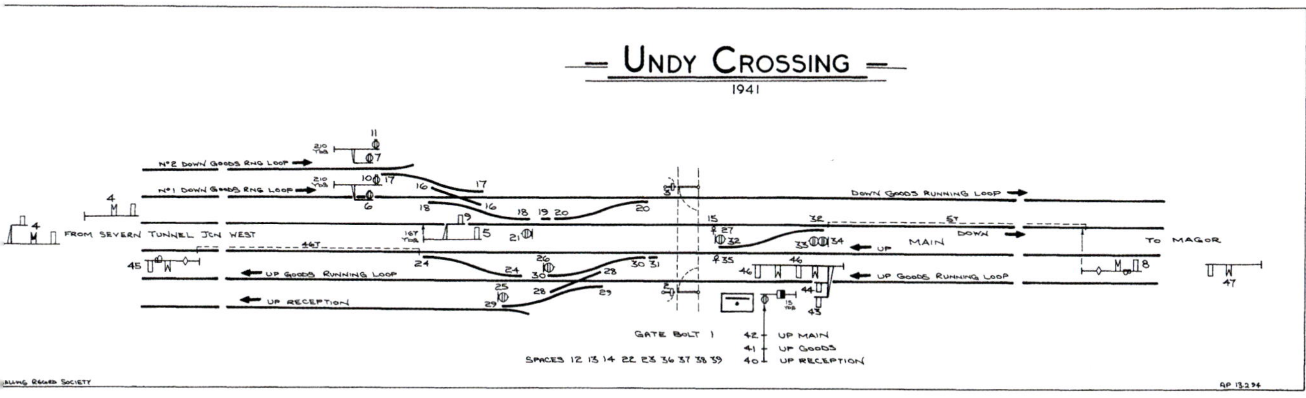

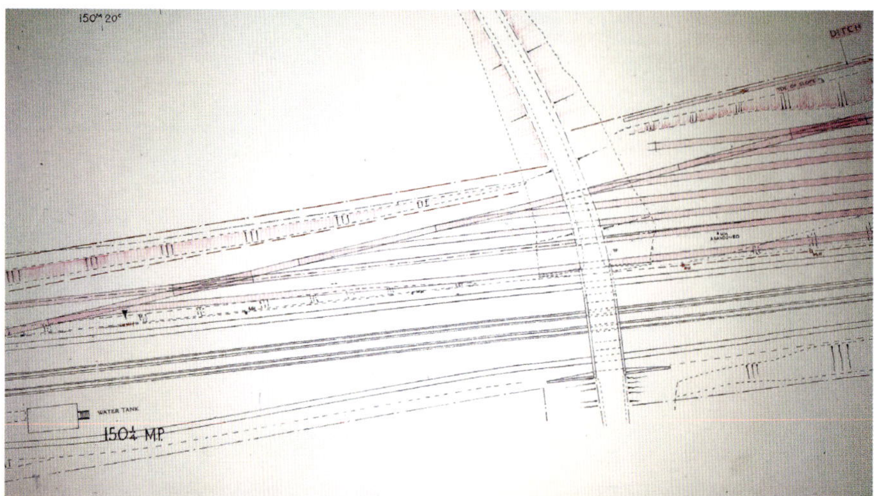

The new entrance to the Up side yards. This is 0.75 miles (1.2km) further away than Undy Crossing. The water tank for Magor troughs is indicated. WILTSHIRE HISTORY CENTRE

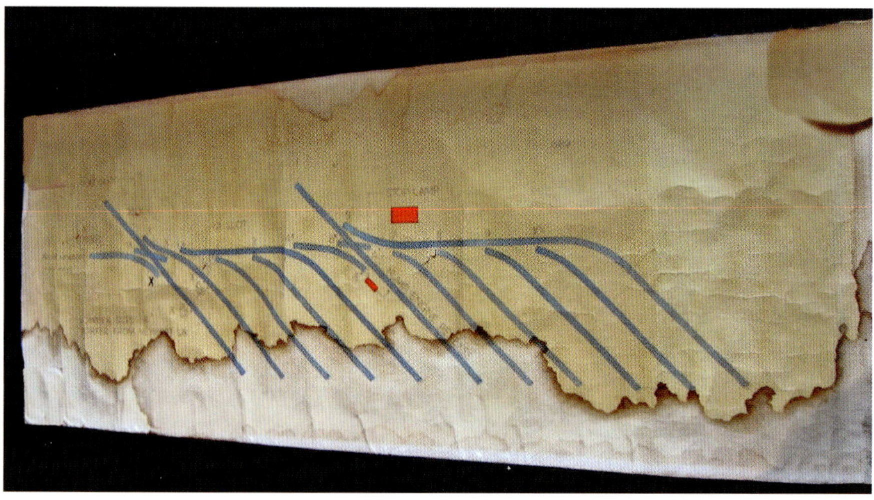

The signalling diagram from Undy ground frame: the main line connection is on the lower left-hand corner. The diagram has been damaged by water after closure of the yards. STEVE SHARP

nalman who was required to use a bar to move the points, clipping (clamping) them after each move. This was because they were initially not connected to a signal box. By the end of the weekend they would be connected to, and operated from, Magor signal box.

A new Undy ground frame was installed. This was in effect a ground-level signal box in all but name. Constructed in similar fashion to the (then) latest BR 'Type 37' signal boxes, it had a short brick base on which the wooden structure was built. It contained a lever frame of twelve levers. Although officially named 'Undy ground frame', this structure was always known to staff as 'Elmsbridge', after the local name for nearby Church Road overbridge.

This new yard was known as the 'Undy yard' and the ten new reception sidings held 582 wagons.

A casualty of the work was a small house that stood east of the road leading to Undy crossing and north of the main and goods lines. This house was originally built for the Undy Crossing keeper in the early days of the South Wales Railway. It was similar in design to crossing keeper's houses built elsewhere, such as those at Green Lane and Ableton Lane crossings on the Pilning–Severn Beach line near Avonmouth. Now, however, the new reception sidings were to be laid here and the house, like Undy signal box, stood in the way. Both were demolished.

Changes to Sidings

Throughout the yards, water cranes and hydrants were resited, shunters' and examiners' cabins moved and some of the old air raid shelters were demolished. In the existing Up reception sidings, Nos. 19 and 20 sidings were to become dead-end sidings and were provided with buffer stops at the Undy end. Access to the Up hump was no longer possible from these sidings. Siding No. 21 was lengthened and also became a dead-end siding. Sidings 22 and 23 were lengthened and would become part of the new storage sidings. A new connection at the east end of No. 23 siding led to a further five new storage sidings, making ten in all. The ten new Bristol yard storage sidings would be brought into use at the end of the work. These could accommodate 712 wagons as follows:

No. 1 storage siding: 57 wagons, loco and brake van

Nos. 2 and 3 storage sidings: 80 wagons, loco and brake van

No. 4 storage siding: 84 wagons, loco and brake van

No. 5 storage siding: 81 wagons, loco and brake van

No. 6 storage siding: 76 wagons, loco and brake van

No. 7 storage siding: 68 wagons, loco and brake van

Nos. 8 and 9 storage sidings: 59 wagons, loco and brake van

No. 10 Storage Siding: 68 wagons, loco and brake van

These sidings were officially designated 'Up storage sidings' but were always known as the 'field sidings', even appearing as such in later working timetables.

A new, trailing, connection was laid leading from the existing Up goods running loop to No. 2 Up goods line. It remained temporarily out of use. The Up goods running loop was renamed 'No. 1 Up goods line'.

Stop lamps were provided at the Magor end of the hump engine release line and at the hump summit – where they applied respectively to the summit outlet of the Up reception sidings and the hump engine return line. Moves beyond the Magor end stop lamp were controlled by the reception sidings shunter, and those of engines released from incoming trains, by the Up hump foreman.

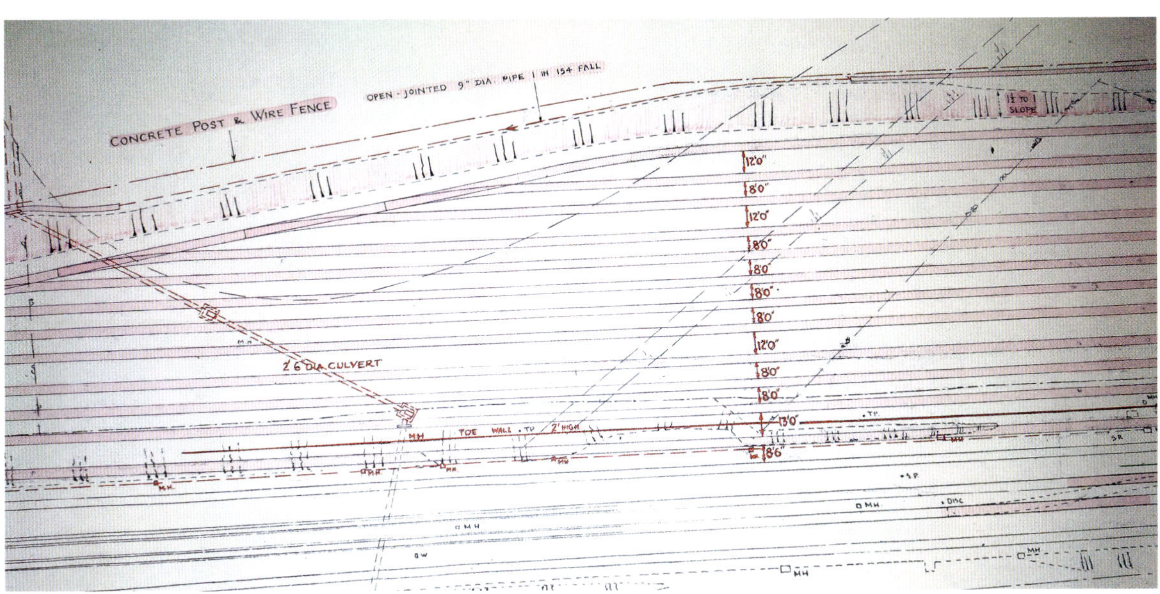

The BR 1958 plans for the new Undy yard. WILTSHIRE HISTORY CENTRE

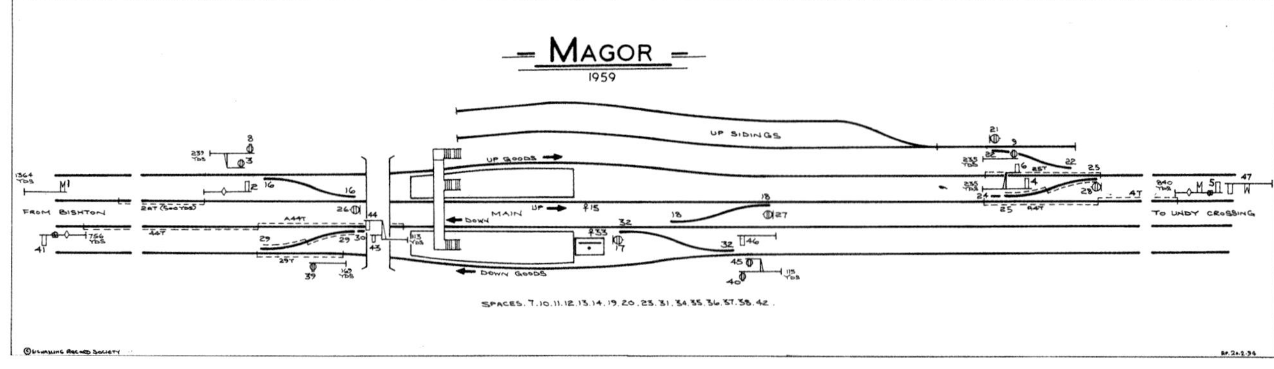

The signalling diagram from Magor box, after wartime quadrupling. SIGNALLING RECORD SOCIETY

At Severn Tunnel Junction West signal box, all levers were temporarily placed out of use and the interlocking 'disarranged' by technicians. All points were disconnected from the box and temporarily worked by hand signalmen. Hand signalmen were also appointed to give verbal instructions to drivers of trains stopped at signals which were fixed at Danger for the duration of the work. Six new storage sidings were laid in on the Down side, east of the station and connected to No. 3 section shunting spur. The new sidings could accommodate 383 wagons in total.

Here, too, movements were controlled by a new stop lamp. The signalman at West box had to give permission before moves could be made past the stop lamp from the engine road and No. 1 Up goods line towards the hump summit.

At the exit of No. 3 section shunting spur and the outlet of the six new sidings, noticeboards were provided which read: 'STOP. Telephone for instructions.' Movements beyond these boards towards the signal that controlled access to the Down goods loop could only be made with the permission of the signalman at Severn Tunnel Junction West box.

At the end of the work, new point motors, manufactured by the Westinghouse Brake and Signal Co., were fitted to points leading from the Up goods line to the Up main; from the hump reception line to No. 1 Up goods loop and from the Down goods loop to the Down goods line.

Some lines had been renamed: No. 2 Down goods running loop became the Down goods loop; No. 1 Down goods running loop became the Down goods line; and the Up goods running loop became No. 1 Up goods.

Changes to Signals

Many signals were altered, replaced or renewed as a result of the work. To list every signal change would be inappropriate here, so these are just the main line signal alterations. At Magor, that box's

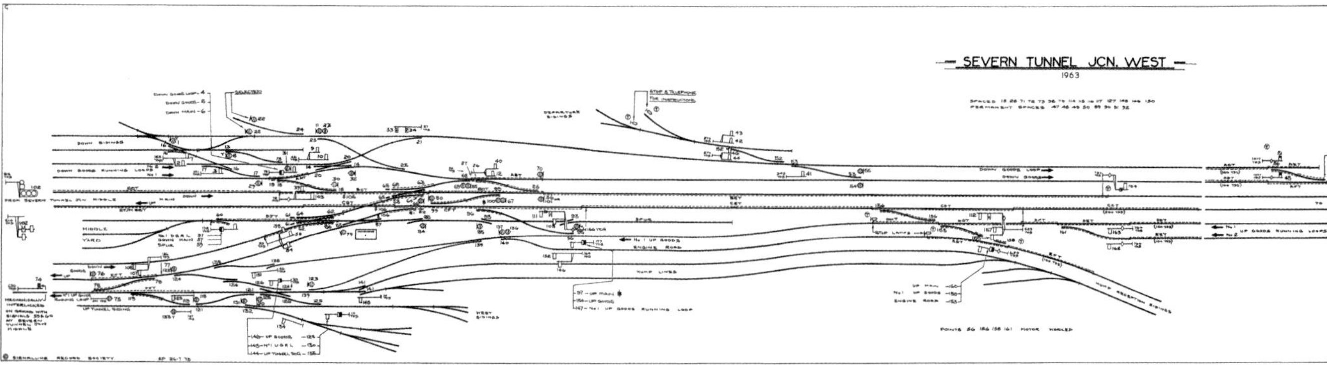

The 1963 signalling diagram from Severn Tunnel Junction West box. SIGNALLING RECORD SOCIETY

Down main distant signal, previously a lower arm on the same signal post as Undy Crossing's Down main starting signal, was moved to the top of the post when Undy's signals were removed. At Severn Tunnel Junction West, The Up goods line home signal was renamed Up goods line inner home. The Up main home became the Up main inner home, whilst the Up main home to Up goods signal was renamed Up main inner home to Up goods.

At Severn Tunnel Middle box, the Up main distant was renamed the Up main inner distant. The layout remained thus for almost three years.

Four Separate Yards

By 1962, then, there were four separate yards at Severn Tunnel Junction; the Down hump yard and the Down yard, with on the up side, the Undy yard and the Bristol hump yard. Undy yard had ten reception sidings from which traffic was 'humped' into the two-section Bristol yard (sometimes called the Undy hump yard.) Bristol yard consisted of twenty-one sidings plus a further ten dead-end sidings north of there, called the 'field sidings'.

On the Down side there were seven reception sidings (later increased to eight) before the hump, plus two goods loops and one Ifton siding, plus a further eighteen sidings in two 'sections' beyond the hump. A further three sidings were allocated to the wagon repair works, and behind that there were a further two dead-end roads (Nos. 20 and 21) and two more through roads: twenty-three in all. West of all the Down sidings were the storage sidings and six dead-end roads.

On both the Up and Down sides were 'cripple' sidings for wagons awaiting repair, engine release roads, hump engine 'return' roads and the Up and Down goods loops and reception roads. On the Up side was a brake van siding; this was where brake vans were kept until they were need to go onto trains before departure, when the van would be allowed to run onto the rear of the train under gravity – just as long as there was a guard or shunter on board to operate the brake.

Further layout changes took place in December 1962, when the panel box at Newport extended its area of control eastwards. Following Great Western practice, the relief and main lines between Newport, Magor and Severn Tunnel Junction West had been 'paired' since quadrupling in the war years; that is to say, the lines ran thus: Down relief, Down main, Up main and Up relief. This layout made it difficult for trains to enter and leave the new steelworks sidings at Llanwern

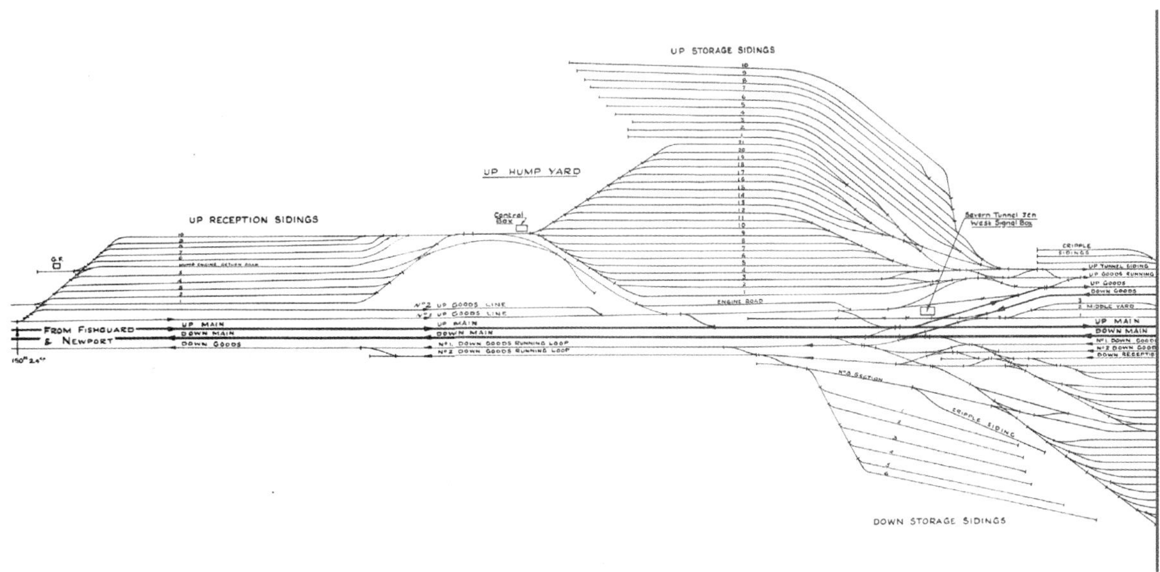

After the 1960 extensions: the west end of the new layout. Undy yard is to the left. BR/AUTHOR'S COLLECTION

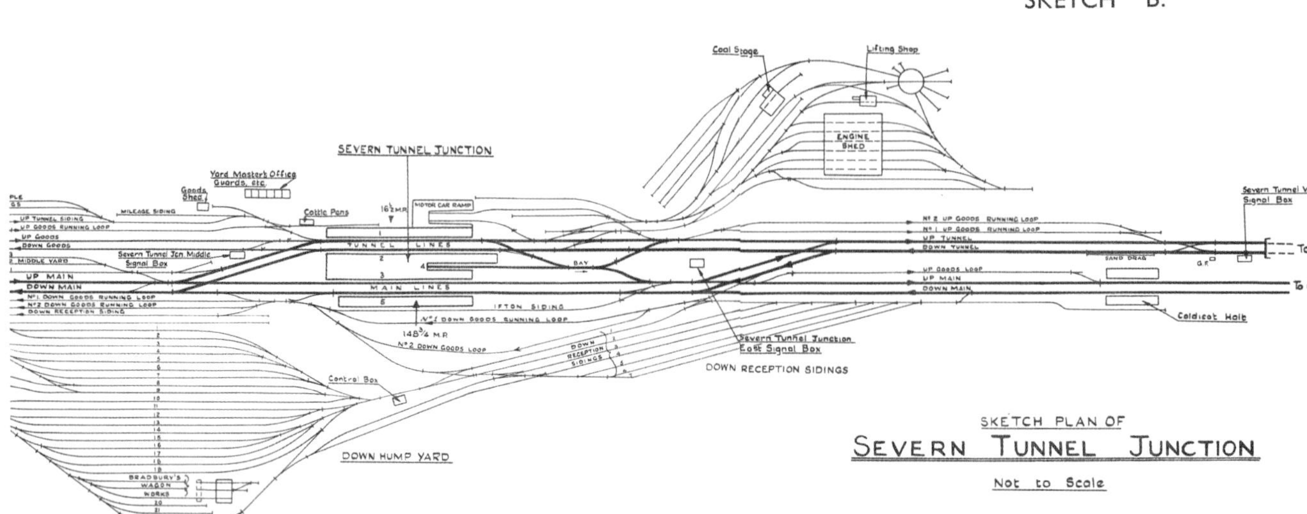

After the 1960 extensions: the east end of the new layout. BR/AUTHOR'S COLLECTION

from Severn Tunnel Junction yards without crossing all four tracks; the same applied at the Newport end of the steelworks, there being junctions to and from the plant at west and east ends.

Therefore, when designs were considered for layout changes for the planned resignalling of Newport and the opening of a new electronic control signalling centre there, a new track layout was planned between Bishton and Severn Tunnel Junction. Under the resignalling, the tracks between the west end access to Llanwern works and Newport were to remain Down relief, Up relief, Down main, Up main. At the east end of the steelworks, the double tracks from the works formed a junction with the Down relief and Up relief lines before crossing a works access road at the level crossing controlled by Bishton signal box (which was reduced to ground frame status under the resignalling). Continuing east, the formation of the relief lines swung south in a wide arc. Here a new flyover was built between Bishton and Magor to allow the Up relief line to cross the Down and Up main lines and resume the 'pairing' of tracks onwards to Severn Tunnel Junction, the four lines all coming together again. This enabled trains to

leave the steelworks and cross directly to the new Undy reception yard without interrupting the flow of traffic on the Down main line and vice versa.

At Magor, the Up siding was used by a cement company for movements of bulk cement in 'Presflo' wagons. A ground frame, released by Magor signal box and operated by a guard or travelling shunter, allowed cement trains to leave the siding and run directly to Severn Tunnel Junction Undy yard via the Up relief line.

Stretching from Caldicot Halt in the east to Undy in the west, the Severn Tunnel Junction marshalling yard complex was over 2 miles (3km) long. Over 1,760 wagons could be accommodated in the Down yard and Down storage sidings. The Undy yard had a capacity of 712 and Bristol yard could hold over 1,700. In all, over 4,000 wagons could be accommodated at Severn Tunnel Junction yards.

Six pilot locos or shunting engines were needed to carry out the shunting duties: No. 1 pilot was the Down hump pilot; No. 2 pilot worked No. 2 section in the Down yard and No. 3 pilot worked No. 3 section. Pilot No. 4 worked the Bristol Yard, Pilot No. 5 was the Undy hump pilot. The sidings north of Bristol yard, the 'field sidings' were worked by

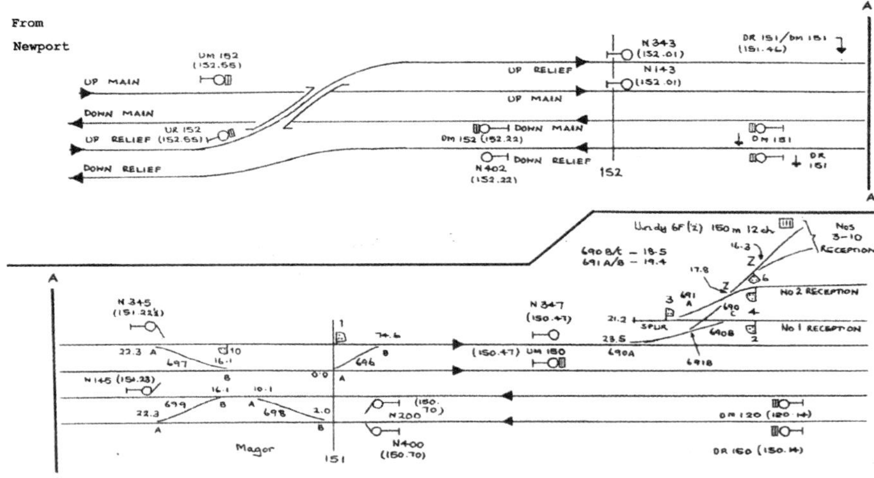

The approaches to Severn Tunnel Junction from the west after the 1968 resignalling and provision of the Bishton flyover. BR

No. 6 pilot (which also covered shunts to the Ford siding). In steam days, pilot duties were usually carried out by the ubiquitous and immensely strong GWR pannier tanks. Diesel days saw duties allocated to the equally strong diesel shunting locos of class 08 and 09: 08932 and 08078 were two of the yard pilots towards the end of the yard's life.

Staffing Roles

Pilot drivers recalled include Arthur Tuck (No. 1 pilot, Down hump in steam days) and Howell David, also Down hump. The job was part of a rotating roster for drivers in the later years of the yards.

As was to be expected, there were many shunting staff employed at the yards over the years. Staff who worked here up to the 1960 expansion included: Percy Jones, Ernie Yorath, George Greening, Bert Bryant, Les Sanger, Harold Francis, Robert Wylie, William Meyrick, George Brown, Eric Workman, Edward Hodges, William Bowyer, Bernard Williams, George Drinkwater, Rob Smith, William Maynard, Edgar Parton, William Stock, J. Hughes, William Kerslake and Harry Carter Selwood.

Thomas Carter, E. C. Evans and Ivor Tomms were head shunters.

Traffic inspectors at the yards in the period up to and including 1940 included Richard Hancock, Percy Cornaby, Horace Edwards, and John Davis. In later years, yard inspectors included Len Wilson, Bert Bryant and Bill Kerslake (Down side), Ken Llewellyn, Eric Wheeler and Stan Shorey (Bristol yard), Jack Price (Up yard) and Jerry Allaway as one of the Relief Inspectors.

Albert Jennings was a traffic foreman.

Tom Thomas and Bert Bryant were goods checkers in the 1940s.

After 1960, extra staff were needed to look after the new sidings. Many stayed there for years, the Junction being known as a good railway community to work in. Staff employed in the 1960s–1980s included 'runner' shunters Billy Marshall, John Turner and Gary Williams, along with head shunter Adrian Price and Undy hump chargeman ex-guard Peter Payne. Specific to the Undy yard and Bristol yard were head shunter Pat Ryan, chargeman (Bristol yard) ex-guard Roy Davies (always known as 'Dai Dawr') and two under shunters.

The yards covering such a large area and distance, several cabins were provided for the use of shunting staff. There was one for the Down yard and this was situated next to the Down hump control box. Another was sited close to the Middle signal box and a further cabin was at the west end of the Down yard, near the Down storage sidings. There were further shunters' cabins at the Undy yard; close to the Up hump control box and at the bottom of the built-up area of the Up hump, adjacent to the Up reception lines. Other cabins were provided at the west end of the Bristol yard and near to Railway Terrace. This last location also had urinals and WC closets for staff. New accommodation was built in the late 1970s.

Pointsmen

As mentioned above, the job of operation of the hump yard control boxes and Undy ground frame (Elmsbridge) was for the grade of a 'pointsman' rather than signalman. Most of the men who took these jobs were 'green card' men; these were men who, through one reason or another, were medically unfit for normal duties and were allocated to light duties. Working in a signal box – even a small box – could be busy at times and some levers were heavy to pull: at STJ the ideal jobs for 'green card' men who didn't wish to have office jobs was the hump control box, where there were control panels instead of levers. It was still quite a demanding job, though, requiring a lot of concentration.

In the 1930s Albert Meacham was a pointsman at one of the hump control boxes. In the 1970s and 80s, Bert Edwards and Frank Coleman were Down yard pointsmen, whilst Tom Jones worked the Undy hump control box. 'Elmsbridge' was worked by pointsmen Wilf Powells and Bert Rogers. Edwards was 'green carded' because he had a false leg.

Economic Downturn

Nonetheless, in spite of the local optimism, generally the economic climate in the UK was not good. The Conservative government had put British Railways under the chairmanship of one

> **EXCERPT FROM THE 1954 CLEAN AIR ACT**
>
> (1) Subject to the provisions of this section, no furnace shall be installed in a building or in any boiler or industrial plant attached to a building or for the time being fixed to or installed on any land unless it is so far as practicable capable of being operated continuously without emitting smoke when burning fuel of a type for which the furnace was designed, and any person who installs a furnace in contravention of this subsection or on whose instructions a furnace is so installed shall be guilty of an offence.

Dr Richard Beeching, and his report on the state of the railway network was under preparation. Large parts of BR traffic were about to be handed over to the powerful and influential road transport lobby. All the recent modernization at Severn Tunnel Junction was not just for the Spencer steelworks, but was also a prelude for plans to equip the South Wales main line with multiple-aspect signalling west of the Severn tunnel. Now, however, freight traffic receipts countrywide took a tumble. Coal, normally a staple of goods traffic, especially in the traditional mining areas – of which South Wales was one – was slowing down. After the winter of 1960–61, this mineral traffic dropped off. By March 1961, goods traffic receipts were down by almost £1 million from the same period in 1960. By the beginning of the last quarter of 1961, freight revenue on BR had fallen by £5.3 million. This was, in part, because of the Clean Air Act of 1954, which had been introduced as a result of the great smogs of the early 1950s. Coal as an industrial and domestic fuel was nonetheless polluting the atmosphere and coke, as a less polluting fossil fuel, was being more widely used. The Clean Air Act also specified 'Smoke Control Areas', sometimes known as 'Smokeless Zones'. In many new homes, the coke or smokeless fuel 'Parkray' fires became popular.

For coal traffic, the writing was on the wall.

CHAPTER 6

Methods of Working at Severn Tunnel Junction

As can be imagined, the working of such a huge complex as Severn Tunnel Junction required a plethora of different instructions to staff to enable safe and efficient working of the yards, station and loco sheds. For example, after the closure of the steam sheds and the takeover of the site for vehicle storage, the Ford company leased a siding at the east end of the station. This was the old line that used to lead to the loco shed. Cartic four-car carrier wagons leased by Silcock and Colling brought in Ford cars and lorry cab/chassis to be stored here for distribution. Wagons arrived on the 09.40 Dagenham–Severn Tunnel Junction service, which ran to either No. 1 or No. 2 reception roads on the Down side from where No. 6 pilot (also known as 'Ford's pilot') would detach the cartics and take them over to the upside via Severn Tunnel East ground frame. In order for rail vehicles to be shunted to this siding, there was a requirement for the car carriers to be propelled between Severn Tunnel Junction Middle and the Ford company's siding. A special instruction was issued to shunting and signalling staff enabling this move to take place.

A Cl. 46 waits on the Down goods line with a train of oil tankers in 1982, whilst No. 6 pilot waits on No. 1 Down reception (east) to move a train of empty 'cartics' across to the Ford siding. Note the old steam shed still standing in the top right-hand corner. TIM RENDALL

No. 6 pilot has moved onto No. 2 Down reception (west) and now propels its train of empty cartics back up the Down goods to cross to the Down tunnel line thence to the Ford siding via the Up side. TIM RENDALL

Working of the Hump Yards

Each hump yard consisted of reception sidings for arriving trains. Wagons to be sorted into different loads for forwarding would be 'humped', that is gravity shunted into different train formations. This was done by means of the pilot engine pushing the wagons up to the hump summit, from where they would run down under gravity to the appropriate siding. The moves were controlled by the hump control box, operated by a pointsman.

The Hump Control Box

The control box was equipped with electro-pneumatic controls for points. Compressed air for the operation of these was supplied by a compressor housed in an adjacent building. Normal working pressure was between 30 and 40psi. The points and signals were operated from a Westinghouse Brake and Signal Co. control panel mounted on a wooden 'desk' arrangement on the operating floor of the box. On the left-hand side of the control panel was a pressure gauge, which indicated the pressure in the air pipes. Should the air pressure fail, then an alarm bell would ring continuously and the signal and telegraph lineman was immediately sent for.

The control panel could be worked in two ways: automatic and unit system. A push button was provided to enable the method of working to be changed from one to the other. This same button was used for cancelling routes which had been incorrectly set up.

When in automatic mode, the system acted in 'route setting' manner. The pointsman (they were not called signalmen) pressed the appropriate one of twenty metal plungers at the front of the panel. This operation set up the route from the hump summit signal into the siding required. Each set of points was track circuited and the plunger remained depressed until the wheels of the wagons in the shunt movement had passed clear of the switch track circuit, when the plunger would be released.

Operated in unit system mode, the panel worked as follows: At each the position of each of the points shown on the control panel was a white switch, or 'key'. These keys were normally set in mid-way position for automatic working (which was the default method). Turning the key operated the points. If by accident someone attempt to move a switch during automatic operation, an alarm bell would sound.

Inside a Hump control cabin. This is the Down hump, as the station water tank is visible outside. BR/AUTHOR'S COLLECTION

The Westinghouse Brake & Signal Co. control panel used in the hump cabins. BR/AUTHOR'S COLLECTION

A close-up of the control panel: the point above the operator's second knuckle is the K-point. BR/AUTHOR'S COLLECTION

All the points in the hump sidings that were controlled by the hump control boxes were track circuited. Indicator lights were provided on the panel and these lit up when the shunt move occupied the track circuit and went out when the movement was in the siding, clear of any fouling point on an adjacent siding.

It was normal to use the automatic method of working during ordinary hump shunting; unit system was only resorted to when 'ordinary' shunts (shunting with a loco attached) were required.

Trains Through the Hump

Before the 1960 alterations, the points leading to the entrance to the Up goods lines had been operated by Undy signal box. After that box was abolished, the control of these points was taken over by Magor signal box. The connections were: Up No. 1 goods line to Up No. 2 goods line and to Nos. 1 and 2 reception sidings. It was the duty of the Magor signalman to advise the reception sidings shunter of the details of all Up freight trains approaching that were booked to terminate at Severn Tunnel Junction. All such trains were to be turned onto the Up reception sidings. Here was Undy ground frame (Elmsbridge). The pointsman employed there would be advised of the destina-

tion line for the approaching train and operate the necessary points. He would call up the Up hump control cabin on the phone and advise (for example), 'Got the Abercwmboi coming up No. 6 road.' Once on the reception road in the sidings, drivers were only allowed to proceed as far as the stop lamp at the east end of the reception sidings unless instructed to proceed further. On arrival at the required reception road, the train would come to a stand and the loco uncoupled. The driver would be advised as to the loco's next move and meanwhile the guard would hand his train list (tally) to the hump foreman.

The checker would then walk along the train to check that the load tallied with the guard's tally. Once the loco was released, it proceeded to the shed area and the guard would report to the Severn Tunnel Junction timekeeper's office, situated in the amenity block near the station.

Once the train engine had been released and the checker was satisfied that the train was in order, the shunter would take charge and when ready, the hump shunting pilot loco would run round and be attached to the rear of the train by the reception sidings shunter.

The train was now ready to be shunted into different sidings in order to be marshalled into new

A general view of the Down hump from Moors Road bridge. AUTHOR'S COLLECTION

trains. Each batch of wagons to be shunted into the same siding was known as a 'cut', and the shunter chalked the siding number on the leading wagon of each cut. Now they were ready for the hump signal to be cleared for the shunt move.

The hump signal was a two-aspect light controlled from the hump control box. There was a plunger fitted to the hump summit shunter's telephone post that enabled the shunter to replace the signal to 'Danger' when required, thus enabling him to control the movements of the hump pilot loco.

The hump pilot could now start to push the wagons over the hump summit. The gradient up to the summit from the reception sidings was 1 in 600 rising; once over the summit, the gradient changed to 1 in 138 falling. Contrary to many expectations, hump shunting was not carried out at any great speed. Walking pace was normal. Older wagons, with white metal axle box bearings that were grease lubricated, would run slower than newer wagons with roller bearings and this needed to be taken into account when allowing moves to take place, especially when wagons with oil-lubricated roller bearings were likely to follow older wagons down the far side of the hump. No more than six wagons coupled were allowed to gravitate over the hump at any one time. During fog or falling snow this instruction was modified to three wagons coupled at a time.

Wagon speeds were regulated by shunters (known as 'runners' because they ran alongside the moving wagons) applying the handbrakes on the leading wagons in the case of batches of wagons gravitating down the hump into the marshalling yard sidings.

In the hump control cabin, the pointsman had a list of the cuts to be made. He set the road accordingly for the first move on his cut list, which would read, for example, '4 for 10, 1 for 2, 6 for 5' and so on, meaning 'Four for road 10, one for road 2 and six for road 5'. Once the cut of wagons was on the move into the siding, the pilot stopped. The wagons needed to pass beyond the 'K-points' and, once they had, a green light would appear on the control panel, indicating to the operator that the points were clear and he could make another move.

It was a difficult job sometimes – in darkness, poor weather or bad visibility – for the pointsman to see what the next cut was. Should he set the road wrong and the cut ran into the wrong road, then time was lost as the pilot needed to go over the hump and retrieve the wagons.

The yards beyond the hump summit were split into two sections. These each began at the first point after the hump summit, which was known as the K-point. On the Up side, the Bristol yard consisted of the 'short leg' section 1 – sidings A, B, C then 1–6 – and the 'long leg' section 2, which was sidings 7–18. On the Down side, section 2 consisted of the stop block road and sidings 1–8. Section 3 consisted of sidings 9–23. There was no section 1, this being the area occupied by the wagons works.

With the hump summit shunter supervising moves from the top of the hump and another shunter walking alongside cuts ready to slow or stop them as necessary by means of the lead wagon's handbrake, shunting was quite a slick operation, if a little heavy on manpower – one pointsman, a pilot loco driver and two shunters were required: something which would be viewed with horror by today's financial controllers. Nonetheless, with the heavy traffic moves at the yard during busy times, these staff were needed to keep traffic moving. At its height and not long before closure, the Undy hump dealt with ten to fifteen trains per shift. This went on 24 hours a day, seven days a week.

Special Circumstances

Additional instructions were issued for when wagons containing fragile loads – such as carboys of acid or similar brittle loads – were to be hump shunted. The shunter who uncoupled the wagon first tested its brakes before allowing the shunt to take place (this instruction was later amended to apply to all single wagon moves over the hump). A shunter would then accompany the wagon as it was hump shunted and control its movement with the handbrake to ensure it did not come into sharp contact with other vehicles. In the case of a wagon containing livestock, hump shunting was not allowed. The wagon could pass over the hump but had to remain coupled to the pilot loco until the wagon was placed in the appropriate siding. (These instructions also applied to the Down hump.)

Further instructions applied specifically for working during fog or falling snow: Should the visibility be affected to the extent that the points-man in his control box be unable to read the siding numbers chalked on the leading wagon, then he was to advise the yard inspector who would in turn arrange for the siding numbers to be announced over the tannoy system before the cut of wagons left the Hump summit. In the case of the Down hump control box, should the view of the nearby Moors Road overbridge be obscured by fog or falling snow, then hump shunting speed must be slowed even further. Wagons were to be braked from the hump as far as the K-point, after which the brake would be taken off and the wagon allowed to roll under gravity into the requisite section siding.

A special siding was allocated for the storage of brake vans. Known as the 'Van Byte' (nobody recalls why…) the siding was beyond the hump and brake vans were able to roll out of the siding and downhill onto their train or siding. Brake vans were not allowed to run down the hump unless there was a man riding in the van who could apply the brake.

If a train formation was made up and there was still room for another train formation to be built up on the same siding behind the previous one, then a wagon or brake van would be hump shunted into the siding and stopped short of the train already there. The brakes would be firmly applied and the shunter would advise the pointsman 'Number XX road empty to you'. The pointsman knew he was now able to use that siding again, with the van or wagon acting as a stop block between the existing train and the next load.

At the Up hump, 'stop' lamps were provided at various locations to control movements. Lamps were provided at the Magor end of the hump engine return road. All movements beyond this lamp towards the reception sidings came under the control of the reception sidings shunter. Further stop lamps were provided at the hump control box end and the hump engine return line end of the reception sidings as follows: between and applying to Nos. 1 and 2 reception sidings; between and applying to Nos. 3 and 4 reception sidings; between and applying to No. 5 reception siding and the engine return line; alongside and applying to No. 8 reception siding and between and applying to Nos. 9 and 10 reception sidings.

After the opening of Newport panel signal box in 1962, it became practice for the Newport signal-man to advise the Severn Tunnel Junction yard inspector of the yard destination of approaching trains. Eastern and Western valleys traffic went to Undy yard for sorting. Most Down freight trains were signalled onto either No. 1 or No. 2 Down reception lines and, if required to be moved to the Bristol yard (which was on the Up side) then when the train engine had cut off and there was sufficient margin between main line traffic, the Bristol yard pilot would proceed to the Down reception road and take the traffic across to the Bristol yard for sorting.

Severn Tunnel Junction East Ground Frame

It was not unusual for Up trains arriving at the yards to be booked to terminate in the Down yard. Such trains would be booked to arrive at the Junction via the Up goods loop. To transfer to the Down yard from the Up goods required the train to cross to the Down side via Severn Tunnel East ground frame. This latter frame was situated just east of Severn Tunnel Junction East signal box. It controlled the connection Down main to Down goods crossover at that spot and was released by an interlocking lever – No. 23 – in that box.

When the guard of the train had obtained permission for the move to take place, the signal from Up goods loop to Up main would be lowered and

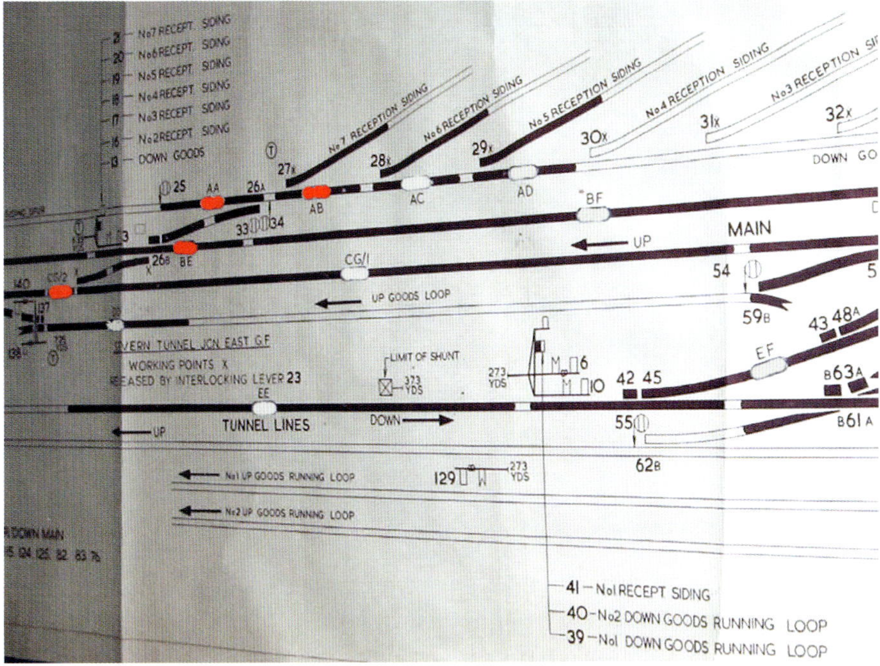

A section of the signal box track diagram from Severn Tunnel Junction East box; the red lights simulate a move backing from the Up main to No. 7 reception siding.

the train proceeded onto the Up main. When the last vehicle was clear of the spring points trailing from the Up goods loop, the guard would signal the driver to halt. The poor old guard would then fetch a point clip from nearby and clip the spring points in the 'normal' position. Meanwhile, the hump 'runround' shunter would have obtained the permission of the signalman at Tunnel Junction East and been given a release of the East ground frame. The shunter would now set up a route from the Up main into the Down reception sidings and advise the guard that this had been done. The guard, travelling on the brake van, would now hand signal the driver to set back slowly into the reception sidings.

Once the train was 'in clear' of the main lines, and as the guard was now a train's length at least away from the points, it fell to the runround shunter to remove the point clip from the spring points, restore the ground frame to 'normal' and advise the signalman that the move was now complete.

These moves also applied as far as necessary in the reverse direction for traffic from the Down side to Up side, as per the Dagenham–STJ working mentioned earlier.

(Note: Prior to the November 1968 resignalling of the Severn Tunnel Junction area, the East ground frame had been brought into use along with a new trailing crossover from Up to Down main lines. After the resignalling, the release of the ground frame was transferred from Severn Tunnel Junction East box to Newport panel box.)

Freight Train Working

In early days the yards were very busy; in addition to the usual type of freight traffic, it was not unusual for special trains of racing pigeons to arrive at the yards – usually at weekends. The pigeons were for release at STJ. In 1972, an average of ninety-six Up trains used the yards at Severn Tunnel Junction every day.

Of these, fifty-seven started from or terminated at Bristol yard. Two were booked to use the Up hump and four Up trains shunted to the Down yard for marshalling into other forwarding services. Sixty-five Down trains were booked to use the yards; forty started from or terminated at the Down yard. Fifteen others were through trains, which called mostly to attach or detach

Having attached a 2-6-2 banking engine at the yard to assist it through the Severn tunnel, a freight train headed by an unidentified Hall class now runs through Platform 1 on its way to Bristol. AUTHOR'S COLLECTION

wagons and change crew. ('Daily' trains, such as 'Wednesdays only', are not counted.) Fifty-two were not fully fitted; in other words the vacuum brake was not operative on all the vehicles in the train and a guard's brake van was provided. Down trains arriving from the Gloucester direction could directly access the Down hump yard, which lay to the east of the station (and was the first of the four yards to close when hump shunting ceased).

Trains came from Swansea Burrow sidings, Runcorn, Bescot, Bristol, Eastleigh, Gloucester, Hereford and Carlisle as well as more local services from Radyr, Ebbw Vale, Cardiff and Barry. There were many other places where traffic originated. Coal came from the South Wales pits. Traffic at the yards included coal, coke, iron ore, scrap metal and bananas, which were moved from Barry Docks to Severn Tunnel Junction Bristol yard and forwarded to destinations from there. Examples from the 1960s include 6C17 – 13.15 Severn Tunnel Junction to Norwood; 4E35 – 13.10 Barry Docks to Temple Mills (which sometimes called at STJ to collect other traffic) and 6A19 – 23.15 Severn Tunnel Junction to Taplow.

Night-Time Working

Even at night, the work of the four yards continued unabated. The following is an example of a few hours of the night shift in the Up yards. A typical night turn would start around 22.00, when the 18.15 Llandilo Junction to Paddington, train number 7A07, would arrive and shunt to the field sidings to put off traffic. Then 8C92, the 21.05 Radyr to Severn Tunnel Junction, would arrive at the Undy reception sidings to be dealt with at the Up hump. Train 8O57 would depart for Hither Green at 22.20 and 7C23, the 21.40 from Cardiff Long Dyke yard, would arrive via the Up relief line at 22.30 and terminate at STJ, with 8C17 from Hereford running close behind it also on the Up relief line and arriving at 22.35. Ten minutes later, and 7M91, the 21.40 Cardiff Tidal sidings to Wolverhampton, would arrive on the Up reception and shunt to the field sidings to work. Then there was a gap as far as freight arrivals or departures was concerned until 7A07 would be calling up, ready to depart from the field sidings after exam, for London at 23.47. Then 7M91 would be ready to leave, also from the field sidings, for Wolverhampton via Gloucester at 23.55. As it pulled out at the east end of the yards, 8C55 was arriving at the west end and would terminate at STJ. This was the 22.50 from Cardiff Tidal sidings.

At one minute past midnight, 4E32 was due to leave the Bristol yard with empty car transporters for Dagenham. At the same time, 6E46, the 20.15 from Swansea Burrows sidings to Dagenham, was arriving on the Up goods. Right behind it on the

It's 1982 and locos 47163 and 47250 wait their next duty at STJ; a train of ferry wagons is seen in the Down yard. AUTHOR

For many years, coal mined in South Wales was one of the major commodities moved to yards like Jersey Marine and thence to Severn Tunnel Junction for marshalling into block trains. This is the colliery yard at Cynheidre pit in the 1980s. AUTHOR

Tower colliery: another pit that sent coal to STJ. AUTHOR

INSTRUCTIONS FOR CROSSING FREIGHT TRAINS, SEVERN TUNNEL JUNCTION EAST

Up freight trains terminating in the Down Hump Reception sidings must, when permission is given, proceed from the Up Main Goods Loop to the Up Main line and come to a stand at the luminous marker board at 147m 63ch.
When the Up Goods Loop exit points have been restored to 'Normal', the train must set back and come to a stand on the two rails' length track circuit on the Caldicot side of the crossover for a period of two minutes and the Hump 'Run Round' Shunter must then obtain permission from the Newport signalman to operate Severn Tunnel Junction East Ground Frame and arrange for a route to be set into the appropriate Reception siding. When the route has been set up, the train must set back into the Reception sidings, the Guard travelling in the brake van and hand signalling to the Driver as necessary.
British Railways Western Region, Cardiff Division Sectional Appendix, April 1969

goods loop 4A19 was due to arrive at 00.10 for crew change, departing at 00.13. This was an air-braked working from Ebbw Vale to Park Royal and carried steel products. No sooner had 4E32 left than 8C43 arrived at the Bristol yard at 00.20, being the 21.55 departure from Jersey Marine yard. Then 6E46, having been examined before travelling through the Severn Tunnel, was ready to depart at 00.40. Train 8A09 departed for Taplow at 00.55 and 8O98 arrived from Llantrisant at 01.10 and shunted to the Bristol yard. At 01.25 the 19.22 Croes Newydd to STJ, 8V78, arrived on the main line and after coming to a stand, reversed across into the Down yard. Once it was clear, 7M81 departed from the field sidings at 01.50 to Brierly Hill via Gloucester. Then 7C65, the 01.35 from Newport, Alexandra Dock Junction, arrived at 02.05 and performed a similar move to that of 8V78 earlier.

Most, if not all traffic from Llantrisant was coke from Cwm Coke Works. Traffic from Swansea's Jersey Marine yard was inevitably coal, collected from the pits in that area.

Train 8B30 departed from the Bristol yard for Gloucester at 02.05 and 6B62 arrived at 02.20.

This was the 23.10 from Margam sorting sidings and was booked to stop for 'tunnel exam'. Behind it was 8O94, which arrived at 02.25 from Cardiff Long Dyke sidings. Train 7E36 left the Bristol yard at 02.45, running to Temple Mills via Gloucester. Service 6B62 departed for Swindon at 03.00 after its exam and ran via the tunnel and Badminton. Then 8O67, the 00.37 Jersey Marine yard to Eastleigh, arrived on the main line at 03.04 and stopped for tunnel exam. It left at 03.14. Next to arrive was 8M65 from Radyr. This was a company block train running to Corby and also stopped for a tunnel exam. It arrived at 03.16. Whilst 8M65 was being examined on the Up relief line, 8V00 arrived from Carlisle and shunted across to the Down yard. At 03.25 the 02.30 from Cardiff Long Dyke sidings, 8A94, arrived and terminated. At 03.30 8E67 left the Bristol yard bound for Sheffield Tinsley. The 02.10 from Radyr, 8C80, arrived at 03.33 and also terminated at STJ. Next, 03.35 saw the departure from the Bristol yard of 8O70 to Eastleigh. Having been examined, 8M65 departed for Corby at 03.45 running via the Severn Tunnel and Badminton, stopping again at Swindon, this time for change of train crew.

8B24 left the Bristol yard at 04.05 bound for Exeter. Ten minutes later the 01.35 Llandarcy to Melksham company block train, 6B32, arrived on the Up relief line and stopped for exam. It would leave again at 04.45. At the same time, 8M70, the 04.15 Bristol yard to Bescot, drew out of the yard and headed off up north, followed 5 minutes later by 7B21, the 04.20 Bristol yard to Bristol, Kingsland Road sidings. Meanwhile, 8M44, the 02.10 Jersey Marine yard to West Drayton, arrived at 04.20 and, after examination, left at 04.30, using the relief line.

Train 6B32 departed at 04.45 and 8A21 took its place. This train, the 02.40 Jersey Marine sidings to Acton yard, was booked for exam between 04.50 and 05.11. Train 8C38, the 02.50 Jersey Marine to STJ, arrived at 05.10. The 23.25 Warrington to STJ arrived at 05.55 via the relief line and was crossed to the Down yard, reporting number 7V22. Finally, 8O68 arrived at 06.00, being another Jersey

An unidentified class 46 heads a Down passenger train from the Gloucester direction through Platform 5.
TIM RENDALL

Seen in the mid-1970s, Western class loco No. 1053 'Western Patriarch' leaves Platform 5 with a train for Swansea.
AUTHOR'S COLLECTION

Marine sidings departure, this time at 03.40. It was bound for Wimbledon and was booked for a tunnel exam and departure at 06.15.

Thirty-five Up freight trains used or called at Severn Tunnel Junction yards during the eight-hour night shift in 1972. On the Down side, thirty-six freight trains called at or used the yards during the same shift, so in total Severn Tunnel Junction yards dealt with a total of seventy-one freight trains in those eight hours.

While all this was going on, passenger and parcels trains were passing through or calling at the station.

Even as late as 1970, new methods of improving the efficiency of the various freight services were tried. The steelworks ran a special test train between Llanwern and Swindon to try out new iron ore wagons (see panel). The train naturally used the yard at Severn Tunnel Junction for a tunnel inspection.

TRAIN NOTICE DATED SEPTEMBER 1970

28 September to 2 October 1970
Iron Ore Train (Test) from Llanwern Steelworks
to Swindon.
Comprises: Locomotive; Inspection Coach; Spacer
wagon (platefit); 1 Test wagon; Spacer
Wagon (platefit); 1 Test wagon; Spacer Wagon
(platefit) and Fully Fitted Brake Van.
Runs daily.

Speedlink

The freight service post-Beeching demanded faster freight trains in order to compete with other longer-distance carriers. As part of the necessary modernization of freight services, British Rail had begun to develop up-to-date wagons with roller axle bearings and longer chassis. Some wagons were equipped with air brakes. These vehicles gradually replaced the time-honoured four-wheel short wheelbase wagons and boxvans which had white-metal axle bearings and which had been in use for decades.

In 1977, a new freight service was launched in the UK. Known as 'Speedlink Freight' it ran to fixed timetables. This in itself was nothing really new. Freight trains had run to timetables for years: older folk remembered when one could set a watch or clock by a freight or passenger train. Speedlink was faster, however, and most of the dedicated wagons were air-braked. Trainloads ran between destinations, rather than the old pick-up goods trains with mixed wagon loads.

Severn Tunnel Junction became a 'network yard' and the hub for the South Wales Speedlink services. In 1986, of the seventy-nine Up trains booked to use Severn Tunnel Junction yards, seventy-two started from or terminated at the yards. Of these, thirty were dedicated Speedlink services.

Of the sixty-six Down trains booked for the yards, forty-two started from or terminated at the Down yard and nineteen used the Undy yard; thirty-two of those trains were Speedlink services. These included 7C38, 08.35 Kingsland Road to Severn Tunnel Junction, and 6C36, Swindon to Severn Tunnel Junction via Bristol and Avonmouth. Forty-seven of the sixty-six were fully fitted with the vacuum or air brake.

Traffic brought in from outlying destinations was marshalled into wagonload trains that would depart, according to timetable, for destinations across the country.

Speedlink days, and class 37 locos dominate the scene. Note the 'Rail 150' mural on the wall of the amenity block. AUTHOR'S COLLECTION

A train of coal leaves the Bristol yard headed by a class 46 diesel in 1982. TIM RENDALL

This picture shows just how close Railway Terrace ('the Barracks') was to the yards. Loco 47502 brings a short Speedlink train of Polybulk grain hoppers and a few tanks into Bristol yard. BR, AUTHOR

Oakdale colliery: trains ran to STJ to and from this pit almost until the end of the yards. AUTHOR

Speedlink days again: a civil engineer's empty ballast train headed by a class 37 has returned to the yard and waits on the Down goods loop. In the background a class 47 scuttles off towards Bristol. The steam sheds have now been demolished. AUTHOR'S COLLECTION

In the 1980s, there were two return trains of empty wagons for Oakdale colliery, which were despatched towards Severn Tunnel Junction within an hour of each other and these Oakdale returns were often running down the Lydney line from Gloucester only an hour apart. Oakdale could only handle one at a time and so the first was generally allowed to run through STJ to the colliery while the second was signalled into the Down reception line until the first train was loaded and ready to return to the Bristol yard. At that stage the second train would be allowed to leave for Oakdale.

Oakdale colliery was one of several South Wales coal mines whose traffic passed through Severn Tunnel Junction. The coal strike of the 1980s followed by many pit closures reduced this type of traffic considerably, to the detriment of the railway. Oakdale colliery outlived Severn Tunnel Junction yards; it closed in 1989, two years after the yards.

Severn Tunnel Junction staff often said that the Up yards were always full except for two weeks around the time of the South Wales collieries' annual holidays. For the first week of the holiday, coal trains loaded at the pits prior to the holiday were still being worked from colliery yards to the Junction and trains already at STJ were being forwarded to their destinations. During the second week of the holiday, no coal trains were sent from the colliery yards and, with the loaded trains gone, the Undy and Bristol yards had many empty sidings. This situation continued during the first week the miners were back at work as they had to cut the coal and wind it to the surface for screening and loading. So it was the second week after the miners' return when loaded trains again filled the sidings at Undy and Bristol yards.

Conversely, whilst the Up side yards were empty, the Down side yards were filling up with coal empties destined for the collieries once the holiday was over.

The yards were also used by civil engineering traffic, including ballast trains to and from New Forest quarries at Tintern and Tidenham. Loaded ballast trains returning to Severn Tunnel Junction from the quarries would usually be routed into the Down goods line and from there shunted across to No. 11 road in the Bristol yard. This road was mainly used for Tidenham, Tintern and Sudbrook traffic. It was also where red-and green-carded wagons for repair were stabled, awaiting repair or trip to the wagon works.

By 1983, Speedlink claimed to be in profit and it was hoped that Channel Tunnel freight traffic could be tapped into. BR looked forward to the continental traffic. The government of the time had privatization of the railways in mind, however. In

Another civil engineer's train, in this case a long-welded rail train, has arrived at STJ and stands on No. 2 reception road. The driver is phoning for further instructions. AUTHOR'S COLLECTION

37147 has the road away from the Down goods loop. Weeds are now beginning to encroach the reception roads… AUTHOR

the mid-1980s, two railway coaches were shunted into the old car dock siding at the station. These housed clerical and management staff who were engaged on a project. They were there to look into the possibility of turning Severn Tunnel Junction into a Freightliner terminal under the auspices of a new sector to be called 'Railfreight'. Rumour had it that prospects looked good for the yards and employment. It didn't happen, however, and after the yards had been closed, Speedlink was amalgamated with Freightliner into a pre-privatization 'company' and renamed 'Railfreight Distribution' in 1988. This was preparation for selling off those sectors which could be made profitable. Speedlink

still maintained its individual identity for a while. Sadly, attempts to get the Channel Tunnel traffic for Speedlink failed, and as the recession of the early 1990s began to bite, Speedlink profit became a £28 million loss. It was eventually shut down in 1991.

Before the introduction of BR's Total Operations Processing System (TOPS) in the 1970s, an earlier method of sending a train list, or consist, was carried out. At STJ this was tasked to a young lad, whose job was to walk the length of a made-up train and recite the wagon numbers into a small tape recorder. Once this was done, he went back to an office in the amenity block and wrote up the train consist. This list was then sent to the destination. Following the introduction of TOPS it was possible to create an automatically generated shunting instruction on shunt lists. Each road in the yard could be allocated to a specific traffic, destination or shunting tag. A shunting tag was an instruction for the routing of traffic. For example, a 21t hopper of coal for Exmouth Junction CCD (TOPS code 83441) stood at Toton, would have a tag of 760 (Severn Tunnel Junction). On arrival at Severn Tunnel Junction the tag would become 830 (Exeter Riverside), then on arrival at Riverside it would become a local shunting tag.

All this working depended on close co-operation between the four yards. If, for example, a train from the West Country arrived in the Down yard with some traffic for the Midlands in its formation, it would be booked to work at the Down yard before going over to the Undy yard to terminate with the Midlands traffic. The Down side chargeman would straight away advise his colleague at the Undy yard that the train had arrived. Once the Undy yard chargeman had given the information that he could accept the train, the Down side traffic would be shunted out. The train could then proceed as booked to the Undy yard. Meanwhile, the Undy yard chargeman would have spoken to his opposite number at the Bristol yard to advise that once the train had been broken up and 'humped' at the Up side hump, there would be some wagons on a particular siding for him. The Bristol yard man could then arrange for the pilot to collect the wagons and place them in the field sidings for attaching to further traffic and form the departure to, say, Sheffield later that day.

Carriage and Wagon Examination

It was a provision of the GWR (and later BR) rule books that all freight trains should be examined before entering the Severn Tunnel. Carriage and wagon examiners were based at Severn Tunnel Junction for this purpose. All freight trains that

A wagon label indicating that the vehicle has a defective brake.

started from the yards at STJ would be examined at the Bristol yard and the examiner, when satisfied that the train was fit to proceed, would contact the signalman and advise him of that fact. It was the examiner's duty to inform the train guard that his train was fit to proceed. Should the examiner find any defect which required urgent attention, he would write out a 'red card', which would be attached to the vehicle. A red card meant 'Vehicle NOT TO GO'. The wagon would need to be removed from the train straight away. If the defect was of a minor nature, then a 'green card' would be made out and attached to the vehicle, meaning that the vehicle could proceed but must be attended to at journey's end.

Other freight trains starting elsewhere in the district were examined at East Usk junction or Newport Alexandra Dock junction. William Richards, Robert Sealy, Fred Puckett, Albert Hughes, William Lines and Herbert Haskins were all carriage and wagon examiners based at Severn Tunnel Junction.

As with shunters, cabins were provided for the use of the carriage and wagon examiners. Cabins were sited close to the Middle signal box and adjacent to the Down hump cabin. A further cabin was sited near the shunters' cabin by Railway Terrace.

Tunnel Exams

Whilst it was necessary to follow the instructions to examine certain trains before they left the Junction, other trains had specific instructions that a full examination of not just the usual running gear, brakes and so on, but the entire load as well had to be undertaken. The latter duty was carried out by the train guard, and the idea was to ensure that every freight train that passed through the Severn Tunnel was safe to travel. For example, in 1960 the 20.08 Manchester to Plymouth (Friary) goods arrived at Severn Tunnel Middle at 05.18 the following morning and was allotted 10 minutes for the tunnel exam. The same applied to most freights booked for exam, but some others, which had extra work to do, such as attach a banker, would be allowed 12 minutes.

One regular working for many years was a train of empty coke hoppers from Avonmouth National Smelting Co. sidings to Severn Tunnel Junction. The working for this service began with the loco crew and guard booking on at Bristol, Bath Road depot. After preparing the engine they ran light to Hallen Marsh Junction, where they ran onto the smelting works sidings. On one particular occasion, the guard was carrying out his inspection of the train to ensure all brakes were off and the hopper unloading doors were closed, when he was joined by a carriage and wagon examiner. The examiner advised the guard that he had already been round the train and all was OK. The guard thanked him but said he still needed to check the train as it was to pass through the Severn Tunnel. The examiner was fine with this and in due course the train set off. Reaching Filton West junction, they were routed to Stoke Gifford instead of taking the chord line to Patchway. For some reason the chord was out of use, so they had to run to Stoke Gifford loop and run round the train before departing for Severn Tunnel via Patchway.

All went well and the train duly arrived in the Down reception sidings at Severn Tunnel Junction. One of the STJ yard examiners arrived and proceeded to check the train over whilst the loco was cut off and run across to the Up yard for its next working. The guard was collecting his kit together in his van when the examiner appeared and demanded to know why the train had a red-carded wagon in it.

The guard was unable to answer this, knowing full well he'd checked the train before it left and there had been no red card anywhere in the train.

A very puzzled guard made his way across to the Up side and reported to the yard office. Next day, the guard was called into the manager's office at Bristol Bath Road and asked for an explanation, as taking a red-carded wagon through the tunnel was a serious offence. In due course of time the truth was discovered. When the train had pulled into Stoke Gifford loop, the Stoke Gifford examiner had assumed that it was a train terminating there. So he had examined it and found a 'defect' – as he thought – and red carded the wagon. However, he failed to check if the train really was terminating and so he didn't tell the train crew.

The guard was innocent after all and the 'please explain' landed on the Stoke Gifford examiner instead.

Staffing Provision

Locomen and guards were based at Severn Tunnel Junction and had accommodation in the amenity block. This was originally a single-storey wooden cabin sited near the goods shed in the yard close to Rogiet Road overbridge. It housed, amongst others, train crew waiting for onward trains or to relieve the crew of trains passing through, the all-important timekeepers and guards. In or around 1967, the old wooden amenity block in the Bristol yard was replaced by a new, two-storey amenity block that contained offices and facilities for the train crews and clerical staff. The timekeepers were based here as before; Bill Andrews was one of them, while other clerical staff included J. Davis, G. H. Evans and G. Davis.

During the time that the new amenity block was being completed, staff were housed in a couple of redundant Pullman coaches, which were stabled

Having left its train at the hump yard, this named class 45 has paused at the amenity block for the guard to report to the timekeeper's office. TIM RENDALL

A train of tankers, probably returning to Milford Haven, has stopped on the Down goods for train crew relief.
TIM RENDALL

on the cattle dock siding. The Pullmans were past their best, however, so the accommodation wasn't as luxurious as the title suggested. In the new block, the area manager had an office on the upper floor. One of the last area managers was Mr Griffiths; his assistant was Chris Taylor.

Among the guards known to have been based at Severn Tunnel Junction yards over the years are the following: John Parry, James Parry, Frank Payne, Len Price, Frank Porter, George Fillibrook, Victor Davis, Will Edwards, Arthur Pitt, John May, Fred Baker, Peter Payne and Roy Davies – all goods guards. Jack May was a yard foreman.

SEVERN TUNNEL JUNCTION – TRAINMEN'S RELIEF ARRANGEMENTS

Trains requiring relief must stop at the undermentioned signals:
Down Goods Line signal N594
Up Main Line signal N153
Up Tunnel Line signal N181

CHAPTER 7

Repair and Maintenance

With early wagons being almost all of wooden construction on metal underframes with wheels running in white-metal axle bearings, and these wagons being in heavy use, it was inevitable that a wagon repair presence would be needed at a busy goods yard. By 1924 there was a wagon repair facility at Severn Tunnel Junction. It was situated at the east end of the Down sidings and was owned by Bradbury, Son and Co. under an agreement dated 29 March 1924. This agreement was amended when the sidings were extended in the 1930s and this was reflected in another agreement dated 9 May 1930. The works were transferred to the ownership of the Cambrian Wagon Co. Ltd in an agreement dated 25 March 1936. Further alterations took place in 1937 during the preparations ahead of World War II.

The wagon works was based in a covered building to the south side of the Down hump sidings. It was accessed from the road to 'the Moors' (as the land between the yards and the river was known.) By the late 1960s, the works was inside a corrugated-iron and wood shed owned by Powell-Duffryn Engineering, wagon repairers and builders who ran the works after the 1950s before which it passed to the Cambrian Wagon and Engineering Co. Ltd. Inside, there was certainly a concrete floor later, but originally this may have been a wooden floor. There were three sidings on the west of the works, but the two northernmost of these sidings terminated at stop blocks before the shed. A traverser spanned all three sidings to give access to the three roads inside the works. A weighbridge was placed on the southernmost of the three sidings at the west end.

The history of the Cambrian Wagon Co. is convoluted. The company was registered in 1906 and took over the works at East Moors, Cardiff, Glamorgan, of the bankrupt Cardiff Rolling Stock Company (originally registered in 1888.) The company was initially concerned with building railway wagons, but in 1919 it also began to repair wagons. In 1931, the Cambrian Wagon Co. Ltd and Central Wagon Co. used a company called the Welsh Wagon Works Ltd to take over the works of Hall, Lewis & Co. (then in liquidation) at Maindy, Cardiff, and elsewhere in South Wales. The company subsequently became part of the firm Gueret, Llewellyn and Merrett, then of Welsh Associated Collieries. In 1934, the Cambrian Wagon Co. Ltd bought out the Central Wagon Co.'s shares in the Welsh Wagon Company, but in 1935 both the Cambrian Wagon Co. Ltd and the Welsh Wagon Works went into voluntary liquidation and a new company, the Cambrian Wagon Works Ltd, was set up as part of Powell Duffryn Associated Collieries. In the early 1950s, the name of the company was changed to the Cambrian

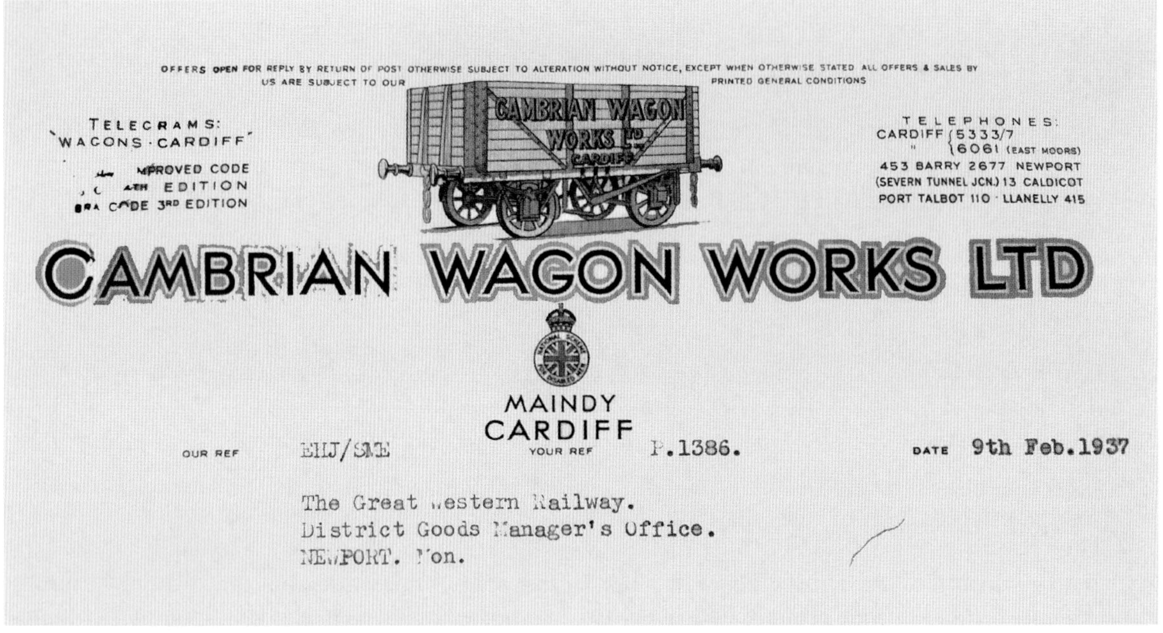

The letterhead of the Cambrian Wagon Works (slightly damaged). AUTHOR'S COLLECTION

Wagon and Engineering Co. Ltd, and in August 1959 it was changed again to the Powell Duffryn Engineering Co. Ltd. In 1965, as part of the reorganization of the Powell Duffryn group, the Powell Duffryn Wagon Co. was set up to take over the wagon repair and wagon hiring activities of Powell Duffryn Engineering Co. The company went into liquidation in 1967.

British Rail carried out a review of their wagon maintenance facilities in South Wales during the early 1970s and, in September 1972, the Chief Mechanical and Electrical Engineer's department at Paddington wrote to Powell Duffryn as follows:

Dear Sirs,

We are currently carrying out a series of area reviews in which I am rationalizing my wagon maintenance facilities. The most recent review has taken place in the East Wales area in which it is proposed to withdraw all colliery outstations and to concentrate repair work at a few strategic points.

This situation has been brought about by a considerable reduction in the wagon fleet size, *but in addition, it is proposed that the maintenance concentration points will provide a good pre-serviced and maintained supply of empty mineral wagons for our customers. In view of this I propose to withdraw wagon repair facilities for BR wagons at the following locations manned by your staff by the 31 December 1972…*

The locations included Severn Tunnel Junction.

As promised, wagon repairs for British Rail-owned vehicles stopped at STJ in December 1972. Severn Tunnel Junction's wagon works closed. In March 1973, BR again wrote to Powell Duffryn, stating that, as there was no longer the need for BR wagons to be repaired at STJ, it followed that there was no longer the need for the private siding agreement of 1924 to stand. 'Would you please,' said the letter, 'accept this letter as being notice of the Board's intentions to terminate the agreement of 29 March 1924' – and went on to say that although six months' notice was to be given on either side, the agreement would be considered as terminated from December 1972.

Powell Duffryn's reply was to state that as the private sidings were originally laid down for the movement of wagons to and from the repair shop, and the repair shop was no longer to be used for wagon repair work, there was no longer any need for the workshop. They agreed with the removal of the sidings and reminded the BR board that they (the board) had the option to purchase any of the wagon works buildings on termination of the lease. BR had no interest in the buildings.

Staff known to have worked at the wagon works include Charlie Rake, a wagon painter, Charlie Scantlebury, a wagon letterer, Edward Hill, carpenter, Harry Carter Selwood, wagon repairer and Henry Chandler, wagon repairer. William Heal was a foreman.

Permanent Way

There were many permanent way staff employed at and around Severn Tunnel Junction over the years. Their job was to keep the acres of trackwork in good condition for both main line trains and those in the yards. There was more than one 'P-Way' gang allocated to the yards: there was a Downside gang, a Bristol yard gang and the main line gang. During the 1960s–70s, ex-fireman Dennis Barecroft was the supervisor, Jan Castellari the ganger. Bill Little, Tommy Watkins and Norman Vaughan were in the main line gang. Dennis Hopkins was the lookout man and Tommy Baker the P-Way van driver.

Some of the staff who worked here over the years include: gangers Sam Nicholas, William Cooper and Thomas Harris; sub-gangers Evan Counsell and J. Arthur; lengthman William Turner and platelayers John Pendre, Harry Howell, Reg Price, Harold Price, William Preece, Ern Hughes, William Jackson, James Holloway, Arthur Tetly and Thomas Pritchard.

As well as track work, the P-Way staff were also called out for snow duties, which entailed clearing snow from points and track fittings so they could be moved for the passage of trains. To facilitate this work, six flame guns were kept at Severn Tunnel Junction, in the permanent way cabins.

Steam lances, which attached to the front of locomotives and were coupled to the engine's steam heating pipe, were kept in the following Severn Tunnel Junction signal boxes: East, Middle, West, Up hump and Down hump. The lances could be used on steam or diesel locos.

CHAPTER 8

Severn Tunnel Junction Loco Sheds

The First Steam Shed

From the opening of the Severn Tunnel in 1886, it was obvious that some sort of locomotive servicing facilities would be required at what had become an important junction. Plans belonging to the National Records Office at Kew show that plans for a locomotive shed at Severn Tunnel Junction were drawn up in 1886 and submitted to the GWR board on 4 September 1886. This was nine months after the first train ran through the newly constructed Severn Tunnel. The shed consisted of two dead-end roads under the roof, with a further dead-end siding on the north side of the building. Accommodation – presumably for shed and loco

staff – was built against the northwest corner of the shed. Near the east entrance stood a water tank. The site of the shed was to the north side of the station. All three 'shed sidings' came together and joined the main line near Severn Tunnel Junction East signal box, the distance between the entrance to the shed and the junction with the main lines being marked as 528ft (160m). A siding served a turntable to the east side of the shed.

Unfortunately, there don't appear to be any plans with details of the shed building. On the ground plan, reference is made to further details of the shed, water and coal facilities being found on 'Drawing No. 6199', but I was unable to trace the whereabouts of this drawing. On OS maps of

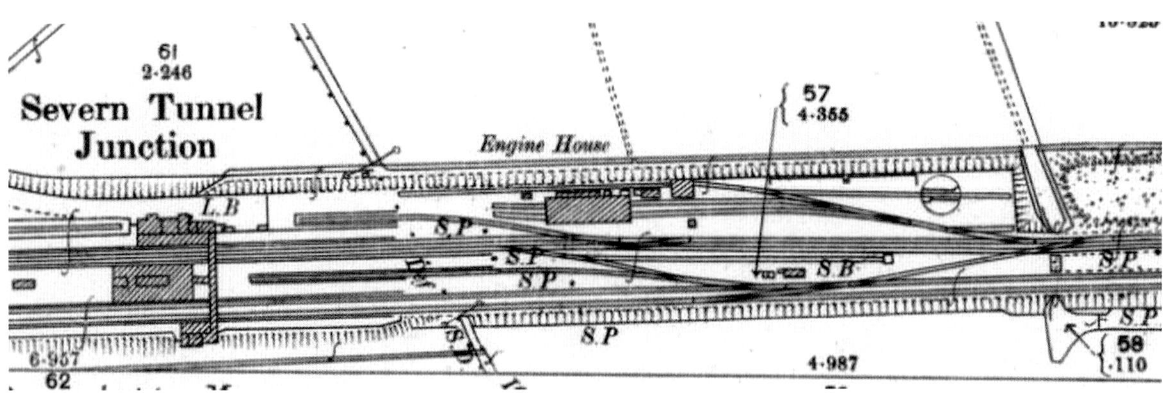

This extract from the 1902 OS map of Rogiet shows the 1886 loco shed and turntable at STJ. (Reproduced with the permission of the National Library of Scotland under a Creative Commons licence.)

Plan of the original loco shed at Severn Tunnel Junction, recently found in the Wiltshire History Centre. WILTSHIRE HISTORY CENTRE

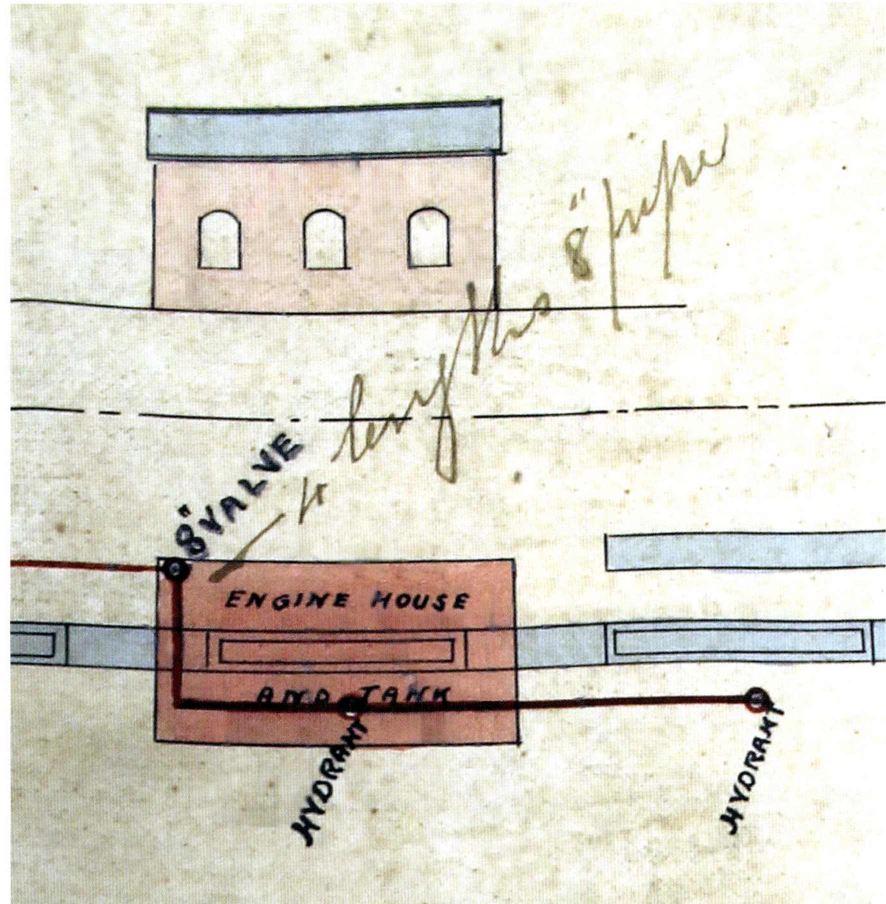

BELOW: *This plan, dated 13 September 1888, shows the site for the installation of the turntable.* WILTSHIRE HISTORY CENTRE

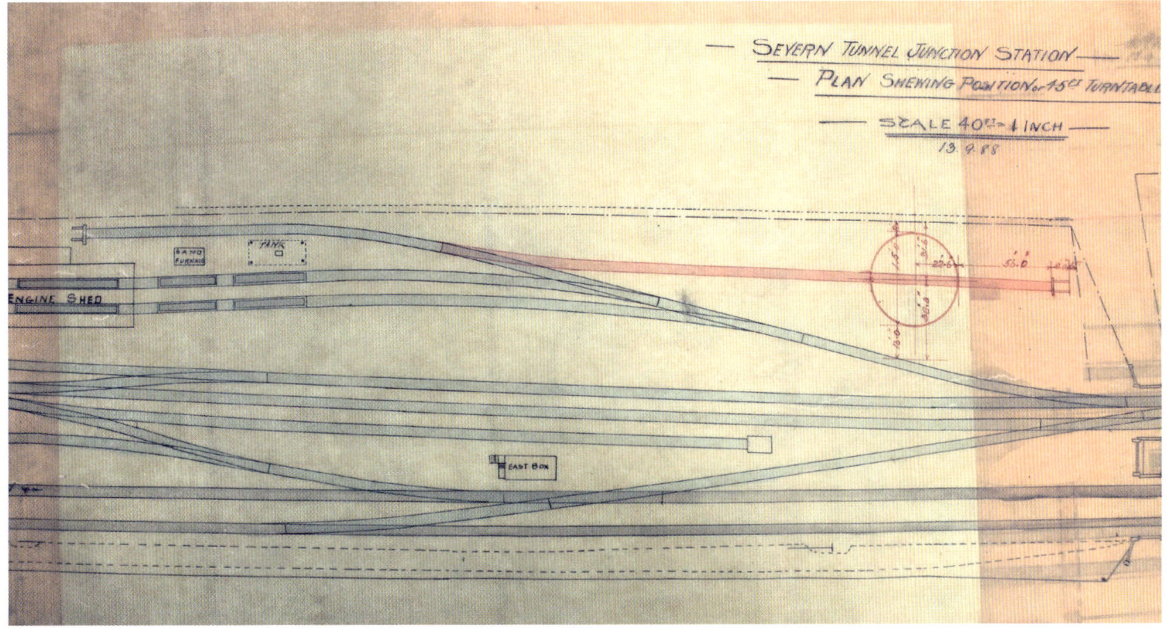

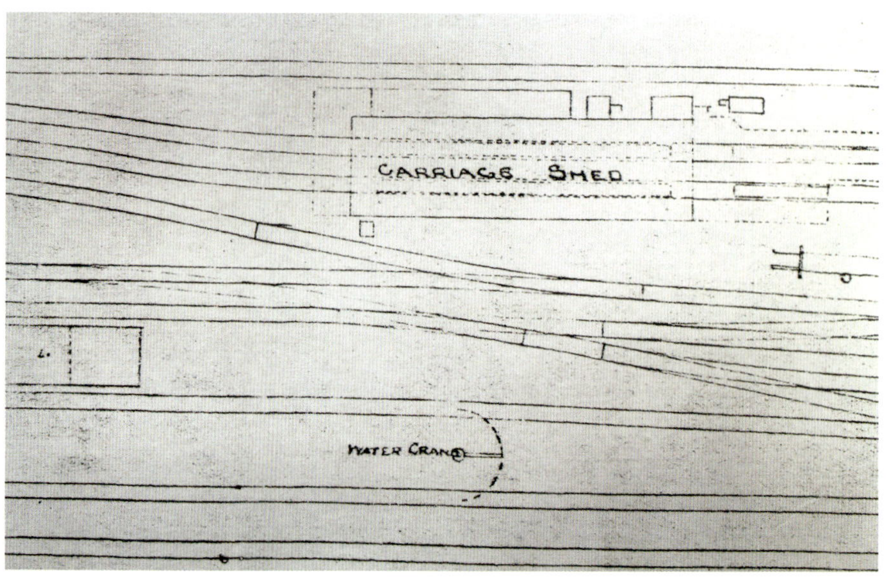

The 1886 loco shed seems to have become a carriage shed in this 1921 plan.
WILTSHIRE HISTORY CENTRE

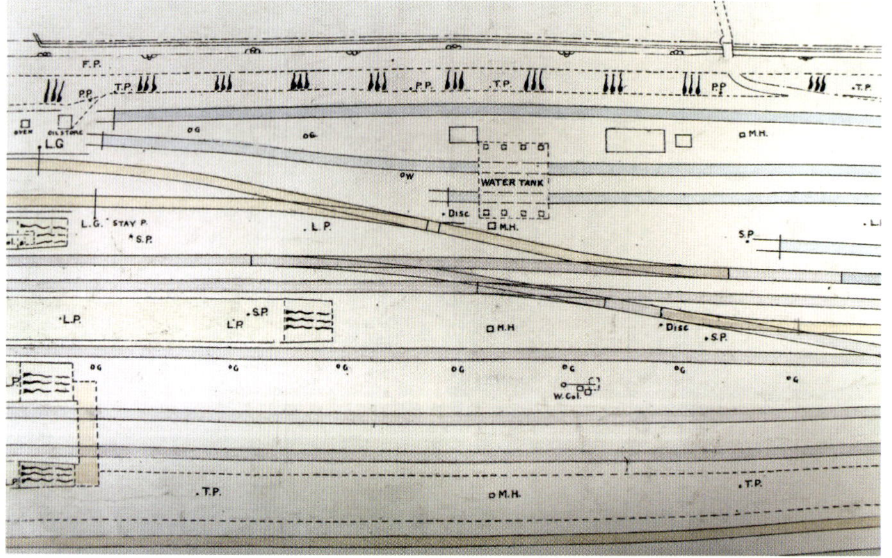

Where the carriage shed and 1886 loco shed once stood now stands the well-known water tank at the east end of the station.
WILTSHIRE HISTORY CENTRE

the station area dated 1901, details are shown of the shed site and it's marked as 'Engine House'. Later maps show a carriage shed on the site. They may be one and the same building, adapted for different use when the new loco shed was built.

Development and Expansion

However, with the increase in traffic brought about by the tunnel, it was very soon obvious that a much larger loco shed would be needed. During the early years of railways there was little in the way of standardization for anything. The GWR was one of the first companies to address this with regard to locomotives and, during the reign of Chief Locomotive, Carriage and Wagon Superintendent William Dean, some degree of standardization was also applied to the building of locomotive sheds. Until Dean, timber, being plentiful in many areas, was used extensively in the construction of locomotive depots. Dean rebuilt many old sheds and several new ones, in stone and/or brick.

By the time George Jackson Churchward became Chief Mechanical Engineer of the GWR in 1902, the facilities at Severn Tunnel Junction were in need of modernization. Plans were drawn up for the construction of a new depot. Churchward had continued with Dean's standardization ideas, building a huge, four-turntable shed at London's Old Oak Common. He built many sheds of this type – known as 'turntable' sheds because the turntables were under the main roof – across the GWR system. Most sheds were of a 'straight road' design and constructed with further expansion in mind. It was one of these sheds that was planned for Severn Tunnel Junction

Accordingly, a new loco shed was built on a site to the east of the station and on ground at a slightly lower level than that of the main lines. It was built of brick with a pitched roof and comprised four roads with a turntable on the north side of the depot. There was a standard GWR coal stage on the north side, with a coal tip each side. Sand-drying facilities were provided along with a fitters' workshop and offices. The local water coming from limestone beds was hard and therefore a water-softening plant was added.

The allocation of locomotives was mainly goods engines, as was to be expected. A few engines were stabled there for the purposes of assisting heavily loaded trains through the Severn Tunnel and up the steep gradient to Patchway or, in some instances, to Badminton. Additionally, some engines were for local passenger working, such as the Wye Valley services. This main steam shed opened in 1908. After the opening of the hump yards and with extra locos needing servicing, coaling and watering, Churchward's forethought in designing a shed expansion-ready meant that when the time came, it was fairly easy to add an extra two bays to the building. In 1931 the depot was extended to six roads. Water cranes were provided for four of these roads. At the same time, the coal stage was given a corrugated iron extension and the coal tips increased to two on the south side, with 65ft (20m) between the centre of each tip. A 'standard' GWR loco repair shop was added on the north side of the main shed. This building had a 35-tonne hoist and a 68ft-long (21m) inspection pit. There was a mess room provided for the lifting shop maintenance staff in the northeast corner of the building. A further extension to the

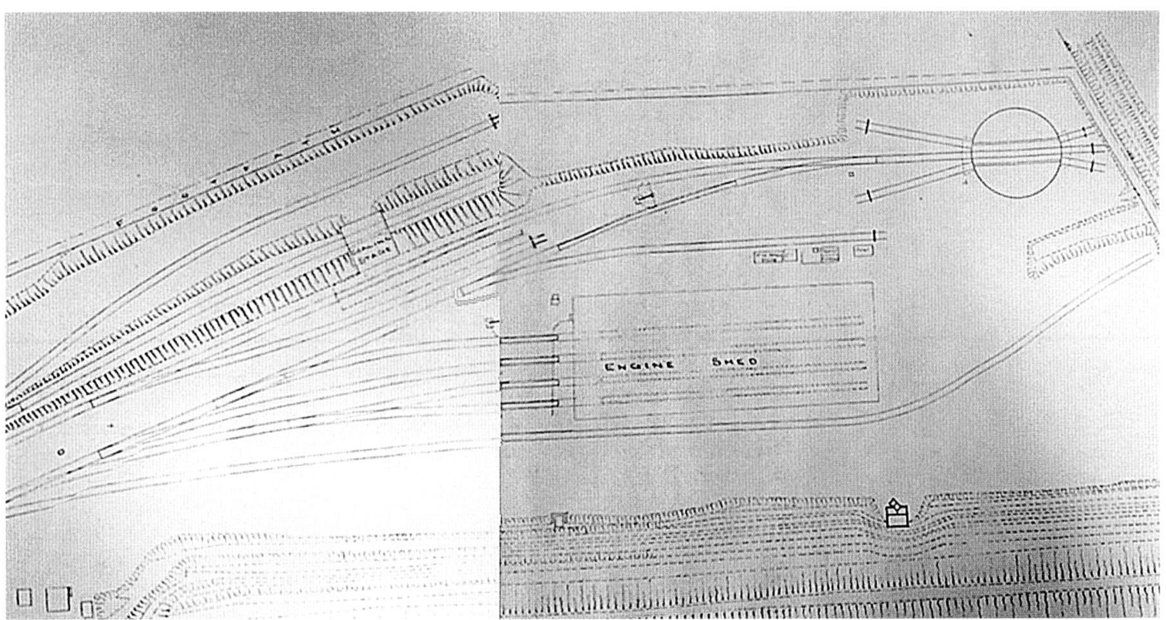

A composite plan of the 1908 Churchward steam shed at STJ. WILTSHIRE HISTORY CENTRE

coal stage was made on the north side, adding an extra coal tip.

As was fairly common practice, a large reserve stack of coal was built near the coal stage. This was intended to hold approximately 3,950 tonnes of coal and would stand 10ft (3m) high.

The building and opening of the loco shed in 1908 added to the Severn Tunnel Junction layout and working. The Great Western gave the depot the shed 'code' of 'STJ'. For administrative purposes it was known as '136' and it became '86E' under British Railways.

Locomotives

In 1947, five 4-6-0 locos were allocated: one Saint class and four Grange class. In addition, there were seventeen 28XX 2-8-0, two 43XX 2-6-0 and one 'WD' 2-8-0 tender engines; ten 72XX 2-8-2 tank engines, four 42XX and 52XX 2-8-0 tank engines, thirty 31XX 2-6-2 Prairie tanks, a couple of ex-Taff Vale Railway 0-6-2 tanks of 56XX and 66XX classes and a variety of the ubiquitous Pannier tanks. There was also an oddity in the form of an old Armstrong 0-4-2 loco, No. 3751. The total locomotive allocation was ninety-three.

A favourite of many train crews at Severn Tunnel Junction was the 28XX class. These locos were renowned for their ability to pull heavy loads in long trains; admittedly the average speed was slow – around 20–25mph (32–40km/h) – but their great ability to keep moving was much appreciated.

For those interested, the Saint class loco was 2952 'Twineham Court'. The Granges were: 6815 'Frilford Grange', 6834 'Dummer Grange', 6871 'Bourton Grange' and 6873 'Caradoc Grange'.

In later years, many BR standard classes could be seen at STJ; class 4 and 5 as well as the mighty 9F 2-0-0 were visitors, although the bulk of the locos were usually ex-GWR types. Seventy-five engines were allocated there in 1950.

It wasn't only GW and BR locos seen at the depot. As it lay at the end of the lines from Gloucester and the Forest of Dean, MR and LMSR engines also appeared at STJ from time to time; 4F 0-6-0 were a common sight and occasionally smaller shunting engines would also appear.

Steam locomotives required water, and there were a lot of steam locos using Severn Tunnel Junction until the end of steam and closure of the steam shed. Large water tanks were built in and around the yards to facilitate this need. Other than the water tank over the coaling stage at the depot, there was a large tank at the east end of the station and one at the Up hump. One was sited in the Bristol yard close to Railway Terrace. There being water troughs between Undy and Magor, a water

2-6-2 tank loco No. 5137 stands outside the shed at STJ. This was probably 1930s. AUTHOR'S COLLECTION

ABOVE: *2-6-0 No. 5336 stands in the shed yard at STJ. The photo taken in 1962, judging by the inscription on the cab side.* AUTHOR'S COLLECTION

Hall class No. 6946 'Heatherden Hall' stands on the coal stage road at STJ, along with a Pannier tank and a 2-8-2 tank. AUTHOR'S COLLECTION

tank was provided on the Down side of the line at 150.25 milepost.

In 1958, as diesel shunting locos were taking over shunting pilot duties, it was decided to provide facilities for the filling of diesel shunter radiators. A 1in (2.5cm) pipe was provided at the water columns at both the Up and Down humps to enable the radiators to be filled.

Many services required assistance through the Severn Tunnel, and engines for this purpose were based at Severn Tunnel Junction shed. The line through the tunnel climbed steeply halfway through and continued to climb on the English side until the summit was reached at either Badminton (on the direct line) or Patchway for Bristol-bound trains. Generally, assisting engines came off the train at Patchway and were returned to Severn Tunnel

Junction as soon as possible (the rules said 'immediately' but this was not always possible, given the heavy traffic on the line between Patchway and Severn Tunnel West). Trains from South Wales or from the Pontypool Road direction that required assistance would stop at Severn Tunnel Junction station to attach a banker, or pilot engine. The GWR Rules required the train engine to be at the head of the train, which meant that the train engine was detached, the pilot attached directly to the train and the train engine reattached to the front of the train. In BR days this was relaxed and the pilot was attached to the front, except that if the train engine was a diesel and the assisting loco a steam engine, then the diesel had to travel on the front to prevent dirt and coal dust from entering the diesel's system. Goods trains generally had the banker at the rear.

'Hall' class No. 6969 'Wraysbury Hall' stands under the coal tip at STJ. Note the corrugated extension to the coal stage. AUTHOR'S COLLECTION

SEVERN TUNNEL INSTRUCTIONS.

Clause 9 on page 129 is amended to read as follows :—

When assistance is required for Up South Wales trains, or trains from the direction of Pontypool Road, it will be provided at Severn Tunnel Junction. Pontypool Road or Newport, as the case may be, must, as regards trains stopping at those Stations, and for which assistance is required through the Tunnel, wire to Severn Tunnel Junction, giving the class of Engine and load of train and the point to which the assistance will be required. The advice must be sent as early as possible before the trains leave the Stations, the loading and class of Engine from Hereford or Cardiff (according to the direction from which the train is running) having already been telephoned or telegraphed to Pontypool Road or Newport. In the case of trains not stopping at Pontypool Road or Newport for which assistance is required, the necessary advices must be sent direct to Severn Tunnel Junction by Hereford or Cardiff.

Unless Assistant Engines on Up trains are required to work beyond Patchway, they must be detached there and be returned from that place immediately.

GWR instructions for banking engines.

Severn Tunnel Junction would be advised in advance by Hereford or Cardiff stations of the class of loco on the train and the load, plus the point at which the banker would be required to be detached. With the advent of diesel traction, the steam shed was home to various diesel classes as well as steam. Closure to steam locos has been reported in some circles as being in November 1965. However, *Railway World* maga-zine reported in their April 1966 edition that in February 1966 an Eastern Region B1 4-6-0 loco, No. 61173, worked a special freight through to Severn Tunnel Junction from York. After leaving the train in the yard, the loco ran light to Severn Tunnel Junction shed, where it was turned before running light to Gloucester. The magazine also reported that a 9F, 92089, brought a Banbury–Llanwern train to the yard and, after visiting the shed (presumably for turning as well), it, too, returned to Gloucester.

The End of the Steam Era

At this time the shed was host to various condemned steam locomotives, mostly from the Southern Region. These engines were stored briefly at the shed or in the yard before being taken to various South Wales scrapyards.

Examples of these condemned loco moves include 2-6-2 tank loco 6169, which arrived at Severn Tunnel Junction on 1 March 1966 on the 17.10 Gloucester–STJ freight service and was bound in due course for John Cashmore's scrapyard at Newport. Three Hall class locos and a 2-6-2 tank arrived on 1 May 1966. These were modified Hall locos 7909 'Heveningham Hall', 6959 'Peatling Hall' and 6967 'Willesley Hall' with 6136. All had come from Oxford shed on the 06.00 Oxford–STJ working and were bound for Cashmore's. Later the same day, the 06.30 Oxford–STJ arrived with 'ordinary' Halls 6923 'Croxteth Hall' and 6953 'Leighton Hall', modified Hall 6991 'Acton Burnell Hall' coupled to Grange class 6872 'Crawley Grange'. These four were also bound for Cashmore's yard.

John Cashmore did not have a monopoly on scrap steam locos: 2-6-4 tanks loco 80143 arrived at STJ on its way to Bird's Commercial Motors yard at Risca on 2 November 1967, while classmate 80042 had arrived from Exmouth Junction on 3 April 1965, eventually to be taken forward to Hayes at Bridgend.

Cashmore's, however, was the destination of Worcester's 6165, which arrived at the Tunnel on 28 February 1966. Later that same day, the 17.10 Gloucester–STJ left Gloucester with 2-6-2 tank 6132, 6815 'Frilford Grange', 6944 'Fledborough Hall' and 6844 'Tidmarsh Grange'. The train stopped at Lydney Junction en route to STJ and detached 6132 (which was bound for Bird's at Risca) before proceeding to STJ with its remaining three condemned engines, all destined for Buttigieg's yard at Newport. Number 6132 was

```
28th April, 1966                    -2-                  NOTICE NO. 561

                               SUNDAY 1ST MAY.

(8.Z.02) 05.30 Oxford to Newport A.D. Jcn. (via Swindon & Gloucester).

        Conveys 4 condemned locomotives 7922, 6999, 6849 and 6937 for Messrs. J.
Cashmore, Newport.
        Engines to travel dead on own wheels at a speed not exceeding 25 m.p.h. in
accordance with the instructions contained on pages 97 and 98 of the General
Appendix.
        Special care to be taken when stopping, starting and shunting and the
usual precautions and careful handling to be observed throughout.
        Will be accompanied by Caretakers from Oxford to Swindon, but a brake
van and guard to be supplied at Swindon. (depart approx 07.00).

06/00 EBV Worcester to Honeybourne.
06.30 Spl Honeybourne to Honeybourne South Loop.

        Engine, brake van and guard to be available 06.30 at Honeybourne, attach
loaded ganes and work as required at Honeybourne South Loop.
        Relief required for trainmen.
        Messrs. Cole and Anderson to arrange.
        Costs to Gloucester D.E.
        Signal Boxes to be open specially:- Honeybourne Station South and Honeybourne
East Loop Junction.
        Traffic Inspector to be in attendance.

(8.Z.02) 06.00 Oxford to Severn Tunnel Jcn (via Swindon and Gloucester).

        Conveys 4 condemned locomotives 7909, 6959, 6967 and 6136 for
Messrs. J. Cashmore, Newport.
        Engines to travel 'dead' on own wheels at a speed not exceeding 25 m.p.h. in
accordance with the instructions contained on pages 97 and 98 of the General Appendix.
        Special care to be taken when stopping, starting and shunting and the
usual precautions and careful handling to be observed throughout.
        Will be accompanied by Caretakers from Oxford to Swindon, but a brake
van and Guard to be supplied at Swindon. (depart approx 07.30).

(8.Z.02) 06.30 Oxford to Severn Tunnel Jcn. (via Swindon and Gloucester).

        Conveys 4 condemned locomotives 6872, 6923, 6953 and 6991 for
Messrs. J. Cashmore, Newport.
        Engines to travel 'dead' on own wheels at a speed not exceeding 25 m.p.h. in
accordance with the instructions contained on pages 97 and 98 of the General
Appendix.
        Special care to be taken when stopping, starting and shunting and the
usual precautions and careful handling to be observed throughout.
        Will be accompanied by Caretakers from Oxford to Swindon, but a brake
van and Guard to be supplied at Swindon (depart approx 08.00).
```

Notice of eight ex-GW steam locos to be sent from Oxford to STJ, en route to John Cashmore's Newport scrapyard, 28 April 1966.

```
28th September, 1967               - 2 -                NOTICE NO.    2060

                           SUNDAY, 1st OCTOBER (Continued)

Description      Condemned locomotives 34001, 34013, 34040, 34100 Salisbury to
                 John Cashmore, Newport.

Service          8.X.72   11.45 Westbury to Severn Tunnel Junction.

Westbury                        11.45     Charfield                  14/15
Trowbridge              11/58             Berkeley Road               14/25
Bathampton             12/28             Standish Jcn.               14/45
Bath Goods             12/35             Tramway Jcn.                15/05
East Depot      13002          13005     Gloucester Central  15C08          15C15
North Som.Jcn.          13/10             Bullo Pill                  15/50
Dr.Days Bdge.Jcn.      M13/13L           Lydney Jcn.                 16/10
Stapleton Road         13/17             Beachley Jcn.               16/13
Filton Jcn.            13/30             Severn Tunnel Jcn.  16.40
Stoke Gifford          13/33
Westerleigh West Jcn.  13/47
Yate South Jcn.        13/53

        All the above movements to adhere to the following conditions.

Signalling
Arrangements     To be signalled 2.6.1

Conditions of    Speed NOT to exceed 25 m.p.h.
Passage.

        Special care to be taken when starting, stopping and shunting and the
usual precautions and careful handling to be observed throughout.

                                          TF.14X/3094/3247.
```

ARRANGE AND ADVISE ALL CONCERNED.

for Divisional Manager.

Notice of 4 ex-SR West Country class locos to be sent from Salisbury shed to STJ, en route to John Cashmore's Newport yard for scrapping, 28 September 1967.

An ex-SR Z class 0-8-0 en route from Exmouth Junction to a South Wales scrapyard is temporarily stabled at STJ, waiting to be forwarded to its fate. AUTHOR'S COLLECTION

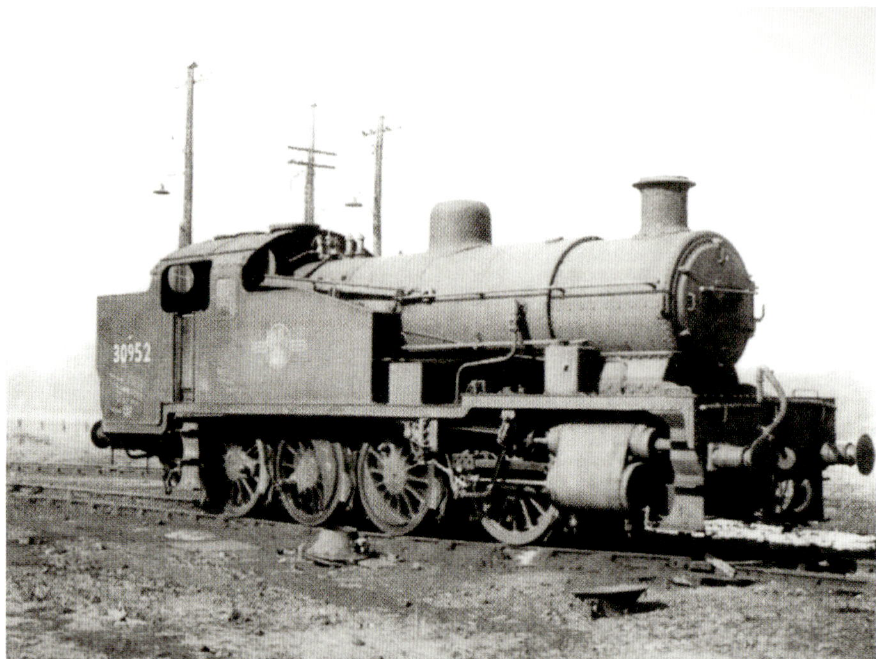

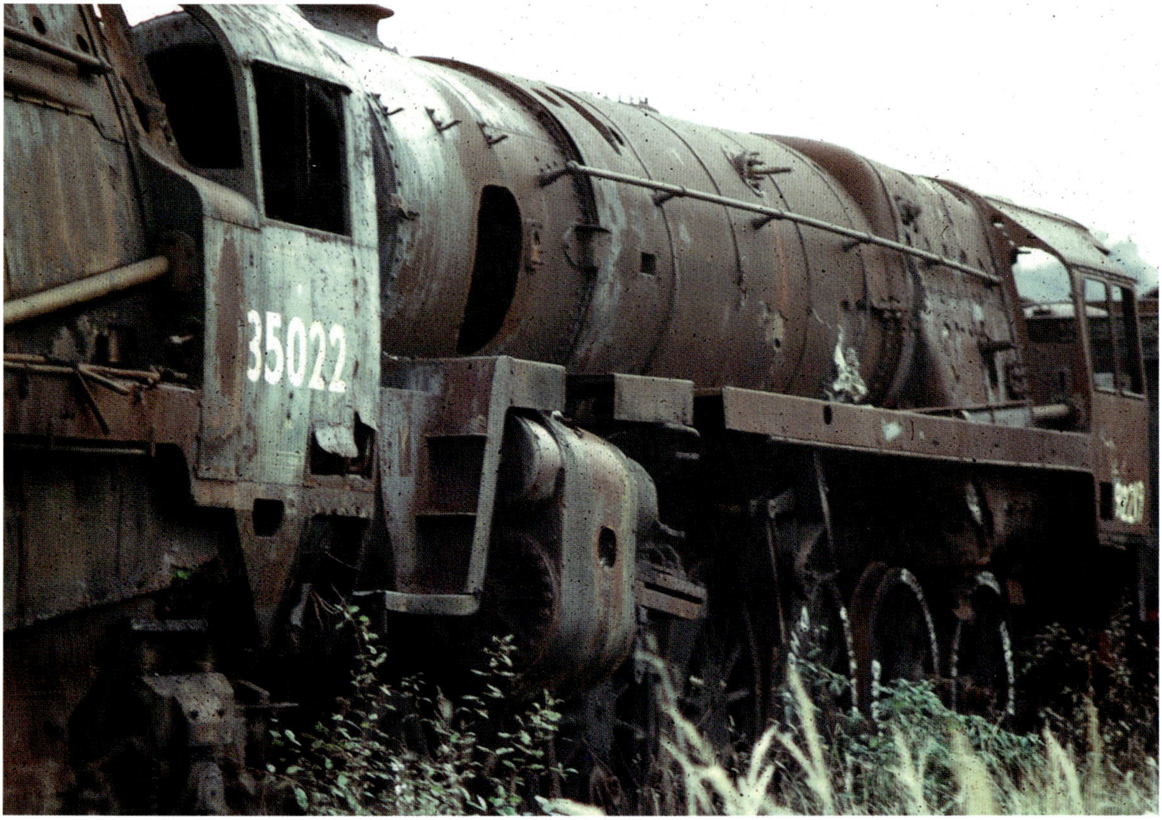

Merchant Navy class 35022 and a BR class 9F stand at Barry scrapyard in the 1980s. TIM RENDALL

BR Standard class 4-6-0 75029 at Barry scrapyard in 1979' Author. All locos passed through Severn Tunnel Junction en-route to Barry.

subsequently collected by a later service, the 17.10 Gloucester–STJ on 4 March and, together with 34085 '501 Squadron' – also from Lydney – taken forward to first STJ, then Bird's.

Ex-Southern Region locos put in an appearance too: on 2 April 1965 ex-SR Battle of Britain class engines 34058 'Sir Frederick Pile', 34067 'Tangmere', 34073 '249 Squadron' and 34081 '92 Squadron' were all conveyed to Severn Tunnel Junction on a special working from Eastleigh, which left at 09.05. All these engines were bound for Woodham Bros. scrapyard at Barry and, ironically, all four survived into preservation.

West Country class 34001 'Exeter', 34013 'Okehampton', 34040 'Crewkerne' and 34100 'Appledore' were conveyed from Salisbury shed to Westbury, and thence to STJ on the 11.45 Westbury–STJ on 1 October 1967. Again, these locos were to be moved on to Cashmore's yard.

All movements of scrap locomotives ran via Gloucester and Lydney, condemned locos being forbidden to travel via the Severn Tunnel.

It wasn't just ex-Great Western and Southern engines which passed through Severn Tunnel Junction on their way to scrapyards, however. Ex-LMSR and BR standard classes were seen at the Tunnel goods yards as well. Nor was it just steam locos: ex-SR electric trains were also seen at STJ on their way to South Wales scrapyards, as were trains of condemned wagons, also for scrap. Even some BR electric locos were seen at the yards. In 1969 electric loco E3044 arrived for exam en route to Crewe after being displayed at an open day at Bristol Bath Road shed; it then went on its way via Pontypool Road, Abergavenny and Hereford. Other electric locos passed through en route to be scrapped at Caerwent in the early twenty-first century.

After final closure to steam locos, the former steam shed acted as a sort of store-cum-distribution centre for motor manufacturer Ford. Trains of cartics and carflats would arrive from Dagenham loaded with Ford Escorts and Cortinas. Often a train would convey wagons for Exeter Riverside yard, and these would be attached to a service bound for Exeter or Plymouth.

The siding that ran from the station and that had given access to the steam shed was now called 'Ford's siding'.

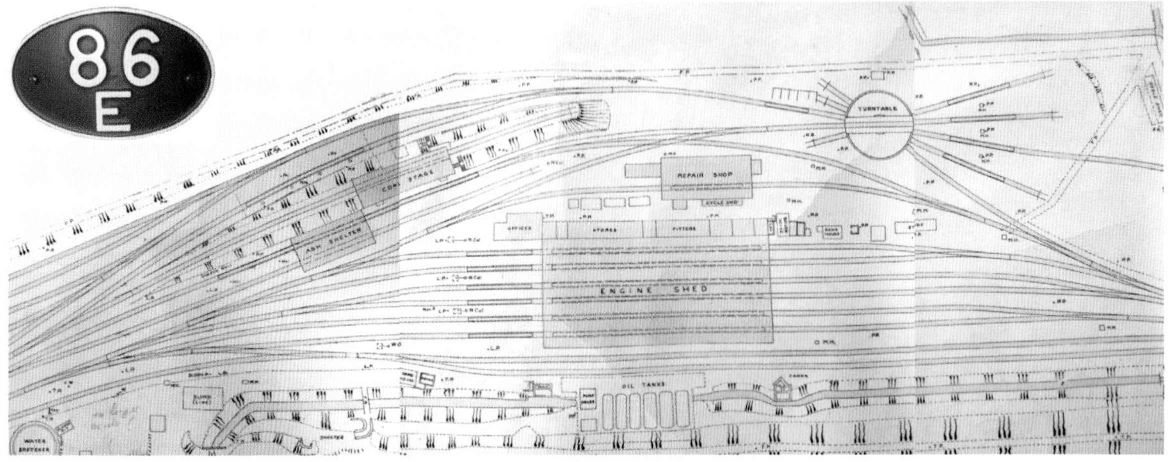

The final layout of Severn Tunnel Junction steam shed: 86E under BR shed coding. WILTSHIRE HISTORY CENTRE

Steam Shed Staff

Over the years many men worked at the Severn Tunnel Junction steam sheds. These included W. E. Andrews, who started as a cleaner in 1899, becoming fireman in 1907; James Wootton, cleaner, 1896; Albert Anthony, Edward Bailey, Harry Hayes, George Bird and Sid Carhays – all cleaners and firemen at the turn of the twentieth century; Edward Anthony, William Brake and Thomas Adams – coalmen. Albert Evans was a shedman (labourer) in 1906, Robert Fear the time-keeper. Augustus Burn was boiler washer's mate in 1907. Joseph Copperwhite and Will Thompson were fitters 1894–1905, Thompson having previously worked at Aberthaw.

Other loco staff included Cecil Rawles, Jack Nurse, Les Jones, Harry Fincham, Frank Wetter, Eric Hackman, Glyn Harris, Roy Powell and T. Margrett. Harry Sims started work at STJ as a traffic department telegraphist in August 1938, transferring to the loco as a cleaner in January 1937. He became acting fireman in July 1939 and resumed cleaning in September 1939. One month later he was fireman again and this time stayed in the grade, making driver in July1951. Harry transferred to a vacancy at Tyseley (Birmingham) in August 1951 and moved again to Plymouth, Laira shed, in April 1952. He was made redundant from Laira in late 1952 and once again moved back to

Severn Tunnel Junction! Between 1942 and 1945 he served in the local Home Guard at STJ.

Charles Dodd started as a cleaner in September 1939 and became fireman in November 1940. He was still at STJ when he became driver in November 1955 and a month later he moved to Old Oak

LIGHT ENGINES RETURNING TO THE SOUTH WALES AREA

British Railways Notice No. 2068
District Operating Superintendent's Office,
9 December 1955

Not more than five engines (excluding 4-6-0 'King' class) may run in steam over the under-mentioned routes, subject to the reservation specified below:

a) PADDINGTON TO SEVERN TUNNEL JUNCTION via BADMINTON
b) PADDINGTON TO SEVERN TUNNEL JUNCTION via GLOUCESTER

On any group of more than two engines speed must be reduced to 10mph [16km/h] when passing over the River Severn Bridge at Over Junction.

Engines must run from Lydney to Severn Tunnel Junction in pairs only, passing over Chepstow River Bridge under the special conditions operative in respect of working coupled engines over this bridge.

Common shed as driver. Walt Rowlands also started as a cleaner, became fireman in November 1940 and moved to Old Oak Common as driver in August 1955.

Sixteen-year old Brian Bond joined the GWR as a cleaner at Severn Tunnel Junction in March 1947. He moved to Southall in July 1947 as fireman and returned to STJ again in November 1947. He was called up for his national service in February 1949, serving until August 1950.

Other drivers include Charlie Curry and Ken Margrett.

It's nice to know that at least two locos that were STJ regulars have been preserved: 2-6-2 Prairie tank loco No. 4160 and 2-8-0 28XX class No. 3850 can both be seen in action on preserved lines.

The Breakdown Train

Severn Tunnel Junction loco shed had a breakdown gang whose job was to attend to derailments in their locality. A tool van equipped with jacks, wooden packing and oxy-acetylene cutting equipment was stabled in the shed yard. The area covered by the STJ breakdown gang was Beachley Junction (inclu-sive), Magor (inclusive), Severn Tunnel West and East, Monmouth May Hill, Wye Valley Junction and the Sudbrook and Caerwent branches. In the event of a derailment occurring in the Severn tunnel, both the STJ and Bristol gangs were required to attend. Water- or oil-filled jacks were used to rerail steam locos, carriages and wagons, but when the diesel-hydraulic locos arrived in the late 1950s and early 1960s, they needed different jacking equip-ment. Hydraulic jacks and special lifting brackets to attach to the locos were made by German company Machinenfabrik Deutschland and were supplied to main depots – Ebbw Junction in the case of STJ. This equipment was known, not surprisingly as 'German Gear' or 'MFD' gear. In the event of one of the main line diesel-hydraulics becoming derailed then Ebbw Junction gang had to be called out to rerail it using the MFD jacks.

Diesel Stabling

So far as diesels were concerned, whilst initially they shared the old steam shed with the steam locos, this was not to be their future home and

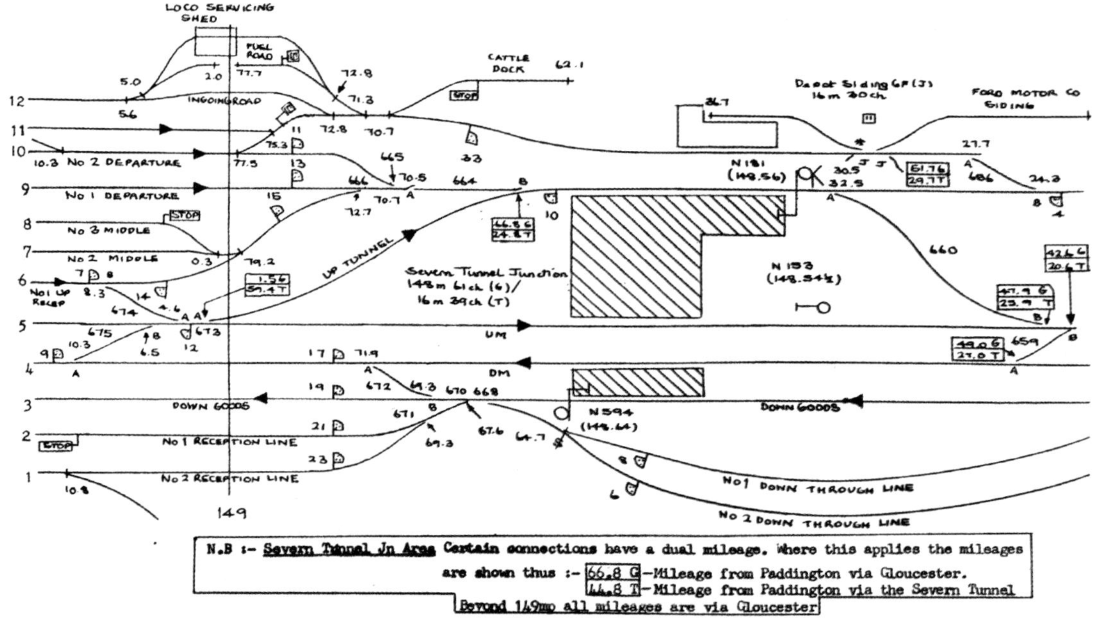

The location of the diesel shed in relation to the station. Note the 'Ford's siding' on the right side of the plan – all that was left of the steam shed layout. BR

In this 1982 view over the yards we can see the Down sidings on the left; in the far left distance is the Undy yard; ballast trains stand on Nos. 2 and 3 middle sidings; in the middle distance is the Bristol yard; at the diesel shed, classes 20, 31 and 47 are in evidence. The field sidings are barely visible above the right side of the diesel depot. TIM RENDALL

The diesel depot at STJ, with classes 31, 37, 20 and 47 in view. AUTHOR

An unidentified class 56 passes the SJ diesel depot as it scuds along the Down main towards Newport. TIM RENDALL

D1941 'Western Prince' stands outside the STJ diesel depot. AUTHOR'S COLLECTION

the function of the old steam depot was taken over by a new depot built to the west side of the station. This was sited on the Up side of the lines, east of Railway Terrace. Opened in the early months of 1966, the new shed consisted of a one-road shed with a through road. Inside was an inspection pit and there were the usual fuelling facilities along with maintenance facilities, oil supply, sand and water, as with other diesel depots. Outside were a couple of sidings for stabling locos. The shed never had a specific allocation of engines as it was a fuelling and inspection point with stabling facilities, although in its early years, some half a dozen class 08 shunters were allocated there as they had yard pilot duties. In September 1968 a class 45 diesel loco, then numbered D76, was based at Severn Tunnel Junction for a few weeks, where it was used for crew training purposes.

For operational purposes, all the lines between the Bristol yard stop lamp (which faced the Bristol yard) and the stop lamps at the east end of the diesel depot, including the cattle pen siding, were regarded as being within the depot limits. All loco movements in this designated area were to be

EXTRACT FROM BRITISH RAIL SECTIONAL APPENDIX TO THE WORKING TIMETABLE AND RULES AND REGULATIONS, 1969

Movements between Sidings near Amenities Block, Severn Tunnel Junction
All movements from the Diesel Depot Out Engine line, Fuel siding, Diesel Depot In Engine line, Shunting Line, Cattle Pen siding and Depot siding, and via the crossover leading from the East end of No. 2 Departure to the Shunting line must be brought to a stand clear of the fouling point with adjoining lines and must not proceed until authority has been obtained by means of the nearest telephone from the person in charge at the West end of the depot siding.

made very cautiously, with drivers being always prepared to stop short of any obstruction. The normal direction of travel over the 'Out' engine line was west to east, and that of the 'In' engine line from east to west. Before any moves were permitted from the diesel depot beyond the stop lamp to the Up tunnel siding, the permission of the Bristol yard inspector had to be obtained.

86E: Severn Tunnel Junction shed plate.

STJ diesel depot seen in 2019. AUTHOR

Locos wishing to proceed towards the depot from the Bristol yard were permitted to pass the stop lamp alongside the Up tunnel siding as long as the driver was satisfied that it was safe to do so.

Severn Tunnel Junction became a mecca for diesel enthusiasts as the extensive yards brought a wide variety of locomotives to the shed. Class 08, 20, 25, 31, 37, 40, 42, 43, 45, 46, 47, 52, 56 along with the sole class 53, 1200 'Falcon', were all seen there. As a point of interest, class 56 wasn't allowed to work on the South Wales main lines until after clearance tests had been carried out. Once the Chief Civil Engineer was satisfied that the tests had been done and no problems found, he authorized the class to work on the South Wales main lines between South Wales and Didcot power station via the Badminton, Box and Hereford routes, on 19 September 1979. After that they were often to be seen on heavy merry-go-round coal trains. In

October 1982, Ebbw Junction loco stabling point closed and the staff transferred to Severn Tunnel Junction. They were to have five years' employment there.

The shed continued to bear its steam-era shed code 86E until June 1968, when it was 'closed' and lost its status as a depot in its own right, becoming a sub-shed of 86B, Newport, until May 1973 when BR renamed the depot. It then became known as 'ST' – to fit in with BR TOPS codes – until final closure on 10 October 1987. William Winter was the roster clerk for locomen, Jasmine John (née Humphries) the roster clerk for yard inspectors, chargemen, shunters and guards.

With full closure of the yards came almost total erasure of all railway freight facilities from the landscape. However, the diesel loco shed survived to be used for other things and was still standing in 2019.

CHAPTER 9

The Caerwent and Sudbrook Branch Lines

As a large marshalling yard, Severn Tunnel Junction was the starting point and reception area for two short but important branches which provided the yards with traffic. One branch – to Sudbrook – dated from the early days of tunnel construction work, the other – to Caerwent – from World War II. We will look at the latter first.

Caerwent Branch

To avoid paralysis of weapons production by enemy action in wartime, the government had adopted a process of moving munitions factories and stores to remote rural areas. North of Severn Tunnel Junction is the small village of Caerwent, and it was here that the government decided to build a weapons establishment. In 1938, the Admiralty acquired a large area of land north of the A48 Chepstow–Newport road. This land was on the south slope of an escarpment and included a tiny hamlet known as Dinham. Local railwaymen engaged on trips between Severn Tunnel Junction and the Caerwent factory always talked of 'going out to Dinham' rather than Caerwent (Dinham itself vanished with the construction of the factory and its site is still within MOD boundaries). Building commenced and the factory partly opened in 1939 as a Royal Ordnance Factory. The premises was used for the manufacture of explosives and storage of ammunition and was controlled by the Admiralty. The rest of the complex became operational in 1941 as the Royal Navy Propellant Factory.

The factory and ancillary buildings were constructed by Sir Alfred McAlpine and Co., who were engaged in the building of several other wartime ammunition depots, such as the underground facilities near Corsham, Wiltshire, and at Dalbeattie in Scotland.

Military Site

The site, which was approximately 2 miles (3km) long and 0.75 miles (1.2km) wide (roughly triangular in shape) included buildings and structures dedicated to a nitroglycerine plant (known as a 'nitroglycerine hill') and provided high-grade propellant for the Royal Navy. It was deliberately located on a hillside so that gravity could be utilized in the manufacturing process. The nitroglycerine plant comprised a mixed acids plant, a refrigeration, compressor and electrical substation, a glycerine and soda store, a brine store, two charge houses, two nitrating houses, three washing houses, a waste acids plant, a paste sheeting and mixing house, three paste drying houses and latrines. The different process areas were separated by earthen bunds and linked by an extensive guttering system.

Some of the remaining buildings of Caerwent Naval Propellant Factory, seen in 2019. AUTHOR

The new factory was served by a new 1 mile 60 chain (2.8km) branch line which ran from a junction with the GWR main line at Caldicot Crossing (soon to be renamed Caldicot Junction) and curved sharply through 90 degrees to head first northwest and then north, crossing the A48 Chepstow–Newport road near Crick by means of a bridge road before entering the factory. (In later years, it crossed the M4 motorway before reaching the A48.) The branch was single track throughout.

There was an extensive railway complex inside the depot. A steam shunting loco fitted with a special spark-arrester at Swindon works was the regular shunting engine at the Caerwent factory. This engine was serviced at STJ. The depot itself had a diesel shunting loco, which arrived in 1964. It was a Ruston-Hornsby 0-4-0 numbered RNPF 3D. This loco (No. 414301) was moved to another military depot in 1972, but found its way back west to the Severn Valley Railway in 1981, where it was used as a source of spare parts for other Ruston shunters.

The entire branch beyond the connections with the main line at Caldicot Junction remained the prop-erty of the Ministry of Defence, who also designed and built the A48 road bridge. Inside the factory complex was an extensive range of sidings. Though well used during World War II and the Cold War period, the site's traffic dwindled during the 1960s and 70s and the branch was seldom used. This led to an instruc-tion being sent out that if no train had passed over the branch for a month, then the track had to be inspected on foot by a permanent way inspector before any train was permitted to travel over the line.

This led to an amusing incident. One day a train was booked to go to Caerwent. The train was ready to go, but before it could depart from Severn Tunnel Junction, Newport panel said they could not signal the train away until the P-Way inspector had walked the branch. It was one very surprised and somewhat disgruntled inspec-tor who answered the phone and was given his instructions! What was even more amusing, was that after a month had elapsed, another train needed to traverse the branch and the same per-manent way Inspector set off on the 1 mile 10 chain (1.8km) walk yet again.

The junction with the main Gloucester–Newport line was, as mentioned above, at Caldicot Crossing. From the junction, speed restrictions for trains over the Caerwent branch were as follows:

Over connections at Caldicot Crossing Ground Frame 25mph (40km/h)

Between Main Road bridge and factory 10mph (16km/h)

Over the loop line at factory platform 5mph (8km/h)

Caerwent factory was, naturally, a place where high security was kept. Train crews who needed to work trains into the base were vetted by the Ministry of Defence and frequently needed to show their MOD passes when they arrived at the gates leading into the factory. On one occasion, a Caerwent-bound train was about to leave the yard at STJ when another driver climbed onto the footplate and announced he was 'learning the road' and wanted to ride with the crew to the factory. Off they set and at Caldicot Junction took the branch to Caerwent. After a slow trundle up the branch they arrived at the closed gates. A couple of MOD policemen arrived to open the gates and asked for the traincrew's passes. Alas, our road-learning chap didn't have one and was forbidden to travel any further! The train was let in but the gates shut behind it. Our man had to stay outside until the train had finished its work and was ready to return to the tunnel yards again.

Towards the end of the factory's life, coal traffic was the usual 'inwards' flow to Caerwent and coal empties by return. Munitions and raw materials also came to the depot from Barry Docks and via Severn Tunnel Junction. The normal working practice in later years was that once 'in clear' of the main lines at Caldicot Junction and the ground frame restored for main line running again, the train for the factory would proceed slowly along the branch until the bridge over the A48 was reached. Here, the brake van would be detached and the train would then proceed to the factory gates where it would be met by the MOD policeman. Inside the gates, the coal wagons were shunted onto a vacant siding as indicated by the factory shunter. Here the engine was detached and moved to the factory end of a rake of coal empties. When this was ready to return to Caldicot Junction and the gates opened, the train would slowly propel the wagons back to the A48 bridge, where the brake van would be attached again. Then the guard would climb back into his van and hand signal the train slowly back to Caldicot once more. At Caldicot the engine would run round the wagons on the branch loop and head off back to Severn Tunnel Junction Down yard. After the removal of the crossover at Caldicot Junction, trains from Caerwent propelled out onto the Up Gloucester line and went to Chepstow to run round via the crossovers there, returning to Bristol yard when there was a sufficient margin in the traffic.

The branch continued to be used sporadically, but the instructions were later changed to state that any train passing over the branch after inspection must stop short of the bridge over the A48 and check if all was safe before proceeding. No one seemed to specify what should be done if the bridge didn't appear safe!

The bridge carrying the Caldicot Junction to Caerwent line over the A48 near Crick. AUTHOR

The Cold War Years

The Royal Naval Propellant Factory (now taken under the ownership of the Ministry of Defence) underwent several changes after the war, with an emphasis on Cold War weaponry in the shape of a static firing bay facility at the new Guided Weapons Scheme Unit. This was built and commissioned in 1959 for proof of concept, investigation and manufacturing control purposes relating to the Gosling rocket booster engines used to power the Royal Navy's Sea Slug surface-to-air missiles. It was located at the northern edge of the factory, on a southwest-facing slope. The installation consisted of a static firing bay, cubicle building, access road and concrete apron, together with the surrounding earthen bunds. The production and testing of the Gosling rocket motors ceased in 1966, being transferred to the Royal Ordnance Factory at Bishopston. The closure of the entire establishment was announced in 1965 to be completed by

1967. Production at the site ceased in 1965 and decontamination was completed by 1968. The US forces took over parts of the site for weapons storage and shipment during later conflicts, in particular the Iraq wars. The United States Army Depot Activity-Caerwent (USADA-C) was in American hands between 1967 and 1993.

The whole missile testing and development site was later judged by CADW (the Welsh equivalent of English Heritage) to be a monument of national importance for its potential to enhance our knowledge of British World War II munitions production and the effort required to sustain a total war. Nitroglycerine plants are a relatively rare monument class.

This factory was one of the last to be built in the UK and represents the next generation on from another scheduled example, that of another ROF site the cordite factory at Holton Heath, near Poole in Dorset.

CAERWENT BRANCH—The "One Train Working" system without train staff has been withdrawn. The line is now worked in accordance with Table C2 of the Sectional Appendix. The Person-in-Charge is the Crossing Keeper at Caldicot LC.
(See Periodical Operating Notice)

Working of the Caerwent branch in 1987. AUTHOR

CADW STATEMENT ON CAERWENT

The survival of the intact plan form, including buildings, guttering, bunds and infrastructure demonstrates the industrial processes at the site. Together the structures form a readily understandable group and possess important group value. The remains of the individual structures are well preserved and retain significant archaeological potential, with a strong probability of the presence of associated archaeological features and deposits…..The monument is of national importance for its potential to enhance our knowledge of British Cold War weapon systems, where there is a very limited survival of evidence overall. The successful development of the Sea Slug missile represents one of the chief British technological achievements during the Cold War period and marked a point of significant escalation in the arms race. It signifies the important transition between the Royal Navy's use of gun ships and the use of missile warships in the modern era. The remains of the individual structures are well preserved and retain significant archaeological potential, with a strong probability of the presence of associated archaeological features and deposits. The importance of the monument is further enhanced by the group value it shares with Aberporth Range Simulated Ship Firing Platform scheduled as CD213.
The area to be scheduled comprises the remains described and an area around within which related evidence may be expected to survive.

In the twenty-first century, part of the site was used by a company called JTL Landscapes, who undertook to carry out the scrapping of ex-BR locos and multiple unit stock. DMUs, EMUs and electric main line locos were scrapped here. Class 87 electric locos scrapped at Caerwent include: 87016 in 2004; 87005/15/24 in 2005 and 87018/24 in 2010.

The parts of the site no longer used or scheduled are still used by the military as a training area for troops and the western part is a trading estate.

Glascoed

It's worth noting that Severn Tunnel Junction not only made up trains to serve the Caerwent branch, but another close by military facility as well. Glascoed munitions depot between Pontypool and Usk was served by the Little Mill–Monmouth branch. Opened in 1940, it had its own railway station and sidings. The depot supplied the filling for bombs and shells and these were taken away by rail. Famous for filling the 'bouncing bombs' used by 617 squadron, the 'Dambusters' in World War II, the base still had two trains per week from Severn Tunnel Junction in the 1970s.

In 1972, Headcode 8A80, a train of boxvans, was timed to leave the yards at STJ at 07.10 weekdays and run to Glascoed via Newport Maindee Junction and Pontypool Road. Formed with vacuum brake vans at the front of the train as a 'vacuum head' to aid braking, the train also ran on Saturdays as 8A80, but timed to leave Severn Tunnel Junction Down yard at 07.30. Weekdays this train was booked to leave Glascoed at 10.15 and arrive back at Severn Tunnel Junction Bristol yard at 11.45. The Saturday return working left Glascoed at 10.50 and arrived back at Bristol yard at 11.45.

By 1985 the Severn Tunnel Junction–Glascoed working was a Speedlink service and as headcode 6A15 and air braked, it left Severn Tunnel Junction Down yard at 07.55. The return working from Glascoed factory was timed to depart at 10.50 and arrived back at Bristol yard at 11.41. The return headcode was 6A25. There was no Saturday working.

With the 1980s changeover to fully fitted block trains of longer bogie wagons, the traffic ceased as Glascoed was unable to cater for bogie vans; the same was true for Caerwent.

Sudbrook Branch

Also forming the junction with the main line at Caldicot Junction was the short branch to Sudbrook, on the western bank of the River Severn. Here was the pumping station built to control the water from the Severn Tunnel. This tall, brick building housed six Cornish steam pumping engines to drain the Great Spring, a natural freshwater spring disturbed in 1883 by the construction of the tunnel. This hard-water spring is constantly threatening to inundate the Severn Tunnel and would do so if the pumps were ever stopped. Water from the spring was pumped to Caerwent munitions factory.

The branch line was used for coal deliveries to the pumping station's Cornish beam engines, which operated the pumps. British Rail replaced the steam pumping engines with electric pumps in 1961 but kept the Cornish steam engines until the annual costs of repairing and maintaining the out-of-use engines was declared uneconomical. In 1966, BR took the decision to scrap the engines. This was decried as an act of vandalism at the time and one which would almost certainly not be permitted today.

This branch was, like the one to Caerwent, operated under the 'One Train in Steam' (later 'One Train Only') system and had no signalling once the train was beyond the main line connections. The branch was 1 mile and 8 chains (1.7km) long, with three level crossings (operated by trainmen): Pulp Mills Crossing at 40 chains (800m) beyond Caldicot Junction, and two other crossings at 61 chains (1.2km) and 68 chains (1.4km) respectively. Maximum speed anywhere over the branch was 25mph (40km).

Sudbrook pumping station.

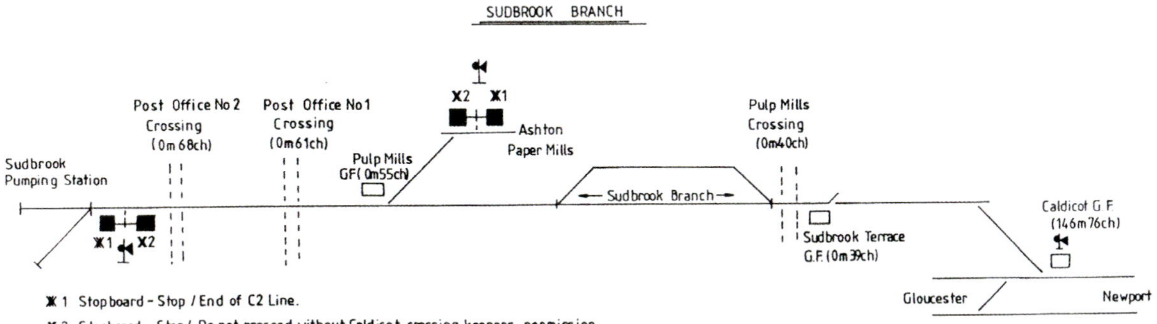

Layout of the Sudbrook branch.

Paper Mill

For years the Sudbrook branch was used mainly for the supply of coal to the pumping station and engineer's trains in connection with maintenance. Other traffic included lime sludge, which was transferred to Sudbrook in old loco tenders and pumped out to sea. Initially the water from the pumps, cleared from the spring at a rate of between 14 and 34 million gallons a day, was returned to the river, but in the late 1950s a company found that it could make use of a steady supply of hard, clean water. The Wiggins Teape group entered into negotiations with British Railways to buy the water from Sudbrook pumping station, on a ninety-nine-year agreement, with the intention of using it in a paper-making process.

The proximity of hardwood forests in South Wales and the Forest of Dean, with the supply of water meant that Wiggins Teape were able to set up a factory to produce good-quality non-carbon bleached paper pulp known as 'Gatecel' in the UK. In an early example of green energy and recycling, the bark, once stripped from the logs, was to be used in a special bark-burning boiler, which in turn supplied some of the steam used for the mill processes.

Sudbrook paper mill was opened in 1958 by Wiggins Teape on a site close to the pumping station. A spur was laid in from the Sudbrook branch and sidings laid at the plant. This enabled trains of tankers carrying sodium sulphite, chlorine and caustic soda – the chemicals used in the pulp-making process – to be discharged at a terminal alongside the mill. These trains were run to Severn Tunnel Junction and then taken to the mill by local trip working. By the 1980s, traffic for the paper mill was moved from Severn Tunnel Junction by local trip working about once a month. Paper pulp was also taken out by train, one destination being Dartford in Kent.

Aerial view of Sudbrook Pulp Mills. AUTHOR'S COLLECTION

Chlorine tankers stand in the sidings at Sudbrook Pulp Mill. BR/AUTHOR'S COLLECTION

SUDBROOK BRANCH—The "One Train Working" system without train staff has been withdrawn. The line is now worked in accordance with Table C2 of the Sectional Appendix. The Person-in-Charge is the Crossing Keeper at Caldicot LC.

New 'STOP' boards have been provided at Sudbrook as shown on the accompanying diagram.

(See Periodical Operating Notice)

Working of the Sudbrook branch in 1987.

Pulp Mills crossing, Sudbrook branch, 2019. The gate is just visible under the foliage. AUTHOR

Soda ash was one commodity that came into the mill via the branch. Another was fuel oil, which, by the mill's final years, was delivered in trains of 100-tonne tankers. The mill used the fuel oil when it was cheaper than gas, changing to gas again when that became cheaper! Goods checker Rob Adaway often supervised the loads.

The mill produced up to around 150,000 tonnes annually of a special form of cardboard casing made from recycled paper and wood pulp. The mill closed in May 2006 after rises in energy costs made the plant uneconomic. At least 135 people were employed there when it closed, with 250 at its peak in the 1970s and 80s.

Passenger trains did not normally use the branch, but over the years it saw several rail tours and enthusiasts' excursions.

The Sudbrook branch has now been lifted and the site has now been redeveloped for housing.

The Severn Tunnel Emergency Train

Vehicles to carry fire engines and rescue apparatus were kept at Severn Tunnel Junction. In the event of any accident or collision in the tunnel, the quickest way to get emergency services personnel and equipment to the site of any incident was by train; walking into the 4-mile-long (6.5km) tunnel was not deemed a sensible option. To this end, two emergency trains were kept for use in the event of an incident. One was stabled at Pilning station on the English side of the river, and the other at Sudbrook, in the pumping station compound. Consisting of two or three six-wheel tank wagons for water, two flat wagons – a carflat and a Weltrol (flat wagons onto which a fire appliance could be loaded) – at Severn Tunnel Junction, two carflats at Pilning and a coach or van for personnel to travel in, these trains inevitably suffered from lack of use. The Pilning train was withdrawn in the 1980s and the Sudbrook train transferred to the old car-loading dock siding at Severn Tunnel Junction station.

After the Severn Tunnel crash of 1991, which exposed flaws in rescue procedures, two class 121 single-unit railcars were kept at STJ for the same purpose and the other rail vehicles withdrawn. The railcars were (thankfully) only ever used for joint services emergency exercises and were themselves withdrawn in 2006 and replaced by road-rail appliances. Today there are three road-rail appliances in use. One is maintained by Avon Fire and Rescue service and is kept at their Avonmouth station. Two others are in the care of South Wales Fire and Rescue service; one is at Caldicot fire station, the other at Malpas. Road access to the railway at both ends of the tunnel was improved to allow easy access for the road-rail units.

Should a permanent way defect be suspected, or a driver report a 'bump' in the tunnel, then the tunnel needed to be inspected. Two special brake vans were kept, one at Severn Tunnel Junction and one at Pilning. If needed, a brake van could be gravity shunted out of the brake van siding and attached to the front of a locomotive. A special tunnel lamp for inspection would be fitted and the brake van propelled through the tunnel. Rules stated that the van had to be accompanied by a movements supervisor or area manager, who would act as the guard. During pile-driving operations in connection with the construction of the Second Severn Crossing in the 1990s, there were numerous incidents where shock waves from the pile driving dislodged the odd brick from the tunnel walls or roof and drivers reported hitting an object. During the ensuing inspection, all trains would be held until the tunnel reported safe for traffic to resume. But what is better? Long delays, or an incident under the river and in darkness?

CHAPTER 10

Signalling

Bishton being the furthest point west in our story, this seems the logical place to start our survey of signal boxes.

Bishton

This box, a Type 28B as described by the Signalling Record Society, was a small, wooden box with outside stairs, sited adjacent to the level crossing. It had a ten-lever GWR stud locking frame, which was replaced by a twenty-four-lever frame in 1919. As it controlled a level crossing, it could not close, and so was not equipped with a block switch.

This box was opened in 1920 and had a twenty-one-lever GWR stud locking frame. It had a block switch.

Both the above boxes closed when the lines were quadrupled in preparation for extra wartime traffic. Bishton Crossing closed on 2 February 1941 and Bishton East on 7 September 1941. Their duties were taken over by a new, brick-built signal box.

This box opened on 2 February 1941, taking over the level crossing and later replacing Bishton East. The new box measured 33ft 4in long by 12ft wide (10m by 3.5m) and stood 11ft (3m) from ground to operating floor level. It had a GWR five-bar vertical tappet locking frame of thirty-eight levers. This box lasted until 16 April 1961, when multiple-aspect colour lights signalling (MAS)

was introduced between Newport and Magor. The levers were removed and the box stayed to operate the level crossing gates when a release was given by Newport panel box. It was then renamed 'Bishton Crossing ground frame'.

Magor

The signal box here was very old box, dating from before the opening of the Severn Tunnel. Known as Type 3, it opened in 1884, and was altered and extended in September 1941 when the lines were quadrupled. It had already been altered in 1936, when its original twenty-five-lever frame was replaced by a GWR three-bar vertical tappet frame of forty-seven levers. This in turn was replaced by five-bar locking in 1960. When, on 16 April 1961, Magor box became a fringe box to Newport panel, a small Entrance-Exit (NX) control panel was added to the box to control new colour-light signals. The box was given the prefix 'MG' which plate was fitted to the front of the box and also to all new signals controlled therefrom.

Undy Crossing (first box)

The box that opened in 1913 was reportedly a timber box that originally came from Margam Moors. It stood on the east side of the level cross-

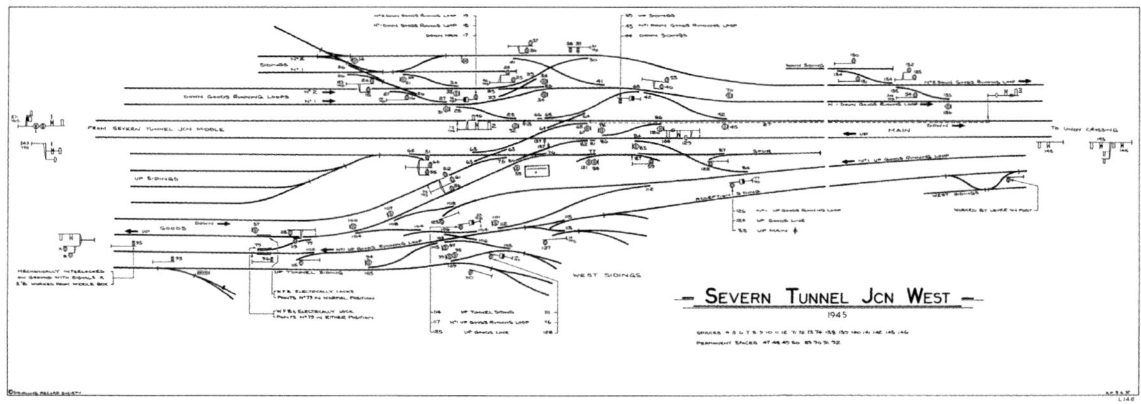

Signal box diagram, Severn Tunnel Junction West (1945). SIGNALLING RECORD SOCIETY

ing at Undy and on the north side of the double track then in place. It had an eighteen-lever GWR stud locking frame which was later replaced by a thirty-lever frame. The box measured 17ft by 9ft (5m by 2.7m) and was a ground-level structure. This box was replaced by a new box in September 1941.

Undy Crossing (second box)

This box was built of brick and reinforced concrete with a flat roof to an ARP design in 1941. The Type 13 box was 33ft 2in long by 12ft wide (10m by 3.5m) and stood 11ft (3m) from ground level to operating floor. It had a GWR five-bar vertical tappet locking frame of forty-seven levers, controlling the (now) four lines and new goods loops. It had no block switch. Undy Crossing box closed on 10 July 1960 and was demolished, when the new storage sidings known as Undy yard were built. New goods lines ran over the site of the box.

Severn Tunnel Junction West (first box)

The first box here was probably opened around 1886 and closed in 1901. It was a timber structure.

Severn Tunnel Junction West (second box)

This box opened in December 1901, replacing the older box. It originally had a ninety-one-lever frame with GWR three-bar horizontal tappet locking, which was replaced by a frame of 130 levers in 1920 as the layout expanded. This box closed in April 1945.

Severn Tunnel Junction West (third box)

This was another Type 13 box of similar construction to the second Undy Crossing box; it was another ARP design but a little later in the war than most other boxes on the GW, which were built to similar design. The box opened in April 1945 and had a GWR five-bar vertical tappet locking frame of 145 levers, which was extended to 162 levers in July 1960 when the yards were expanded. There were twenty-three spaces in the lever frame, giving a total number of working levers of 139.

Just under eight years later, West box closed, on 30 November 1968, when all signalling between Magor and Caldicot Junction (Gloucester lines) and Severn Tunnel West (Bristol lines) was taken over by Newport panel under Stage 1 of the Newport MAS eastern extension scheme.

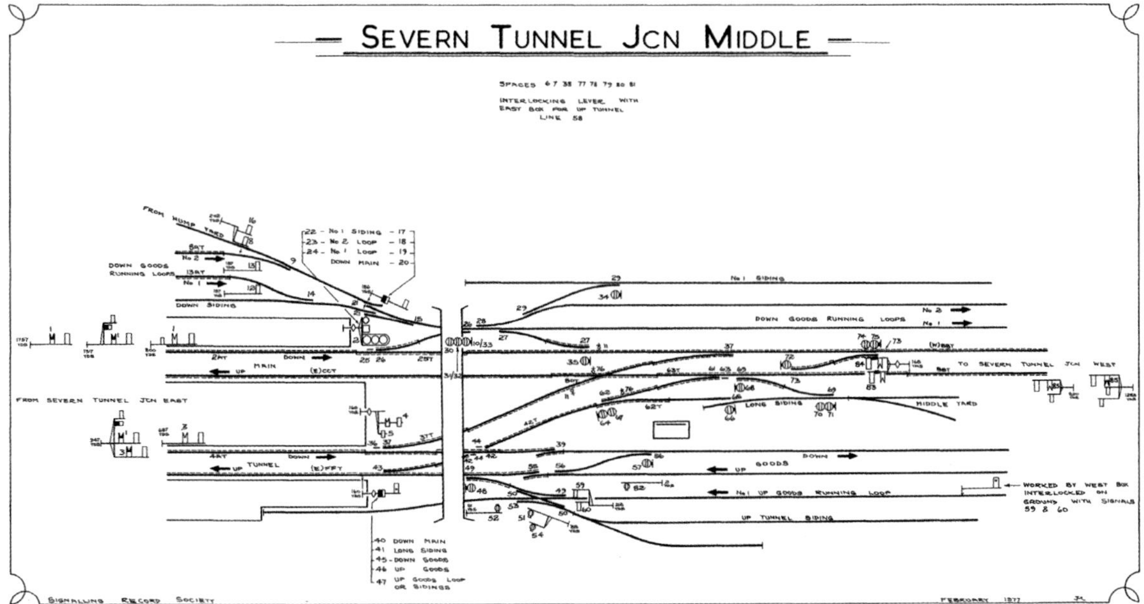

Signal box diagram, Severn Tunnel Middle. SIGNALLING RECORD SOCIETY

Severn Tunnel Junction Middle (first box)

The opening date of the first box here is unknown, but it must have been somewhere between 1886 and 1901. No further details are known at present.

Severn Tunnel Junction Middle (second box) This was a GWR Type 7B and opened in 1901 to replace the first box. The box was constructed of brick and had outside stairs. It measured 38ft by 13ft by 10ft from ground to operating floor. It had eighty-five levers, originally with eight spaces, leaving seventy-seven working levers. By 1955, after alterations, the box had an extra two spaces so had seventy-five working levers when it was closed on 30 November 1968 as part of Stage 1 of the Newport MAS eastern extension. This box did not have a block switch.

One other important function of Middle box was to advise other signal boxes of the running of trains and any delays. In particular, Middle box was the box responsible for contacting Bristol Stapleton Road signal box to advise the train regulator stationed there in GWR days of the departure time from Pontypool Road station of all North to West expresses and perishables trains, plus the departure times from Newport station of all Up South Wales expresses and perishables trains, which would run through Stapleton Road and beyond. Likewise, Middle box would receive from Stapleton Road the departure or passing time of all trains running via the Severn Tunnel as well as necessary information from Pontypool Road and Newport signal boxes.

Severn Tunnel Junction East (first box)

Again, the actual opening date isn't known, but it must have been somewhere between 1886 and 1906. The box had ninety-six levers.

Severn Tunnel Junction East (second box)

This was a GWR Type 7D and replaced the first box in December 1906. It had a 100-lever frame until this was replaced by one of 132 levers with six spaces and GW five-bar VT locking in 1938. When the yards were further expanded in 1960, the frame was extended to 147 levers with twenty spaces. There was no block switch.

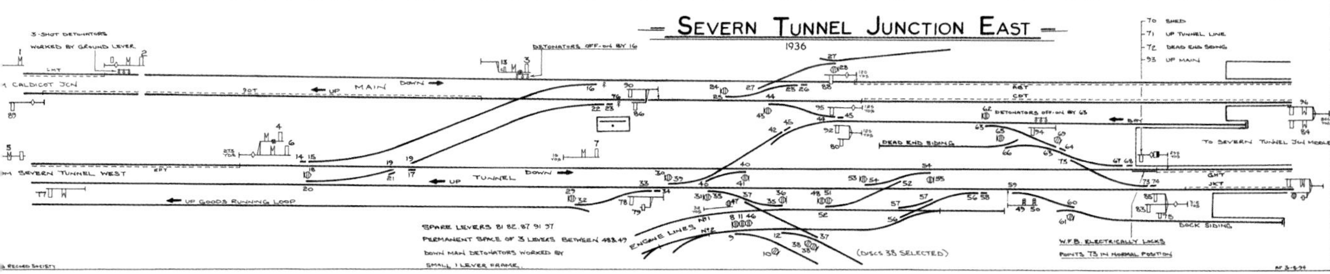

Signal box diagram, Severn Tunnel East (1936). SIGNALLING RECORD SOCIETY

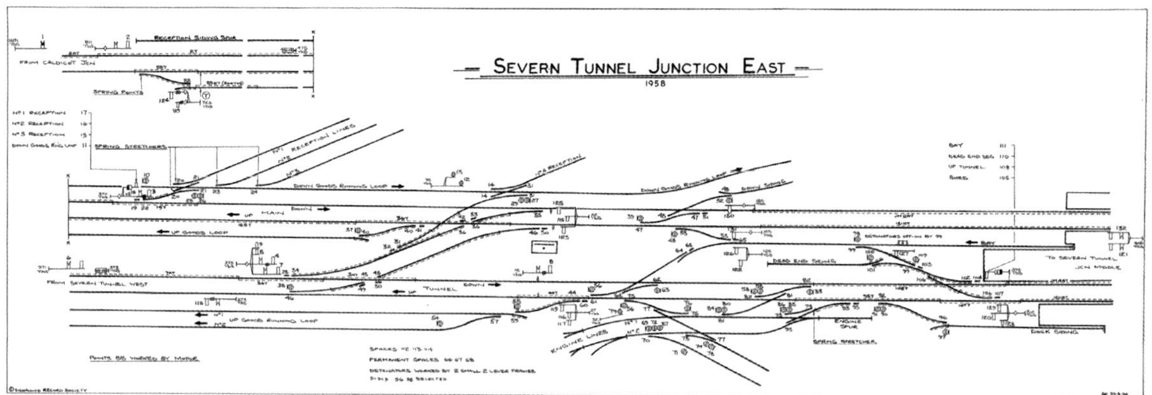

Signal box diagram, Severn Tunnel East (1958). SIGNALLING RECORD SOCIETY

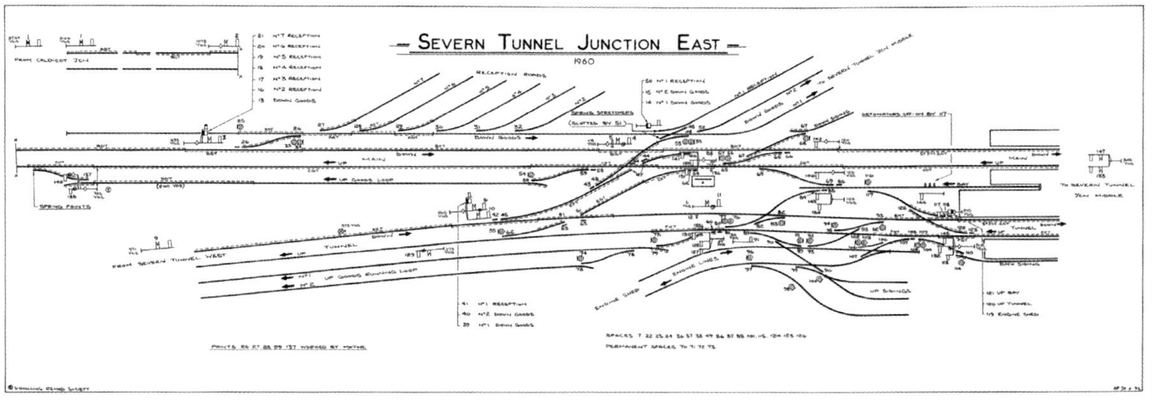

Signal box diagram, Severn Tunnel East (1960). SIGNALLING RECORD SOCIETY

Severn Tunnel Junction Up Hump Cabins

Severn Tunnel Junction Up hump cabin This box opened in 1939. It was a radically different design to other GWR boxes, although there were parallels with the ARP design. It was equipped with a Westinghouse 'thumb switch' panel, operating hump yard points via compressed air motors. It closed on 6 September 1981.

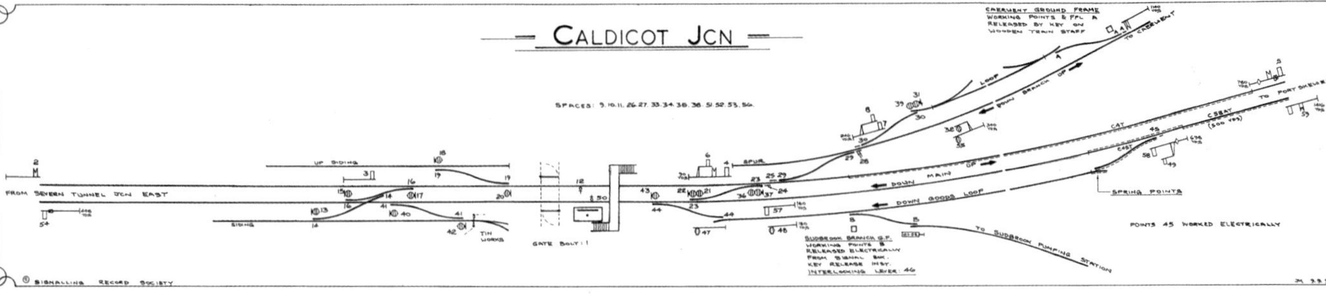

Signal box diagram, Caldicot Junction, showing Sudbrook and Caerwent branches. SIGNALLING RECORD SOCIETY

Severn Tunnel Junction Down hump cabin

The Down box opened on 1 October 1939. Like the Up hump cabin, it was radically different design from other GWR boxes though there were parallels with the ARP design. It was equipped with a Westinghouse 'thumb switch' panel, operating hump yard points via compressed air motors. It closed on 4 December 1982. (This box was the most photographed hump box as it was in full view of the road overbridge and the station.)

Caldicot Junction, Gloucester Lines (first box)

A signal box was provided here in 1884 to control the Sudbrook branch and the level crossing over the road between Caldicot village and Caldicot Pill. This signal box was superseded by a new, larger box (brought from Aller Siding in Devon) on 11 October1927.

Caldicot Junction, Gloucester lines (second box)

Replacing the original box, this new one opened on 11 October 1927. It was a GWR Type 27C box, with twenty-nine levers, equipped with GWR five-bar VT locking. It controlled the level crossing at Caldicot and the entrance to the Down goods loop.

In connection with the wartime expansion of the yards in 1939, the box was extended to 21ft 2in long by 12ft 2in (6.5m by 3.7m) wide and 8ft (2.5m) to the operating floor. At the same time it had the lever frame extended to fifty-nine levers to take on the additional loops and the branch to Caerwent. The box was renamed from 'Caldicot Crossing' to 'Caldicot Junction' at the same time. It was to be the last box on the site

When Caldicot Junction became a fringe box to Newport panel after the extension of MAS eastward in 1968, the box was prefixed 'CJ'.

When the second stage of Newport MAS eastern extension took place, on the weekend of 1–3 February 1969, Caldicot Junction box was one of five signal boxes officially closed. However, it only closed as a signal box; there were still the two branches (Sudbrook and Caerwent) to control, and the level crossing. Remote control of such equipment was not yet sophisticated (or cheap) enough to install and so Caldicot box was renamed 'Caldicot ground frame' and retained levers to control the points and ground signals for the branches, plus a crossover and the level crossing. To use any of these points, signals or the crossing required a release from Newport panel signal box.

Caldicot Ground Frame This was a ground-level cabin, of (then) modern design which was built on the same side of the tracks, but on the Newport side of the level crossing. It replaced Caldicot ground frame (signal box) in 1979. This was closed in 2010 when the crossing was closed.

Severn Tunnel West, Bristol Lines (first box)

Almost certainly opened not long after the Severn Tunnel itself, in 1888, this was a small, brick and timber box sited close to the Welsh side tunnel mouth. The box stood on the Down side of the line, close to the tunnel mouth. It closed in 1901 being replaced by the second box.

Severn Tunnel West (second box)

Opened in 1901, it was a GWR 'Type 7B' box, measuring 21ft x 12ft 8in. It had a GWR stud locking frame with 17 levers. It was closed on 6 July 1968 in connection with the Newport MAS eastern extension.

Out of interest, the English (east) side of the tunnel had been protected by a similar brick and timber box as the first box at 'Tunnel West'. This was replaced by a 'Type 13' ARP box in 1942 which closed at the same time as the Welsh side box.

Newport Panel Western Extension

In December 1962 the immediate area around Newport High Street station was resignalled. All the old signalling was recovered along with the old signal boxes. The tracks through and on the approaches to Newport station were realigned and the whole layout became more flexible for traffic. The plan was to extend the area controlled by the 1962 new panel signalling centre at Newport to cover a wider area. It would eventually link up with Cardiff, Gloucester and Bristol signalling panels, when they were built.

Initial Work

The first stage of the Newport western extension was to take place in December 1968. For months beforehand, preliminary works took place to install new signals, build new points and crossings and put ground frames into place. There was an engineers' occupation of the lines between Magor and Severn Tunnel West on Sunday 28 April 1968, when, as a forerunner to the main works, the Down goods line, Down reception siding and Down and Up main lines were blocked between the hours of 06.00 and 18.00 in order for new points to be laid in. A crane was in use.

On Sunday 7 July 1968, more preliminary work was undertaken, this time at Severn Tunnel West and Middle. At the West box, the facing connection in the Up main leading to the Up goods line was taken out of use. The connection spur–Up goods was also taken out of use and fixed in the reverse position. Similarly, the spur safety point was taken out of use and fixed reverse. The compound points in the Up sidings leading to the spur were taken out of use and fixed normal. The trailing points Up sidings to spur from Down goods were fixed normal

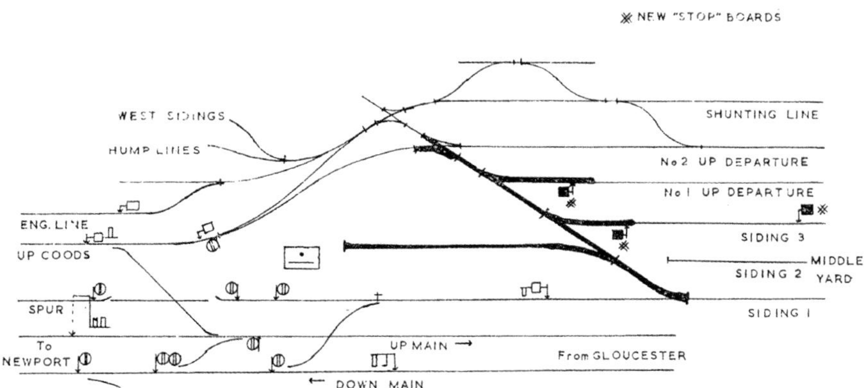

Pre-1968 resignalling: modifications at Severn Tunnel Junction West.

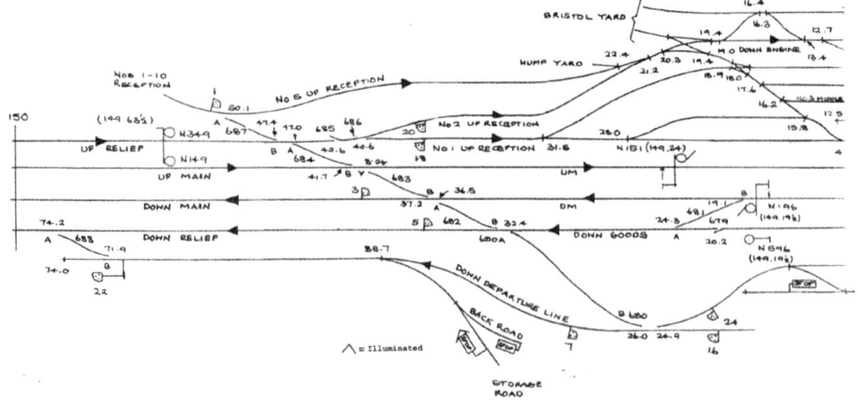

Post-1968 resignalling: the layout in late years. West Junction box stood approximately where the figure '28.0' is on No. 1 Up reception line.

and the Up sidings safety points fixed normal. All associated signals were recovered. New connections were provided from Bristol yard to Up goods or Up main and Up goods to No. 1 Up departure and Nos. 1 and 3 Middle yard sidings. All were hand worked. No. 2 Middle yard siding was shortened at the Newport end. A new cripple siding for wagons was provided at the connection from No. 1 Middle yard to Bristol yard and hand worked.

At Severn Tunnel Middle, the block controls for the Down goods line between there and Severn Tunnel West box were recovered; after the new works were completed, this line would become the No. 1 Up departure siding. The Up goods line was to become the No. 2 Up departure siding. The No. 1 Up goods siding would become the Up shunting line.

At Severn Tunnel Junction itself, there were significant changes to the layout. A new connection was laid in to link the Down tunnel line (from Bristol) to the Down main line (from Gloucester). This connection passed through the Up main line, and at this point 'elbows' or 'switch diamonds' were provided owing to the angle of the crossing. At the west end of the station a new connection between the Up and Down tunnel lines was provided. Three new crossovers were laid in to provide a 'ladder' crossing linking the Down hump yard with the Up sidings, enabling direct shunts and transfers between the Up and Down yards. The immediate connection leading from the Down hump yard was controlled from a new ground frame, Severn Tunnel Junction West ground frame, released by Newport panel.

Weekend Blitz

From 16.30 on the afternoon of Saturday, 30 November 1968, the lines between Magor (inclusive) and Caldicot Junction and Severn Tunnel West (exclusive) were taken over by the Chief Civil Engineer's department and that of the Chief Signal and Telecommunications Engineer. Gangs of permanent way staff descended on the trackwork and began replacing points and crossings. Teams of S & T staff arrived at signal boxes, lineside locations and relay rooms to start work.

From the beginning of this work, the signal boxes at Magor, Severn Tunnel Junction West, Severn Tunnel Junction Middle and Severn Tunnel Junction East were all closed and taken out of use. All semaphore signalling was recovered. Any existing colour-light signals that were not included as part of the new scheme were also recovered.

To the east of Severn Tunnel Junction, on the Gloucester lines at Caldicot Junction, where the existing signal box would stay in use for a while yet, some changes were made. The Up main distant and Up main home signals were recovered and replaced by a three-aspect colour light signal, designated 'CJ3' – the 'CJ' being the prefix for Caldicot Junction (the same prefix method applied to signals worked from all other signal boxes involved, Newport panel box signals being 'N' and so on). The new signal stood on the west side of the level crossing at Caldicot. The existing Up goods line between Severn Tunnel Junction East and Caldicot Halt was renamed 'Up main goods loop'.

At the western mouth of the Severn Tunnel, at Severn Tunnel West box, the Up goods loop was renamed 'Up tunnel goods loop; the reason for

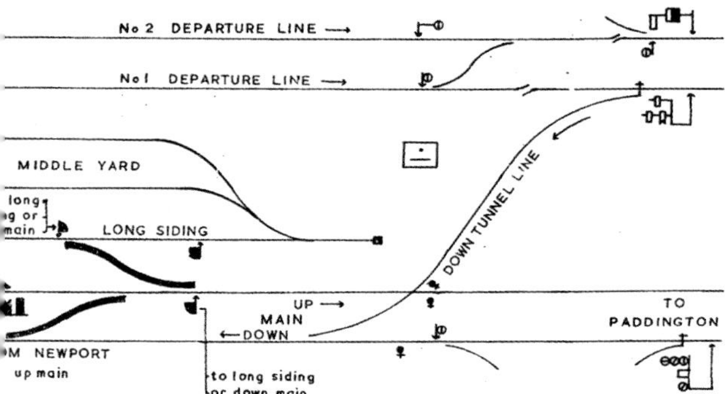

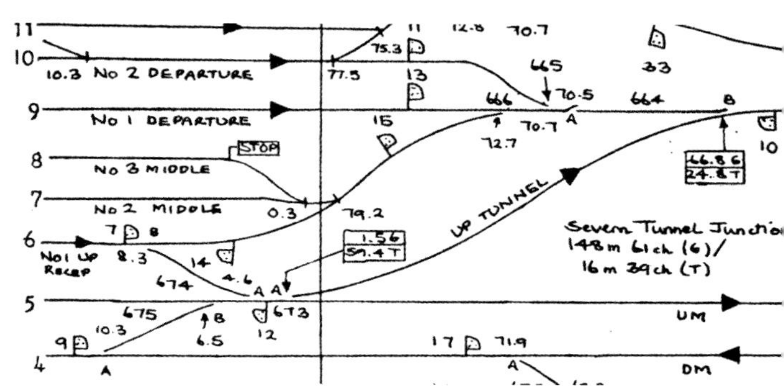

Pre-1968 resignalling: modifications at Severn Tunnel Junction Middle. BR

Post-1968 resignalling: the same area in later years.

the changes of name was that the lines had been renamed: the Gloucester lines became 'Up and Down main' while the Bristol lines became 'Up and Down tunnel lines'. Still at Severn Tunnel West, the Up main home and Up goods home signals were replaced by two three-aspect colour lights signals sited on a bracket. These were designated 'TW2' and 'TW3' respectively. The Down main distant signal was recovered and the Down main home signal, previously renewed as a three-aspect colour light signal, was redesignated 'TW16'.

On the western approaches to the Severn Tunnel Junction yards, at Magor, the signal box was closed. As with the other boxes closed, all semaphore signalling was removed. Existing colour-light signals controlled by Magor – MG44, MG46 and MG47 – were also recovered, being no longer required. Any colour light signals previously operated by Magor but still needed as part of the new scheme were transferred to Newport panel box control.

As the layout at Magor had been provided for the new scheme well in advance, there was no alteration to points or crossings here, most being brought under the control of Newport. One exception was the facing Down main–Up main crossover at the west end of the old station. This was transferred to a new ground frame, Magor West ground frame, which was released by Newport. At the east end of the station, the old cement siding ground frame was renamed 'Magor East ground frame', and was henceforth released by Newport instead of Magor box. A stop lamp at the cement siding was removed. Finally, the Up and Down goods lines between Magor and Severn Tunnel Junction West were equipped for passenger train working and renamed 'Up and Down relief lines'.

The release of the existing ground frame at the west end of Undy yard was transferred to Newport instead of Severn Tunnel Junction West.

A ground frame that controlled the trailing crossover between the Up and Down main lines just west of Caldicot Halt had its release transferred from Severn Tunnel Junction East box to Newport.

In the Down hump yard, new works were carried out to equip sidings on the eastern approach to the Down hump summit with motor points. These would henceforth be controlled from the Down hump control panel, where alterations were made to add sidings 1 to 8 to the layout.

The work, although not without the occasional technical hitch, went well and by the Monday morning everything was handed back for normal working, with a few speed restrictions over new track.

Final stages

To complete the story, three months later, Stage 2 of the Newport resignalling western extension was brought in. Caldicot Junction signal box was closed as a signal box on 22 February 1969. All existing signals were either removed or had their controls taken over by Newport. The control of Caldicot signal CJ13, mentioned above, was transferred to Newport. The box was reduced in status to ground frame, continuing to have control of the points and shunt signals for both the Caerwent and the Sudbrook branches, both of which were still in use.

Stage 3 was implemented on 5 July 1969. Severn Tunnel West and Severn Tunnel East boxes were closed, the entire length of the tunnel now coming under the control or supervision of Newport. All existing signalling at both locations was either removed or transferred to Newport.

After these stages were completed, the only signal boxes still working in their original functions were the control cabins at Severn Tunnel Junction Down hump, Severn Tunnel Junction Up hump and Undy ground frame. None of these, of course, had ever controlled any trains on the main lines.

By July 1969, then, all approaches to Severn Tunnel Junction were controlled from Newport panel signal box.

A further alteration came about over the period Saturday 20 June–Tuesday 23 June 1970, when Severn Tunnel Junction West ground frame was removed. The connection from the Down hump yard that the ground frame had controlled was now motorized and controlled from Newport. Minor but appropriate signalling alterations were made.

Newport panel box thus had full control of the signalling between Pilning on the English side (where it linked to Bristol panel box in 1971) to Severn Tunnel Junction and beyond. This state of affairs continued until the new computer-equipped signalling centre at Cardiff – the South Wales Control Centre (SWCC) – took over complete control of all signalling between Newport (Maindee East), and Patchway on the English side of the tunnel, and to just beyond Caldicot on the Gloucester lines. This occurred over the period up to 4 January 2010. Caldicot ground frame cabin was retained for the time being.

Signalling Staff

There being so many signal boxes in the area, it stands to reason that there were many regular and relief signalmen needed to work them over the years. Severn Tunnel Junction West box was known to have employed regular men Johnny Harries and Roy Thomas. Severn Tunnel Junction Middle box (always known to staff as 'Centre' box) saw David Richards, Stan Evans and George Foulkes. Severn Tunnel Junction West box was always the busiest and had a 'booking boy' and a traffic regulator on each shift as well as a signalman. Ern Sands and Geoff Shenton are known to have worked here as signalmen. Bill Hicks was a telephonist at Severn Tunnel Junction East box, and Walter Jones a signalman.

Another employed as a telephonist was Doug Harris. William Winter was a telephonist in Severn Tunnel Junction East box before he became roster clerk at the diesel depot.

The signal lampman – the 'lampy' – in the 1940s was William Alsop.

At Caldicot Junction, some of the signalmen recalled are Dave Morgan, Phil Taylor and Malcolm Arthurs. Arthurs was later to gain promotion and became an assistant district signalling inspector at Bristol. After Caldicot Junction was reduced in status as a result of Stage 2 of the Newport resignalling western extension, Peter Payne and reliefman Stan Evans moved there.

Other signalmen who are known to have worked in the Severn Tunnel Junction area boxes, but who were relief signalmen or whose specific box isn't known were: Ken Wood, Ted Pippin, Fred Boon, Sid Thorne, Albert Jones, Charles Hughes, Walter Gomm, William Court, William Taplin and Edgar Jarvis, along with Frank Payne, who was a special class relief signalman; Jack Kite, who was also the NUR union representative; and Adrian Baker and George Hare, who were relief men.

In the twenty-first century the Severn Tunnel Junction area was once again subjected to resignalling. This time it was computers that took over the control of the area's points and signals, rather than switches replacing levers. A new signalling centre at Cardiff was opened and took over the STJ area as part of the Newport area signalling renewal from Monday 4 January 2010. The main junction between the Bristol and Gloucester lines, which had previously been situated at the river (east) end of the station, was now resited to the west side of the station. Platform 4 was reopened (the old Platform 1). All new signalling, previously installed, was now brought into use and controlled by computers at the new South Wales Control Centre (SWCC). This stage of the work also saw the SWCC take over control of the lines through the Severn Tunnel and as far as Patchway on the Bristol side.

Severn Tunnel Junction East ground frame was taken out of use.

CHAPTER 11

Railway Housing

From being a place that was home to mainly farm-workers and a few quarrymen in 1871, Rogiet village saw sustained growth with the arrival of the railway, especially after the opening of the Severn Tunnel in 1886. The presence of the new station at Severn Tunnel Junction became a catalyst for the growth of the village. The censuses of 1851, 1861 and 1871 show the main employment to be agricultural, with a few working in the limestone quarries at Ifton. There were no railway workers. The area showed an increase in population of a third in the ten years between 1881 and 1891, from eighty-four to 122 persons.

Brick Terraces

These people needed somewhere to live and new homes were built accordingly. The first phase of new building was the construction of red-brick terraces. These were named Railway Terrace,

Ifton Terrace: one of the early streets in Rogiet to be constructed for railway workers. AUTHOR

Ifton Terrace and (perhaps ironically) Seaview Terrace. All were built towards the river side of the area: Seaview Terrace on the approach road to Severn Tunnel Junction station; Railway Terrace alongside the railway line to the west of the station and Ifton Terrace on the river side of what would become the 'new town' of Rogiet.

A pub was built and named the Roggiet Hotel, a large Victorian-style construction that was perhaps a little oversize for what was then still a small community – perhaps the owners had an eye to the future? The Roggiet Hotel operated as an active hotel, mostly for the farmers and other agricultural workers from the nearby cattle market. There followed a school and the village post office. Ifton Terrace was one of the first streets of houses built. In 1911, No. 12 Ifton Terrace was occupied by Alf Carter, a, GWR timekeeper, along with his wife and family, plus a lodger, Charles Gilford, a GWR railway guard. No. 10 was occupied by

James Dobson, a GWR engine driver, his wife and daughter and they, too, had a lodger: William John Thompson, a GWR foreman fitter. No. 8 was lived in by loco department foreman William Gerrard, his wife, two daughters and two sons. The eldest son, William Junior, was aged sixteen and employed in the loco department stores. Charles Howell, aged sixty-seven, was an inspector on the GWR and lived in No. 6, along with his wife. In No. 4 lived Richard Killick, railway engine driver, and his family. Eldest son Albert was a railway engine cleaner.

Further evidence of the extent to which these early-built homes were dedicated to railway staff can be demonstrated by looking at the occupation of Railway Terrace in 1911.

No. 1 Railway Terrace was occupied by GWR railway inspector Richard Hancock, his wife, Sarah, son Alexander, a railway telegraph clerk, and another son and daughter of school age.

Empty and forlorn in 2019, the Roggiet Hotel. AUTHOR

No. 2 was lived in by Charles Bullock, his wife Emily, son Reg, a carriage cleaner, and thirteen-year-old daughter Elsie. Charles was a GWR goods guard.

In No. 3 lived shunter William Johnson and family, while in No. 4 was another shunter, Anthony Curtis, with his family. They also had a boarder, twenty-six-year-old Horace Webb, a GWR carriage and wagon examiner.

No. 5 was occupied by Edward Hughes, a leading platelayer, with his family, which included son George, who was a loco cleaner, while No. 6 was the home of goods guard William Lines, wife Emma and four sons. They, too, had a lodger: twenty-three-year-old porter William Ayliffe.

In No. 7 lived foreman platelayer Thomas Preece with his wife Maria. Their eldest son, John, was a platelayer. Another son broke tradition by becoming a baker! Here, too, was a lodger in the shape of twenty-six-year-old John Cox, a railway mechanic's labourer.

No. 8 was the home of GWR gas lineman Richard Harries with his wife and school-age son, and last but not least, No. 9 was occupied by goods guard Charles Ball with his wife and daughter, along with a lodger, William Wellings, who worked as a platelayer.

Railway Terrace was not unusual in being railway accommodation occupied by railway employees. Many areas had a row or two of railway houses for staff. What made the Rogiet/Severn Tunnel Junction area as a whole different was the large amount of purpose-built railway housing.

These are just some examples of how almost every house in the town was lived, or lodged, in by railway staff, almost exclusively employed at Severn Tunnel Junction – if not in the station, then in the marshalling yards, engine sheds or wagon repair works. This was to be a town to rival Swindon, albeit on a much smaller scale.

Interestingly, Railway Terrace was known to locals and railway staff as 'the Barracks', although the reason for this name has been forgotten. It may have come from the somewhat austere design of the houses, or perhaps it was because it was occu-

The pub sign still hangs in 2019 but can attract no more customers; at least the brewery had made a good job of the sign. AUTHOR

pied by so many railway staff. It's difficult to think how the people living in Railway Terrace coped with the constant noise of shunting, trains passing and locomotives standing outside, especially once the yards had expanded to their final size by 1960. At least they had help with internal lighting due to the prolific tall yard lights dotted everywhere. The residents were not alone in being liable to disturbance from railway noise: one driver who lived in Seaview Terrace and who shall remain nameless (although still well known to this day), used to complain to all and sundry about being disturbed by loco noise when in bed!

Understandably, the growth of Rogiet slowed when the Great War broke out, but post-war the need for working-class housing in towns throughout Britain became greater. In 1919, parliament passed the ambitious Housing Act, which promised government subsidies to help finance the construction of 500,000 new houses within three years. A noble gesture perhaps, in the light of post-war needs and pressure to fulfil promises to provide homes fit for heroes. Chepstow Rural District Council built some homes in Caldicot Road and Ifton Road as a result of finances obtained via the Housing Act. The building of South Grove was started as well, but in the early 1920s the economy rapidly weakened. Funding for homes had to be cut, and nationally, only 213,000 homes were completed under the provisions of the 1919 Act.

Garden Village Society Housing

Partly as a result of the Act, a new housing scheme for Severn Tunnel Junction took off when an organization known initially as the 'Great Western Railway Severn Tunnel Garden Village Society' undertook, in 1919, to build a further ninety-four houses. Chepstow Council would invest money, and tenants would invest in ordinary shares in the society, whose membership was restricted to railwaymen. The first new houses built by the Society were known to locals as the 'yellow houses' owing to the pale ochre colour of the wash used on the exterior walls. These were in Meadowcroft and Woodland View. They were sturdy houses with a decent garden for tenants to grow fruit and vegetables.

The concept of 'garden villages' and 'garden cities' had its origins in 1899, when the Garden City Association was started by Sir Ebenezer Howard.

Howard had become interested in the poor conditions brought about by the Industrial revolution. Whilst living in towns had certain advantages (mostly for employers) Howard considered that 'human beings became psychologically poor' if they were denied contact with nature and the rural life. In garden cities, all these advantages would be brought together with industry, on the same site. Thus new towns like Welwyn Garden City and Letchworth Garden City came about. Practical, new houses in leafy streets would make the lot of the working man and woman much more tolerable.

On 5 April 1923, architect Thomas Alwyn Lloyd FRIBA (1881–1960) was appointed to design thirty 'cottages' for the Great Western (Severn Tunnel) Garden Village Society Ltd, as it had become. Lloyd was a leading Welsh architect and town planner. He was one of the founders of the Town Planning Institute in 1914 and became its president in 1933. He was also a founding member of the Council for the Protection of Rural Wales. Lloyd's office was in Cardiff. Educated at Liverpool University and Liverpool School of Architecture, Lloyd had an impressive pedigree in the field of designing low-cost housing for working people. Between 1907 and 1912 he was an assistant to

Some more early GW Garden Village houses; these are in South Grove, Rogiet.
FROM AN OLD POSTCARD

Sir Raymond Unwin in the Hampstead Garden Suburb project. In 1913 he had been appointed as consulting architect to the Welsh Town Planning and Housing Trust. Between 1913 and 1914 he had been responsible for designing 205 houses for Wrexham Garden Village. He worked on the Llandiloes Garden Suburb in 1914; Barry Garden Suburb in 1915; and Rhiwbina Garden Village, Cardiff, between 1920 and 1923.

The railway community of Rogiet/Severn Tunnel Junction, living in what would have been described in the 1960s as a 'new town', found itself not just a focal point for the normal 'outside work' community activities, such as football and cricket, but other cultural activities of the sort often proposed by well-meaning philanthropists as being suitable to 'broaden the mind' of working class folk. To give the seal of approval to the new scheme, a cultural event was to be held. Being on the edge of Welsh territory (locals would have thought of themselves as Welsh, but technically were living in the English county of Monmouth), it was decided to hold the 1925 annual Grand Eisteddfod at Rogiet. This was organized by the Severn Tunnel Junction branch of the Great Western Railway's Social and Educational Union. It was held on Thursday 3 September 1925 in a field 'adjoining the Magor and Caldicot main road'. There were musical events, singing and reading. Prizes were awarded for the best reader, violin player and so on. Taxis to and from the railway station could be ordered from Arthur M. Walker. Naturally, the vicar was present to preside over the spiritual side of affairs.

Then, as now, many local businesses advertised in the Eisteddfod programme, giving us an insight into local people. The Roggiett (sic) Hotel was there; John G. Davis ran the 'stationer and tobacconist'; A. F. George ran the general store. The baker was J. Cartwright; the boot- and shoemaker and repairer, J. Marsh. The Chepstow Co-operative Society (Caldicot Branch) had 'vans delivering daily'.

Mr Hall Williams was the appointed secretary of the Severn Tunnel Garden Village Society and in June 1925 they appointed builder J. C. Richards

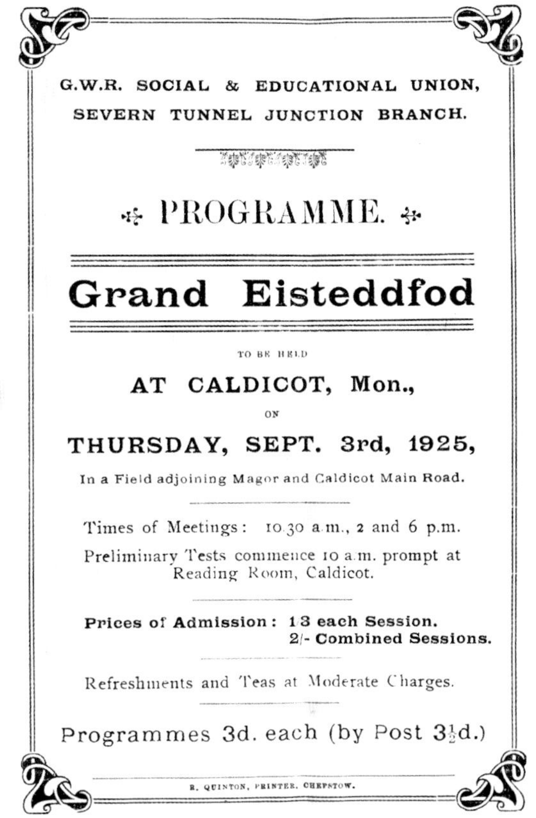

The 1925 Grand Eisteddfod poster. J. NEMETH COLLECTION

to construct the first thirty cottages at Rogiet. Work was slow and there were frequent disputes between the council and the Garden Village Society in respect of funding and how the tenants were to repay money.

In April 1926, the builder, J. C. Richards, applied to the council for permission to extend the local water main to the houses he was building. Oddly, the council refused permission. Then, in May 1926, the Ministry of Health wrote to Chepstow Council asking about the 'present position regards the erection of fifty houses at Severn Tunnel Junction'. These were in addition to the thirty already under construction. At the same time, the GWR asked for permission to renew an existing licence for the storage of 200 gallons (900 litres) of petrol at Severn Tunnel Junction station; this was renewed without question!

The same month saw another letter to Chepstow Council from Hall Williams, secretary of the Garden Village Society. He was undertaking to build a further twenty houses at STJ, but said it would be necessary for the society to negotiate with the GWR before any further steps were taken. This was presumably for extra funding. Once the council had given formal sanction to the building of the houses, further tenders for the work could be obtained. The council had themselves loaned the society the sum of £1,000 under the provisions of the 1919 Act. This money was to be used by the society to reduce the investment that tenants were to make in ordinary shares. The society found it difficult to apply this condition to the twenty houses already sanctioned but the council stood firm.

Now, however, there was a cloud on the horizon. The April 1925 budget overvalued the pound by 10 per cent in order to make the pound as valuable as the dollar. Industry bosses needed to make up this overvaluation and workers' pay was cut. Mine owners were the first to announce wages cuts. On 1 May 1926, one million miners were locked out of work and the General Strike began. The strike was seen by many as the climax of the increasing class struggle in Britain since World War I. For nine days, nearly every inhabitant of Britain was affected as more than four million workers walked out, bringing key industries to a standstill and transport and food supplies to a halt. A state of emergency was declared. Food, coal and petrol were stockpiled. Regional civil commissioners were given dictatorial powers and were ready to go into action at the delivery of a telegram. This telegram was sent on 2 May. Army and Navy leave was cancelled and reinforcements were sent to Scotland, South Wales, London and Lancashire. By the end of the first day of the strike, builders, printers, dockers, and iron, steel, metal, heavy chemical, transport and railway workers were out on strike. This was almost the revolution many had hoped for, but after a week there was little in the way of co-ordinated efforts. The TUC was at odds with the workers' aims and without any idea where they wanted the strike to go, the workers saw no way forward but to go back to work.

How much the state of affairs affected the building of homes for the railway workers can only be supposed. Chepstow Council would have been seen by some as representatives of the 'ruling classes'. Hall Williams advised the council that owing to 'previous industrial conditions', the Garden Village Society were not in a position to erect further houses but that 'as soon as the coal stoppage… had been settled' the matter would be revisited. It would appear that Chepstow Council and the Garden Village Society did not see eye to eye over the housing scheme. The council served a three-day notice on the society in July 1926 regarding a defective drain.

By February 1927, Chepstow Council were writing to the Garden Village Society to enquire as to the previous proposal to erect fifty houses at Severn Tunnel Junction. By March of that year there was still some dispute as to the loan arrangements, which prompted Hall Williams to attend a council meeting in person that April. He told the meeting that the houses could be completed by September 1927 if the loan arrangements could be sorted out.

After much debate, the council made the decision to rescind the previous arrangements and for the loan of £1,000 to be now used by the Garden Village Society for reducing the average investment of tenants throughout the estate.

Building now went on apace, and by November 1928 the Garden Village Society was inviting tenders for the erection of six pairs of houses as an extension to Crossway. Chepstow Council granted assistance under the Housing Financial Provisions Act 1924 in respect of these twelve new houses and the clerk to the council wrote to the Minister of Health for sanction to build the homes.

From then on until World War II, house building continued and more people – mostly railway employees – moved into the area, increasing the population from 136 in 1921 to 234 in 1934. Many

No. 43 Crossway, Rogiet, home of Augusta and May Dodsley. MAUREEN RENDALL

railwaymen still commuted from the other local villages, but for those who lived in Rogiet it was but a 10-minute walk to work.

Typical 1920s House

Let's now take a look at a typical house in Rogiet. No. 43 Crossway must have been there in 1927 and was known as 'Lynwood, 7 New Road'. It was still 'New Road' in 1939 but became 43 Crossway after the war.

Widowed Augusta Dodsley bought the house circa 1926/27 and moved there from rented accommodation at Shirenewton/Earlswood with her daughter May. Elder daughter Sybil, a teacher, moved there in 1927 and married her fiancé in St Mary's church, Rogiet the same year. Sybil and her husband, who was an RAF steward, moved to Middlesex shortly after.

The house was a brick-built two up, two down property. Downstairs the front door led to the small hallway where were the stairs to the upper rooms and a through passage to the kitchen. A door off this passage led to the front room. The kitchen, which was at the rear of the property, was the width of the house. It had a small coal-fired range and a sink. There was no bathroom: the bath was the traditional tin bath and was normally kept covered with a tin sheet, which was used as a work surface. There was room for a small table at which meals were taken. Upstairs there was a small landing from which led doors to the two bedrooms.

A door from the kitchen led into the back garden, where, built on to the rear of the house, was a wooden lean-to which contained the dark and cobweb-infested lavatory, next door to which was the coal shed. Augusta kept chickens in the generously sized back garden.

No. 43 had no electricity supply – a condition which prevailed until after May's death in 1976, when the house was sold.

By 1939, and with the huge expansion in railway traffic at Severn Tunnel Junction, almost every house in Rogiet was lived in by railway staff.

The Dodsley house was no exception; Augusta and May shared their tiny home with two lodgers, both locomen: thirty-nine-year-old Andrew Jackson, a GWR loco driver, and thirty-eight-year-old William Pope, a GWR fireman.

As mentioned in the Introduction, during World War II, fifty prefabs were erected for the use of railway employees. These were built on land on Caldicot Road, to the west of South Grove and on the corner of what is now Meadway/Fford Y Ddol. The prefabs were gradually replaced by modern houses in the 1960s.

Post-War Housing

It wasn't just the state of yard facilities that were called into question in the decades after the war. Along with the other 'Big Four' railway companies, the Great Western Railway had been nationalized in 1948. The new state-owned company found itself the proud owner of many things other than railway infrastructure. Many railway companies owned houses which they rented to employees. At first, the new owners were the British Transport Commission, which later became British Railways (BR). BR was subdivided in regions and these took a while to get organized and recognize their new assets. Thus it was that when BR (Western Region) got round to looking at what it owned, it wasn't always happy with what it found. That's not to say that there was any underhand intent when BR wrote to Chepstow Rural District Council on 10 March 1965 via its appointed solicitors, John D. Wood (Estate Office, Port Talbot):

British Railways Board – Sale of Houses,
Cardiff Division
Dear Sir,
We are instructed by British Railways Board in the matter of disposal of their houses throughout the Cardiff District, and a decision has recently been made by the Board that, before their houses are offered to tenants, or elsewhere, an approach should first be made to your authority to ascertain if, in principle,

they would be interested in purchasing the houses in your district.
In the case of your area, the total number of houses to be sold is 13, with a gross income of £88/15/4p. If your authority is interested in principle in the first instance, the writer, Mr W. Reynolds, would suggest that we should meet you at possibly a sub-committee to discuss the Board's policy, and whether or not it could be furthered at the present time. If this proposal is of interest no doubt you could let us have some alternative dates.
Meantime, we should be grateful if you would be good enough to treat this matter as confidential.

The houses in question were located at various places around Severn Tunnel Junction. In Portskewett were two cottages and all six houses that comprised the terrace called Western Villas. At Severn Tunnel Junction itself was one house in Rogiet Terrace and three others in 'The Pool', Rogiet, and one in Old Row, Sudbrook. All were occupied by tenants. BR wanted £12,500 for the lot.

It would appear that Chepstow RDC were indeed interested in these houses, and replied as follows to John Wood on 15 April 1965:

Dear Sir,
Disposal of Board Owned houses
I thank you for your letter and will write to you further thereon when the Council have considered the report of their officers on the properties included in your schedule.
Yours Faithfully,
Clerk of the Council

Later that month the BRB wrote again to Chepstow RDC on the subject of board-owned houses:

It is understood from John D. Wood & Co., of Eagle House, Port Talbot, the Board's agents, that you are interested in purchasing the properties indicated in the schedule.

Houses at Sudbrook.
AUTHOR

I should be glad if you will kindly note a suitable communication has been sent to all the tenants concerned, that your Council's representatives will shortly be inspecting the properties. No doubt you will advise each respective tenant of the visit so that he can arrange accordingly.

Yours faithfully,
For D. W. Baird
District Estate Surveyor

In a letter dated 5 July 1965, the clerk of Chepstow RDC wrote to the BRB saying that the council had decided to accept the offer to negotiate for the purchase of the properties, and had instructed the council's District Valuer to deal with the matter, and in the meanwhile requested plans of the sites of the properties from BR. Some delays now occurred, with the District Valuer's assessment being held up by John Wood & Co. 'overlooking' the letter requesting plans, which were then forwarded in due course. The valuer got on with his work and by 20 December 1965, the council reported that they were indeed interested in buying the houses 'providing we can do so at a rea-sonable figure' and by 20 January 1966 Chepstow RDC were also showing an interest in some land in Station Road, Caldicot, previously occupied by some bungalows. The BRB informed the council that they hoped to sell the land in the near future.

Six months passed with little progress but by June 1966, the council wanted to speed things up, for reasons that are apparent in the following letter:

To District Valuer Newport, from Clerk of the Council, Chepstow RDC.

BR Houses, The Pool, Rogiet; Caldicot Road, Portskewett; Rogiet Terrace, Rogiet; Western Villas, Portskewett; Old Row, Sudbrook.

With reference to my letter of 20 December 1965, the Council have asked me to enquire whether you can submit your report and valu-ation of the above properties at an early date. The properties need urgent repairs which are not being done by BR as they are disposing of the houses, and the Council are anxious to acquire them to carry out the work.

Things seem to have dragged on for a further year as the next event seems to have been on 26 June 1967, when Chepstow RDC instructed the Chief Public Health Inspector to inspect the properties concerned with a view to serving notices where appropriate under Section 16 of the Housing Act 1957, the properties 'having deteriorated further'.

The houses comprised three two-bedroom dwellings, and ten three-bedroom dwellings, all in need of repair and improvement. By now four were vacant. Most of the houses were indeed in poor condition; most had no electricity and no bathroom. The council estimated that it would cost in the region of £8,000 to put the houses into habitable condition. The annual income from the properties being £88, it would take them years to recoup the costs. However, they had a public duty and weren't giving up yet.

On 2 August 1967, Chepstow RDC wrote to BR as follows

We have received the report of the District Valuer and have carried out a review of repairs necessary to put these houses into reasonable order. In view of the level of rent to cover the purchase, repair and future maintenance, the Council offer £9,000 [for the houses].

It would seem that British Railways had been caught out. The houses were in such a poor state that they were on the verge of being uninhabitable. In October 1967, the council were still attempting to negotiate with BR, but were becoming frustrated by a lack of movement, particularly when the BRB claimed they now had not been able to trace the letter which had contained the offer of £9,000 for the houses. Nonetheless, Chepstow RDC

BUILDER'S ESTIMATE FOR REPAIRS TO A COTTAGE IN SUDBROOK

Newport District Valuer to Chepstow RDC: total value of 13 Properties: £12,500.

1. Take up floor in small front living room. Lay Marley tiles on concrete.
2. Remove wall to form large living room, kitchen at one end. Replaster 5 yards of wall.
3. New doors and frames throughout.
4. New fireplace in living room.
5. Demolish kitchen.
6. Spar [pebbledash] outside walls, and provide with new windows throughout.
7. Demolish all upstairs partitions, provide studding to form three bedrooms and a bathroom.
8. Take down ceilings and hack off all wall plaster. Replaster throughout.
9. Provide electricity.
10. Fix skirting throughout.
11. Provide fuel store, outhouses and external WC.
12. Insulate roof.
13. Decorate inside and out.
Total cost = £1,104

upped their offer to £10,000 but appear to have got little in the way of positive response, even though BR suggested a figure of £10,500, as the following letter from the clerk of Chepstow Council to John Wood & Co. on 28 November 1967 indicates:

The Council have decided that they are no longer prepared to negotiate any further, even at the reduced value of £10,500. No doubt the Board will consider selling to sitting tenants and private purchasers.

Nine public health notices were served on BR in respect of nine of the properties.

CHAPTER 12

Reductions, Closures and the Future

The rapid rate of growth in the area decreased after the World War II, and the population of Rogiet and Severn Tunnel Junction only increased from 1,137 in 1951 to 1,347 in 1971. This was mainly due to the withdrawal of steam locomotives from the railway in the mid-1960s, and the resultant reduction in the staff needed at the locomotive sheds. With the advent of the more powerful diesels, banking of freight trains was reduced. The Beeching Plan's cutting of branch lines saw the loss of more traffic. Freight still remained heavy, though. Four-wheel wagons, one of Beeching's targets for replacement by modern wagons, took a long time to be superseded.

The Collapse of Coal

With the facilities at Severn Tunnel Junction comprising four yards, stretching over 2 miles (3km) long, main and relief lines, goods loops and busy round the clock, who would ever envisage such a huge yard being closed? I remember from my time as signalman at Bristol panel box in the mid-1980s that traffic to and from Severn Tunnel Junction was always heavy. Still, 1984 saw the announcement that the Conservative government was to embark on a mass colliery closure programme.

As we all know, after a prolonged battle between miners, trade unions and the government, the government won. Pits all over the country closed. For those that remained open, road transport (which had been one of the real winners during the strike, when road haulage contractors moved coal and coke that the rail unions had 'blacked' in sympathy with the miners) took a large part of the traffic.

```
Private and not for publication                Notice No. WW.531


             BRITISH RAILWAYS (WESTERN REGION)

       SEVERN TUNNEL JUNCTION  -  CLOSURE OF DOWN HUMP

Severn Tunnel Junction Down Hump will be taken out of use on Sunday,
2 November, and the alterations shown below will be carried out between
2 November and 9 November, or until completion.  A diagram of the
alterations is included with this notice.

Down Reception Sidings

Nos. 1 and 2 reception lines will be retained as through lines
leading via nos. 1 and 2 engine release lines to the down goods line.
The crossover between nos. 1 and 2 lines near the hump, together with
the two connections in the no. 2 engine release line, will be spiked,
clipped and padlocked for through working.

No. 4 reception line will be retained for through working behind the
hump panel box to no. 23 sorting siding.  The compound at the hump end
of no. 4 reception will be spiked, clipped and padlocked in the
direction of no. 23 siding, and the stop board immediately preceding
the compound will be taken away.  The connection between nos. 4 and 5
lines at the back of the hump panel will be spiked, clipped and padlocked
for no. 4 line.  A new stop board will be provided at the west end of
no. 23 siding.

Nos. 3, 5, 6, 7 and 8 reception lines will be taken out of use, and the
connections in the down goods line will be spiked, clipped and
padlocked in the normal position.

All signals worked from the Down Hump Yard Panel (DH) will be dispensed
with, except the ground position light signals shown below :-

        DH11  -  No. 1 reception to down tunnel or spur
        DH13  -  No. 2    "       "    "    "    "    "
        DH4   -  Spur to down goods or no. 4 reception


Down hump sorting sidings

Nos. 1 to 4 sidings will be converted to hand point operation at the
hump end, a spur retained for 2 locomotive lengths, and a temporary
stop block provided.  Nos. 5 to 19 sidings will be converted to
single-ended sidings with access from the west only.
```

BR notice of the closure of the Down hump 1982.

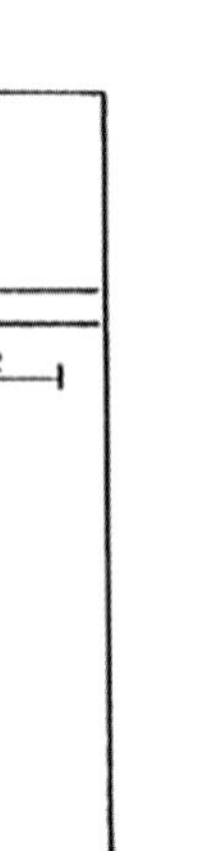

Diagram of the closure of lines at the Down hump.

Inevitably this would lead to a loss of a substantial amount of work for the railway, even though there were pits still using rail to transport coal.

With the reduction in freight traffic came inevitable closures. The Up main goods loop at Severn Tunnel Junction East was taken out of use from 09.00 on Monday 23 May 1983.

The Richard Thomas and Baldwin Spencer steelworks at Llanwern subsequently passed to British Steel, then to the Corus Group and is currently owned by Tata Steel Europe. But by then, the Severn Tunnel Junction yards had closed.

Rundown commenced as early as 1982. In December 1982, the Down hump control box was closed. Nos. 1 and 2 Down reception sidings were reclassified as through lines. The other Down reception sidings and sorting sidings were taken out of use and lifted. All signalling associated with the Down hump box was recovered, except for some ground signals, control of which was transferred to Newport panel box.

As a result of reduced coal and industrial production from the mid-1980s from South Wales, Severn Tunnel Junction goods yard and locomotive depot were closed from 12 October 1987, with residual marshalling moving to Newport railway station. Staff made redundant from the yards in most cases found other work. Some drivers based at STJ moved to other depots. Some staff found work at the Spencer steelworks, echoing the moves made when the plant opened in the 1960s and some railway staff had taken jobs there. Most of the shunters were unable to find railway jobs; shunting was becoming a thing of the past as block trains in fixed formations became the norm. William Winter's letter to staff, reproduced in the Introduction, neatly expresses the feelings held by many when their livelihood was taken away. Many ex-railway employees left Rogiet altogether after the yards closed.

At Bristol, the freight traffic that used to run down the main lines towards the Severn Tunnel and South Wales now reversed direction. Trains that previously had passed through Bristol Parkway and through Patchway junction now travelled in the opposite direction, as Gloucester New Yard had become the new marshalling point for much of the Severn Tunnel Junction traffic. Even that didn't last long.

Trains continued to supply the remaining facilities at Spencer works with raw materials. Suffering from the lack of a deep-water iron ore unloading terminal amongst other difficulties, Llanwern Steelworks ceased to produce steel in 2001 and the Newport 'heavy' end of the works furnaces was demolished in 2004. In 2011, the hot strip mill was threatened with closure but continued to employ 1,600 employees and roll

SEVERN TUNNEL JUNCTION—Down Yard, Down Storage Sidings, Bristol Yard, Up Hump Yard and Undy Yard are closed. All associated Departure and Reception lines, together with the Loco Servicing Depot roads, Emergency Siding and Private (Silcock & Collings) siding have been taken out of use.

(See Periodical Operating Notice) (32)

BR notice of closure of Severn Tunnel Junction yards and diesel depot, October 1987.

1988

A class 37 runs past the sad sight of the closed and derelict Undy yard in 1988.

ROGER GEACH

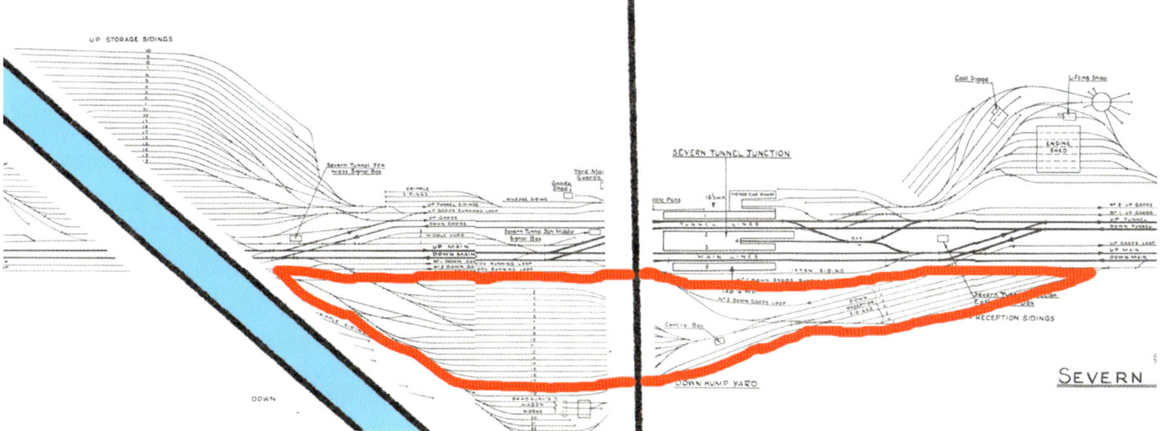

Superimposed on the 1960 plan of the yards is the area of land taken over by Monmouthshire County Council for use as a park (outlined in red): it encompasses the Down reception sidings and the Down yard. The black vertical line represents Moors Road bridge, while the blue line is the M4 motorway. MONMOUTHSHIRE COUNTY COUNCIL

The slightly stylized representation of a steam loco forms the park information board on the site of the Down yard. AUTHOR

'Where have all the trains gone?' Just look at the nearby M4 for the answer…

more than 1.5 million tonnes of steel per year. Since 2006, work on the former steelworks has been undertaken to clear and make the site environmentally safe. From 2010, development has been underway to build 4,000 new homes, primary schools, a 100-acre (40ha) business park, a library, a doctor's surgery, a police station, shops, sporting facilities, parkland, habitats for wildlife and lakes.

In 1994, part of the site of the former goods yard was covered by the new section of the M4 motorway, which crossed the main lines just between the Up hump and the exit from the Down storage sidings. The southern edge of the storage sidings was used for the toll booths for the Second Severn Crossing.

After the tracks were lifted in the early 1990s, the area of land as detailed below was acquired by Monmouthshire County Council by way of a transfer from the British Railways Board on 26 March 1998.

Most of the Down yard became a park, with walks and seats. A signboard next to a relief sculpture of a railway engine shows some pictures of the area as it was

The 2010 Renovations

In 2019, Severn Tunnel Junction station continues to serve the local and wider communities. Improvements were carried out in 2009–10 in connection with the resignalling of the line that saw signalling control transferred from Newport to a new computer centre at Cardiff. To reflect its new lease of life in the twenty-first century, Severn Tunnel Junction will be remodelled in the £150 million first phase of the latest renewal of Newport area signalling. The first phase of improvement work for what is currently the largest rail investment scheme in South Wales marked a new start for thousands of passengers at Severn Tunnel Junction. Sixteen sets of life-expired points and crossings were renewed to create a new layout at Severn Tunnel Junction which improved train movements into and out of the tunnel. The new layout moved the junction between the Bristol and Gloucester lines to a point west of the station, where there was more space for a high-speed junction.

The derelict Platform 4 was restored for trains to Bristol, and the station's passenger facilities

A 2019 view over the remaining facilities at what was once the largest marshalling yard in the Western Region. Compare this with the view earlier…. AUTHOR

Severn Tunnel Junction in 2019. On the right-hand side of the picture a red machine can be seen: this marks the position of the Down hump cabin. AUTHOR

and parking were brought up to current standards. The work was the first phase of the £150m Newport area resignalling scheme which was carried out in several stages up to 2010. It is part of the wider £400m South Wales resignalling scheme which will also see improvements made to the Cardiff area over the period leading to 2016.

To facilitate the new works, rail services between Newport and Bristol and Newport and Gloucester were replaced by coach services between 27 December 2009 and 3 January 2010. The work was carried out over two months and engineers made use of the Christmas period to continue the improvement work up to New Year's Eve, in time for the new timetable on 4 January.

Replacement bus services ran hourly through services between Bristol Parkway and Newport; an hourly service calling at Bristol Parkway, Patchway and Severn Tunnel Junction; two-hourly services calling at Newport, Severn Tunnel Junction, Caldicot, Chepstow, Lydney and Gloucester, and hourly through services between Gloucester and Newport.

Network Rail issued a press statement as follows:

New crossovers, an improved layout and an additional station platform are about to bring Severn Tunnel Junction into the 21st century, as Network Rail continues its £400 million South Wales resignalling.

The junction, where the Birmingham–Cardiff line joins the South Wales main line from Paddington, neatly illustrates recent changes in British rail traffic. The marshalling yards have vanished but the station, once a sleepy wayside halt, is now a popular park-and-ride facility for people working in Cardiff and Bristol. It even has its own, vociferous, passenger action group. Two or three local trains call there each hour. Many others pass without stopping, including freights and half-hourly London–South Wales expresses.

Network Rail seem to have been slightly mistaken: to describe Severn Tunnel Junction station as a 'sleepy wayside halt' is somewhat denying the station's history.

They did, however, get this part right: 'The current layout is a relic of an age when efficient reception and dispatch of freights was an operating priority. Westbound trains from Bristol and London cross the Up Birmingham line on the flat between the tunnel and the station.'

Severn Tunnel Junction Today

The train service for Severn Tunnel Junction today is very different – but then, so are the circumstances of modern-day commuting: people work further from home and in very different conditions than they did forty or more years ago. Today's (2019) network serves the commuter and shopper better than years ago. There are eleven trains per day to Gloucester in the weekday service; the first leaves STJ at 06.38. There are two morning trains between 7 and 8: the 07.06 and 07.34. Then it's roughly an hourly service until 13.39. The next after that is the 15.37, then again an hourly service until 18.35. There are trains every hour from then until the last departure at 23.58.

To Newport and Cardiff there's an astonishing forty trains, commencing with the 06.16 and ending with the 23.54. The same trains serve both stations. Bristol Temple Meads has a lesser service, with twenty-five trains between 06.55 and 23.58, of which sixteen run via Bristol Parkway. Bristol Parkway itself therefore has sixteen trains that go forward to Temple Meads and other destinations, and six that go onward from Parkway and don't go to Temple Meads. The good citizens of Severn Tunnel Junction and surrounding area have, therefore, an excellent train service that would put many larger stations in the shade. The cancelling of tolls on the Severn road bridges has served to make the area between Lydney in the north and Magor in the south a much more attractive place for people to live and commute from; developers too, have seen the opportunities, with new houses going up around Magor and Undy. More will follow.

With the introduction of the Cardiff–Bristol electric suburban services, Severn Tunnel Junction in 2017 showed a 9.1 per cent growth in usage compared with the national growth of 2.3 per cent. Today the station again boasts four platforms, which have been renumbered. Nearest the carpark, the old Platform 1 is now Platform 4, Platform 2 has become Platform 3. Platform 3 is now platform 2 and Platform 5 is Platform 1. The Wye Valley lines having been closed by Beeching, there is no need for the Wye Valley bay platforms. A Portakabin-style booking office and enquiry office stands where the main station buildings of old once were. This is open between 06.30 and 10.30 Monday to Friday. There are toilets provided. Passengers today benefit from new waiting shelters and digitized real-time information system at the station as part of a separate initiative, jointly funded by Network Rail, Arriva Train Wales, Welsh Assembly Government and SEWTA (the South East Wales Transport Alliance). The footbridge has been rebuilt to enable disabled access to all platforms and to cope with the overhead electrification equipment. The lines are now electrified by the overhead 25KV system and, in connection with the electrification, several bridges in the area were rebuilt; these include Moors Road bridge at Severn Tunnel Junction station and the footbridge near the site of Undy Halt. New bimodal (diesel and electric) trains speed through Severn Tunnel Junction. These trains are run by First Group and are painted in Brunswick green with the GWR logo on them. Local services serve the station.

New and adequate car parking facilities for commuters, with plenty of disabled bays, have been put in at the station on the Up side, where the car dock used to be. The NCP-managed car park can hold upwards of 114 cars, although there are calls to extend it further and there's a bike rack for ten bicycles. However, there's no refreshment room any more and commuters wishing to enjoy a quick drink before heading home need to look elsewhere nowadays: The Roggiet Arms has been closed since 2008, leaving the station – and the community – without a pub. Lying at the end of a road that leads nowhere, poor old Severn Tunnel Junction station in 2019 isn't served by any of the commercial bus services. For the fitness fanatic

Looking from the site of the Down hump cabin towards the rebuilt Moors Road bridge in 2019. AUTHOR

Severn Tunnel Junction station in 2019 – a thoroughly modern commuter station. AUTHOR

Electrified lines, real-time information boards, bilingual station signs and a decent waiting room to replace the horrible 'bus shelters' of the 1970s – STJ station in 2019. AUTHOR

At platform level, the station is clean, tidy and boasts disabled access to the footbridge. AUTHOR

it's a 10-minute walk to the station from the bus stop on the main road. Caldicot Halt is still open.

Track-wise, there is a goods loop on the Up tunnel line and another on the Down Gloucester line. The latter runs behind Platform 1 on the same alignment as the old Ifton siding.

Future Plans

At Magor, a group has been formed to press for a new station to be built here to serve the growing community. From being a tiny village in the days when Severn Tunnel Junction was expanding, Undy now has a population of approximately 7,000 people, and under the latest development plans there are proposals to build a further 500 houses. The group called 'Railfuture' has called for a two-platform station to be set on the relief lines between Magor and Undy. The site is 2.25 miles (3.6km) west of Severn Tunnel Junction station and 7.75 miles (12.4km) east of Newport. The proposal is different from 'normal' station proposals as Railfuture wants a 'Community Walkway' station, so called as the station site is within 10–15 minutes' walking distance of the entire population of Magor and Undy and sits perfectly with the recent Active Travel (Wales) Act 2013 which aims to continuously improve facilities and routes for walkers and cyclists – of which access to public transport is a part. The station would be co-located with the proposed Magor and Undy Sports and Leisure Association community centre in the middle of the community to encourage walking to the site instead of car use. The Railfuture website says that 'as with the community centre itself, parking and use of a "parked" car is deliberately intended to be discouraged and only limited parking in the region of twenty spaces provided'. These would be primarily for disabled drivers and those merely wishing to drop off/collect passengers.

There are also outline proposals for another station between Severn Tunnel Junction and Newport, at Llanwern, which is 5 miles (8km) to the west of Magor & Undy Walkway and 2.5 miles (4km) from Newport itself. The partial closure of the steelworks and the redevelopment of part of the site as housing and community use led to calls for a railway station to serve it (the original Llanwern station was a victim of Dr Beeching). Railfuture says that the station is intended to serve the Llanwern steelworks site new housing redevelopment but also to act as a park & ride for road traffic coming south down the A449 from Raglan, Monmouth and Ross off the M50. The Transport Consortia's proposal is again for a two-platform halt on the relief lines and a 380-space car park, but no other facilities apart from a single shelter on each platform. The Llanwern proposal, should it go ahead, is like Severn Tunnel Junction, complementary to the proposal at Magor & Undy Walkway and would be served by the same train services. However, the September 2019 announcement that Tata Steel was to close the plant completely may have put paid to this idea.

In addition, the revamped railway, complete with new track, new layout and modernized signalling technology, is set to improve performance, significantly cutting delays.

What, then of the statement made by that Network Rail director whom I mentioned earlier, who said that the area around Severn Tunnel Junction had suffered years of decline after being bombed during the war? As I've shown in preceding chapters, the area did *not* suffer years of decline; far from it: the yards were *improved and expanded* both during and after the war. The Spencer steelworks added traffic. How one can describe the creation of the Undy yard and the expansion of the other facilities in 1960 as a 'decline' is beyond me. Was the area in 'decline' when it was resignalled with the (then) latest type of colour-light signalling in 1962 and 1968? Once again, the Network Rail man has not read his history correctly; perhaps he's fallen victim to the pseudo-history often found on social media and certain websites. Or perhaps the modern railway likes to think that the old railway was little but a primitive tramway compared to its privatized, modern, electrified service?

Don't rewrite the history of Severn Tunnel Junction, Network Rail: *acknowledge* it.

Reprise

What, then of Severn Tunnel Junction yards today? What remains?

Other than the station and goods loops mentioned previously, very little remains. But a peek over the Moors Road bridge on each side shows some evidence of the old railway presence; the site of the Up yard is still visible, but only comparison with old photos will show where the Down hump cabin stood.

For the railway photographer, the 2019 view from Moors Road bridge holds little of interest. If it did, you couldn't see it for the 'over-engineered' electrification equipment. AUTHOR

New signalling and masts almost obscure the view of the Down goods, compared to earlier pictures. AUTHOR

Once this was a classic view over the yards and diesel depot, but nowadays even the landmark of St Mary's church is difficult to discern from Moors Road bridge. AUTHOR

Railway Terrace in 2019. AUTHOR

The Undy yard in 2019. AUTHOR

Looking towards Newport it's still possible to see the old diesel shed and Railway Terrace behind it.

The Undy yard is wasteland, used by a farmer to gain access to his fields.

And the M4 motorway to and from the Second Severn Crossing (renamed the Prince of Wales Bridge in 2018) severs the site between the Down departure sidings and the Up hump…

Bibliography

A Brief History of Rogiet, online, source unknown-tatasteeleurope.com

BACTEC Ltd, *Explosive Ordnance Threat Assessment in Respect of M4 Corridor around Newport* (21 November 2014)

Benham, Patrick, *The Avalonians* (Gothic Image, 1993)

Booker, Frank, *The Great Western Railway – a New History* (David and Charles, 2nd ed., 1980)

Cadw

Chepstow Town Council minute books 1926–1928 Clarke, C. P. S, *Everyman's Book of Saints* (Mowbray & Co., 1914)

gracesguide.co.uk/Thomas_Alwyn_Lloyd

Great Western Railway, Classification of Signal Boxes and Relief Signalmen's Posts (GWR, 1925)

A Guide to the Industrial Archaeology of South East Wales (AIA,2003)

Hawkins, Mac, *Somerset at War 1939–45* (Dovecote Press, 1988, 1990)

LibCom.org

Lyons, E., *An Historical Survey of GWR Engine Sheds 1947* (Oxford Publishing, 1972)

Marsden, Colin, *BR Motive Power Depots – Western Region* (Ian Allan, 1988)

McCamely, N. J., *Secret Underground Cities* (Pen and Sword (Military), 2007)

Network Rail, Media Centre Press Release 2010

Potts, C. R., *An Historical Survey of Selected Great Western Stations, Vol. 4* (Oxford Publishing, 1985)

railfuture.org.uk

Railway World magazine, various issues (Ian Allan)

Records of Cambrian Wagon Works Ltd and Powell Duffryn Wagon Co. Ltd 1895–1975, Glamorgan Archives, ref: GB 0214 DCWW

Simmons, J. (ed.), *Rail 150* (BRB, 1975)

BR Western Region, Working Timetable Section 7, Swindon and Swansea May 1971–April 1972

BR Western Region, Working Timetable Section PE, September 1985–May 1986

BR Supplementary Operating Notices, various 1961–1995

Wiggins Teape Group, *Sudbrook Pulp Mill – Gatecel* (1958)

bbc.co.uk/history/ww2peopleswar/stories/94/15/10/2014, Dennis Harper's Story

Index